WALKING DARTMOOR'S
ANCIENT TRACKS
A Guide to 28 Routes

Born in the Blackmoor Vale of Dorset in 1914, Eric Hemery trained as a musician. In intervals between his musical commitments, he studied, explored and guided on Dartmoor. On retirement as a teacher, he switched professions and became Dartmoor's foremost writer and lecturer. He is the author of the definitive *High Dartmoor: Land and People* ('the standard work', *Daily Telegraph*) and until his death in early 1986 was the acknowledged world authority on Dartmoor. He is buried in the churchyard of Meavy, the church where he and his family regularly worshipped.

Topographical Books and Guides by Eric Hemery

South West England
Wilderness Camping in Britain
Historic Dart
High Dartmoor: Land and People
Walking the Dartmoor Railroads
Walk Dartmoor
Harvey Mountain Map – Dartmoor (ed. Hemery)
Walking the Dartmoor Waterways

Walking Dartmoor's Ancient Tracks

A Guide to 28 Routes

ERIC HEMERY

ROBERT HALE · LONDON

© Eric Hemery 1986
First published in Great Britain 1986
First paperback edition 1997

ISBN 0 7090 6075 0

Robert Hale Limited
Clerkenwell House
Clerkenwell Green
London EC1R 0HT

2 4 6 8 10 9 7 5 3 1

Printed and bound by Interprint Limited, Malta.

Contents

For my son Gabriel

The Traveller on the Moor

DEVONSHIRE SCENES

One morn I watch'd the rain subside;
And then fared singly forth,
Below the clouds, till eve to ride
From Edgecumb* to the North.
Once, only once, I paused upon
The sea-transcending height,
And turn'd to gaze: far breakers shone,
Slow gleams of silent light.
Into my horse I struck the spur;
Sad was the soul in me;
Sore were my lids with tears for her
Who slept beneath the sea.
But soon I sooth'd my startled horse,
And check'd that sudden grief,
And look'd abroad on crag and gorse
And Dartmoor's cloudy reef.
Far forth the air was dark and clear,
The crags acute and large,
The clouds uneven, black and near,
And ragged at the marge.
The spider, in his rainy mesh,
Shook not, but, as I rode,
The opposing air, sweet, sharp and fresh,
Against my hot lids flow'd.
Peat-cutters pass'd me, carrying tools;
Hawks glimmer'd on the wing;
The ground was glad with grassy pools,
And brooklets galloping;
And sparrows chirp'd, with feathers spread,
And dipp'd and drank their fill
I cross'd the furze-grown table-land,
And near'd the northern vales,
That lay perspicuously plann'd
In lesser hills and dales.
Then rearward, in a slow review,
Fell Dartmoor's jagged lines;
Around were dross-heaps, red and blue,
Old shafts of gutted mines,
Impetuous currents copper-stain'd,
Wheels stream-urged with a roar,
Sluice-guiding grooves, strong works that strain'd
With freight of upheaved ore ...

Coventry Patmore 1823-96

---

* Mount Edgcumb (modern spelling) overlooking Plymouth Sound.

Illustrations

Plates

Figures

Maps

Acknowledgements

Geoffrey Alford of Sourton; Mrs H. Andrew formerly of Ward House, Walkhampton; Reverend P.A. Apps of Lydford; Charles Bennison of Tavistock; Hugh Black, formerly of Widecombe-in-the-Moor; Eric Blatchford of DNPA (Dartmoor National Park Authority); Jim Boddy of Torquay; Keith Brook of South Zeal; Percy Brook of South Zeal; Frank Downing of Yelverton; Ray Downton of Peter Tavy; Miss D. Eggins of Walkhampton; George Eggins of Walkhampton; Dr Andrew Fleming, University of Sheffield; Alfred Garth of Holne; Mrs J. Gillott of Blackdown; The Governor, HM Prison, Princetown; Dr Thomas Greeves; Mrs C. Grigg of Two Bridges; Miss Deborah Hannaford of Widecombe; George Heesem of Plympton; Rupert Jones of Widecombe-in-the-Moor; Will Jordan of Gidleigh; Will Legassick of Sheepstor; Mrs B.J. Lind of West Shallowford; Edward Masson Phillips of Totnes; Ian Mercer, Dartmoor National Park Officer; Miss Sylvia Needham of Widecombe-in-the Moor; George Penrose of Peter Tavy; Dr Nicholas Ralph, University of Sheffield; Ken Rickard of Roborough; Peter Rickard of Blackdown; Mrs M.M. Rowe, Devon County Archivist, Exeter; Mrs J. Slatey of Two Bridges; Dr R.L. Taverner of Exeter; Rosemary Thomas of Meavy; Gregory Wall of South Brent; Bill and Mary Warne of Blackdown; Mrs A.R. Wilson and staff of the Local History Department, Plymouth City Library.

My special thanks are due to my wife Pauline and son Gabriel for their substantial assistance in field work and proof-reading.

Introduction

The best way to become acquainted with wild, open country is to follow recognizable tracks into its interior. These will all have been formed for specific purposes and are likely to provide fine viewpoints and to reveal features of natural and historical interest. While desultory wanderings about Dartmoor can be pleasant enough, they sometimes produce little of real interest for the wanderer, and can lead to the dangers of personal exhaustion, exposure and even hypothermia if mist obscures the return route. The ancient tracks serve Dartmoor as do the blood-vessels the body – arteries conducting the life-blood of its topographical history. They are consequently treated here as exploratory threads penetrating large areas of the granite mass and border-country below.

There is no doubt that ancient travel-routes hold a great fascination for modern man, who wishes not only to follow them physically but also to know of their historical purpose, and so visualize the endless succession of men and beasts that have marked them so deeply through the centuries. Prehistoric and medieval long-distance routes in lowland Britain – those unadopted in modern times – are usually described as 'trackways'; in the highland zones, and in particular on Dartmoor, they are known simply as 'tracks'. All are lines of communication and have come into being over the ages as routes for travellers on foot, in saddle and in horse-drawn vehicles. Some British upland tracks are of great antiquity – certainly prehistoric; most are medieval, some originated during the Victorian Industrial Revolution, while others are modern. Many were formed for the transportation of specific commodities from source to outlet, others for the driving of herds and for the safe guidance of merchants and messengers. In prehistoric upland Britain, settlements were sited according to the proximity of timber and water and to the procuring of shelter from

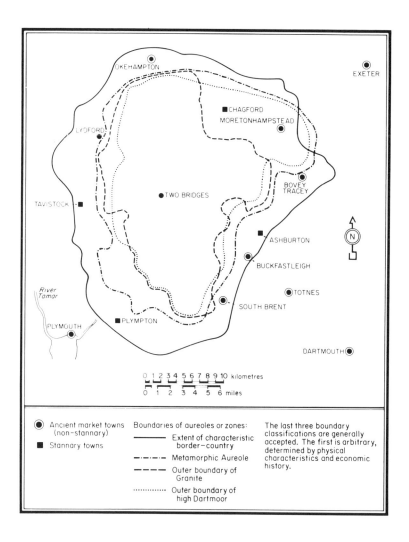

Map A – Topographical Zones Surrounding the Dartmoor Highland

prevailing winds and weather, as well as ground suited to the cultivation of cereal crops and the grazing of herds. It then became the task of the merchant to blaze a trail from his supply source – perhaps a port – to such settlements. A few of these trails have remained in use for up to four thousand years; some were adopted by the Romans and ultimately absorbed into our modern road system.

Professor W.G. Hoskins, in *The Making of the English Landscape*, writes that the importance of such lines of communication 'comes out in the Anglo-Saxon period, for they were, together with the larger rivers, the ready-made routes by which the English colonists penetrated more swiftly and safely into new country than if they had had to hack their way in yard by yard from the edge. There had been, of course, and there still existed, a considerable system of prehistoric trackways, along which settlers and colonists of new land had moved since Bronze Age times, and of which the Anglo-Saxon colonists made extensive use wherever they found them; but these early trackways kept mostly to the higher and more open ground.' The same writer, however, cautions us in his *Devon* against dating Dartmoor's ridgeway tracks earlier than the Iron Age. Indeed, the type of track that particularly concerns this book is not one clinging to the ridgeways but one actually surveyed to follow easy gradients, cross good ground and ford the moorland waters by avoiding deep and unstable stream beds. Such tracks are likely to have resulted from the spread of medieval commerce, when reliability of route, including the bridging of dangerous rivers and avoidance of delay, became all-important. Even by the early thirteenth century, Time had become Money for the wool jobber and tin merchant.

An important requirement on long-distance highland tracks was the provision of rest and shelter for the traveller, as well as feed for riding- or pack-horses, a factor that seems previously to have received little attention from Dartmoor writers. The tradition, even in some places the still existing buildings, of such points of rest helps in several cases to determine the line of a route which might otherwise remain conjectural. Classic Dartmoor examples of this are the trans-Dartmoor monastic way, the Lych Way, and the commercial and general travel routes from Ashburton and Chagford to Tavistock. Along these old ways, over at least four centuries, the Stannary jurats (tin-miners' area representatives) converged on Crockern Tor to attend the open-air Stannary Parliament. Tough though our ancestors must have been, flesh and blood, both human and horse, can stand so much and no more. It is educative for the hardiest walker to imagine himself in the position of an eighteenth-century packhorse-train driver or a Crockern-bound stannator and realize that their journeys, unlike his own, were undertaken not as physical recreation or a challenge in expedition style but as a part of their daily life and work, hopefully to be accomplished with the minimum of danger and hardship to both man and beast.

Distinct contrasts exist between the travel-route patterns of mountain country and a large-scale moorland such as Dartmoor. Precipitous mountain slopes and peaks restrict routes to passes parallel with and connecting 'back-to-back' river systems; typical examples are the Hardknott and Honnister Passes of the Cumbrian Mountains, and in the Scottish Highlands, the Pass of Glencoe, General Wade's Military Road through Glen Garry and the pass through Glen Torridon to Kinlochewe. However harsh may be the weather conditions encountered in a locality of 3,000-4,000 foot peaks, it is virtually impossible to lose the way where wheels, hooves and feet of centuries have trundled and trodden between mountainside and stream. On Dartmoor, however, it is the very absence of towering peaks and scree-covered slopes that allows, in addition to valley-floor travel, inter-transverse valley routes. So on the high plateaux the tracks become stranded and comparatively indeterminable, and in severe conditions of mist and high wind – common meteorological features in Britain's south-west peninsula – can cause disorientation with the unpleasant consequences mentioned in the opening paragraph of the Introduction. The twenty-eight tracks described here are selected from a great number of old Dartmoor ways, as historically the most important.

William Crossing (1847-1928) was the first true topographer of Dartmoor and his work is invaluable in studying the ancient tracks. In his Guide of 1909 he wrote a detailed description of the Moor and over one hundred itineraries for the walker. Mention of the house he occupied in Blackdown at the end of his working life will be found here on page 131. Others of his valuable studies of Dartmoor are *One Hundred Years on Dartmoor, The Ancient Stone Crosses of Dartmoor and its Borderland* and a collection of his articles published in *Western Morning News* and edited under the title *Crossing's Dartmoor Worker*. The author was buried with his wife in Mary Tavy churchyard.

The title of the present book precludes description outside the

Dartmoor country of portions of trans-*county* tracks such as the Mariners' Way (from southern to northern seaboard of Devon) and the Trans-Dartmoor Track via the north central basin (from Exeter to Truro), in which cases description begins and ends in the border-country at the foot of the high moor.

Note: Each track is described in one direction, indicated at the head of the 'Following the Track' section. Where uncertainties may arise in walking in the opposite direction, appropriate notes are inserted in *italics* and headed according to direction. These notes should make it possible for the walker to choose either direction of travel without insuperable problems.

Tracks are usually sunken and sharply defined on hillsides, or wherever movement has been in any way confined; in crossing open tracts of firm, dry ground they often become divided into strands through the choice of movement open to the traveller. Such lengths of tracks are here described as 'stranded'.

In cases where I have received authentic information about tracks in use up to two centuries ago, I have given the sources of information under the heading of each chapter. Such cases are, in the main, those that have faded or are fading fast and have not previously been researched and recorded. Others, perhaps ill-defined or almost lost in the mists of Time, which cannot so readily be supported by living or recent tradition, I have researched from sources available in earlier books and maps and by work in the field covering many years. I have been enabled to describe in detail the course of each track through the kind co-operation of landowners through whose property certain portions pass. In several cases the owners are not willing to admit the public without prior agreement, when conditions of entry will be found in the text. It is the author's hope that long-standing confusion over certain track-name and routes might be dispelled by this study. Numerous place-names in the book will be found to be at variance with OS versions, many of which are regrettably corrupt. The most satisfactory map to use in conjunction with the book is the *Harvey Mountain Map – Dartmoor*, which contains authentic names and several tracks described here.

For map references in the border-country (beyond the borders of the Harvey Map) the OS one-inch Tourist Map is convenient for handling.

Mileages are correct within a quarter of a mile.

Access: Every effort has been made to clarify rights of way and privilege of access. If any doubt should remain in the reader's mind he or she should, if at all possible, seek out the owner of the land to be entered and request permission to pass over it. Readers will the more readily be accepted as bona fide walkers if they are able to produce a copy of this book.

Warnings: Inherent dangers on Dartmoor are frequency of mist (low cloud), undue exposure in wet, cold or windy weather – conditions common to the highest land in southern England where an oceanic climate exists – mire (valley swamp) and military live-firing on three ranges. These are Okehampton (north), Willsworthy (west) and Merivale (immediately north of central basin). When firing is in progress red flags fly from prominent tors and hills in each range area. Firing programmes for each week are displayed at post offices in the Dartmoor border-country and should be consulted before setting out to follow a track entering a range area. These are as follows:

Track	Range
2	Okehampton
17	Nears, but does NOT enter, the Merivale boundary on Roos Tor where the red danger flag will fly NORTH of the line of the track between the Steeple Tors
18	Merivale, and Okehampton
19	Okehampton
20	Okehampton
21	Willsworthy and Okehampton
22	Merivale and Willsworthy

Always carry a reliable map – of a scale not smaller than one inch to one mile – a compass, and emergency rations. ALWAYS leave details with a relative or friend of your proposed itinerary. Dartmoor is vast: an accident or exhaustion in the case of the lone walker who tells no one of his plans can cause very serious delay to the Dartmoor Rescue Service with possible dire consequences to the victim. Be properly clothed and equipped. Never go without a woollen garment – even in midsummer, when a cloud-bank can herald a chilly wind, as well as mist.

Key to Maps

——— Roads	Deep valley, gorge cleave or hole	*River Tavy* (italic) — Waterways
– – – – Normal access	Embankment	*BLACK TOR* (italic) — Physical features
–·–·– Route of no access or conditional access	Leat	OKEHAMPTON — Settlement
==== Modern road on line of track	✚ ◌ ■ Features of interest of human origin	Teignhead Farm — Human features
·········· Original route now impassable	△ Tors, hills	
Track 19 Intersecting tracks or important tracks not described in text.	Reservoirs & pools	
	Camps	
╫╫╫╫╫╫╫ Railway	Woodland–deciduous	
≈≈≈≈ River or stream	Woodland–coniferous	
◌ ● Towns and settlements	Mire or Marsh	

Note to Readers

This key applies to all maps in the book. Some additional symbols are explained on individual maps.

Part I

Trans-Moorland Tracks

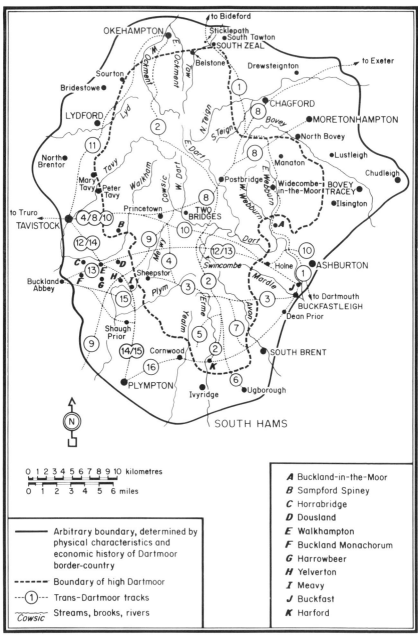

Map B – Disposition of Trans-Dartmoor Tracks. Note: Tracks 5, 6 and 7, although strictly inter-moorland ways and shown on Map C, also appear here because of their historical importance as branches of Tracks 2 and 3.

TRACK 1

THE MARINERS' WAY: HOLNE BRIDGE — SOUTH ZEAL   20 miles

Portions of route according to tradition received by Emmie Varwell of Throwleigh, and others received by the author from Ted and Deborah Hannaford of Natsworthy, Will Jordan of Moortown and the late Jack Rowe of Frenchbere.

A tradition exists, some centuries old, that seamen landing at Dartmouth in south Devon or Bideford in the north, and wishing to change ship, were accustomed to walking between those ports, once of great commercial importance, over a route later dubbed 'Mariners' Way'.

Bideford
The town received its charter of incorporation from Queen Elizabeth I in 1573 'at the instance of the great Sir Richard Grenville' (W.G. Hoskins) and a considerable trade developed with America which lasted until almost the end of the eighteenth century. In the previous century 'Bideford merchants were importing wool from Spain for the flourishing Devonshire textile industry and in 1663 Bishops Quay was built by the corporation.' The port also had a large share in the (Dartmouth-founded) Newfoundland trade, sending out more ships in 1699 than any port except London and Topsham. The tobacco trade in particular (with Maryland and Virginia) flourished from about 1680 to 1730, after which it dwindled over the next thirty years.

Dartmouth
An historical sketch of this ancient port appears in the author's *Historic Dart*, and the commerce of both Bideford and Dartmouth,

21

with their contrasting trades, certainly strongly supports the old tradition of sailors travelling over the trans-Devon path. To follow Mariners' Way entailed an overall walk of about seventy miles. The middle stage of the journey threaded a natural pass in the eastern highlands of the high moor and passed through the Dartmoor border-country and lowlands to the north and south. Crossing states that rest-houses occurred at intervals, and Emmie Varwell in *Throwleigh* (1938) strengthens the tradition by recording what she had learned from aged people about the use and route of the track. Also in TDA 79 of 1947, extracts are given from the Churchwardens' Accounts of Gidleigh parish, as follows:

| 1760 | Gave a sailor that had a pass | 1s. |
| 1774 | Giv'd Alms to Sailor | 6d. |

D. St Leger Gordon, in *Under Dartmoor Hills*, gives these items from the Churchwardens' Accounts of South Tawton:

1670	To Two seamen as shown by their certificates suffered shipwreck	2s. 0d.
1670	Given to James Wallis and his family having had Losses at Sea by the Turks and for Ransoming of some taken by the Turks	2s. 0d.
1670	Given to Oliver Faully and Edward Dollyton, who came from sea as shown by their certificates	2s. 6d.

It is possible that similar entries remain to be discovered in the accounts of others parishes along the way. It may be, too, that the ancient house at West Coombe was a hostel for walking seamen four or five centuries ago when the Tudor shipbuilding industry flourished at Bideford and crews were recruited for new vessels. Totnes, near the southern seaboard and occupying a strategically important position at the head of the navigable Dart, also was a busy port where ships were built for England's anti-Armada fleet and crews recruited; sailors intending to walk between Dartmouth and Bideford could therefore save themselves ten weary foot-miles by gaining passage up or down the tidal river on one of the many vessels plying between Totnes and Dartmouth.

The path entered the Dartmoor border-country at Holne Park and

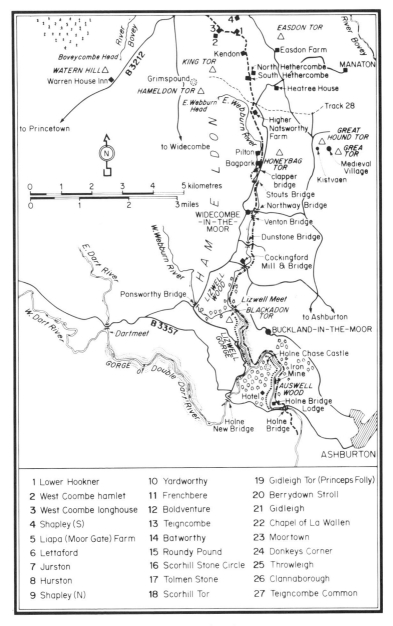

1 Lower Hookner	10 Yardworthy	19 Gidleigh Tor (Princeps Folly)
2 West Coombe hamlet	11 Frenchbere	20 Berrydown Stroll
3 West Coombe longhouse	12 Boldventure	21 Gidleigh
4 Shapley (S)	13 Teigncombe	22 Chapel of La Wallen
5 Liapa (Moor Gate) Farm	14 Batworthy	23 Moortown
6 Lettaford	15 Roundy Pound	24 Donkeys Corner
7 Jurston	16 Scorhill Stone Circle	25 Throwleigh
8 Hurston	17 Tolmen Stone	26 Clannaborough
9 Shapley (N)	18 Scorhill Tor	27 Teigncombe Common

Track 1 – South

ran via Buckland Woods and Lizwell Meet to Cockingford Mill. In the Widecombe area I have been fortunate in discovering oral tradition preserving the use of the title 'Mariners' Way', for paths beside the East Webburn river which had been open to the public until the years between the two world wars.

The route from Holne Bridge to Natsworthy Gate includes practically no public right of way (except where coinciding with a public road) and is consequently unmarked by the DNPA, whose efforts to have it opened have been unavailing. In view of the national heritage character of the woodlands and riverside paths, this can only be regarded as very regrettable and a sad reversal of the situation prevailing in Greenwood's day (1827) when he was able to mark both Dart- and Webburn-side tracks as public roads.

Every field is numbered in the text in a northward direction according to its relative position in a group of fields separating the numerous farms encountered on the walk. In view of these circumstances, the initial stages of the walk cannot be along the actual track – which passes through land worked by two private forestry firms and includes a shooting lease – but will follow an alternative route from which the original way is visible throughout.

Landowners and tenants concerned have kindly allowed the author to follow the original route in order to record its passage through their 'no-access' land. In the interests of historical accuracy, therefore, I include a description of the route here, numerous points on which are referred to in the guiding text as they become visible from the alternative route open to the walker. The reader also is asked to note that passage through farm fields entails the careful closing of all gates and of keeping dogs under strict control during lambing and calving times. Most – but not all – of the field paths have been fingerposted and marked with their conventional yellow dots by the DNPA. Map references are given in 'Following the Track' sections for initial, and in some cases intermediate car-parking locations. The walker following the longer tracks is left to decide personally on his or her walking and motoring stages.

Original route of riverside portion
Track 1 enters the gate of the drive to Holne Bridge Lodge (north end of bridge), passes behind the Lodge and climbs to a high shelf above the river – here an alarming torrent when swollen. Cleft Rock, a high crag literally split, or cleft, by the old copper-miners, towers above,

and tree-covered Holne Chase Iron Age fort rises above the river's right bank. The way then switchbacks into a hollow and passes the former Auswellwood Iron Mine.* After passing an island and Foster's Pool, the great loop of Dart is seen below with an impressive swirl of the oncoming river. Another hollow is formed by a bend above the strong sound of the river, and Lovers' Leap comes in sight. The track then fords a stream descending from Buckland Court grounds and runs to Warren Bridge, where it crosses Ruddycleave Water and continues onward beside the broad Dart.

The track leaves the riverside through the gate at Buckland 'Lowen' (properly 'Lower') Lodge, passes before the house and enters Mistress's Piece and Great Lot Wood. Now a grass track, it climbs to a shelf on the precipitous hillside and maintains a considerable height above the River Webburn, here approaching its confluence with Dart at Spitchwick Meet. Soon there comes into view above the opposite, high valley-side the tower of Leusdon church and the buildings of Lower Town; then follows the first sighting of Blackadon Tor, with crags breaking out from the steeply opposing hillsides. Suddenly the converging valley of West Webburn opens between wooded and picturesque interlocking spurs. The Mariners' Way now passes beneath the outcropping crags and makes its first entry upon the Dartmoor granite. A large clitter lies below a beetling crag as it descends yet again to the valley floor at the beautiful union of the Webburn rivers, Lizwell Meet. East Webburn cascades towards the confluence, and a branch of the track crosses the river at a wide, sandy ford. Passing an island, the track again branches this time to Lizwell Bridge, its stone arches linking each back to an island in this truly romantic glen.

Some 400 yards above Lizwell Bridge is another and even more picturesque crossing place, where a fine set of 'steps' (river stepping-stones) and a shallow, sandy ford constitute a crossing once used by local farm-folk. Eventually the woodlands and magnificent river scenery end at a gate opening upon the fields of Cockingford Mill Farm. The track passes from the gateway through three fields and reaches the Widecombe-Cold East Cross road at Cockingford Bridge beside the scenic, former cornmill; crossing the road, it then becomes impassable as it follows East Webburn's left bank through the fields of

---

* A detailed description of all features mentioned between Holne Bridge and Buckland Lower Lodge may be found in the author's *Historic Dart*.

four different farms and emerges at Chittleford.

Following the permitted Track (northward)
Call at the Holne Chase Hotel (722708, west of Holne Bridge) and request the permission of Mr or Mrs Bromage to follow the riverside path, which their goodwill has made possible. Readers may like to note that the hotel, with its bar and restaurant, is open all the year round. If anyone should wish to lead a group or party along the Holne Chase path, they should make prior application to the hotel. Lastly, also note that this concession is available only between 1 October and 31 March. Show your copy of this book when calling at the hotel.

Descend to the river; turn right and view Track 1 (beyond the opposite bank) approaching and passing behind Holne Bridge Lodge. Turn about and walk upstream, noticing Cleft Rock and Track 1 passing below it. Beyond an island and Foster's Pool a perpendicular crag will come in view above the opposite bank; this is Lovers' Leap, at the downstream end of the river's great loop in Holne Chase. From the top of the crag, legend claims, a medieval monk of Buckfast Abbey and his sweetheart – this was obviously an affair of the heart contrary to the monk's vows – together leapt to their death in the swirling waters of Dart when confronted by the maiden's antagonistic guardian flourishing a drawn sword.

Walk to the edge of the river bank at the head of the loop with its impressive swirl of water. Above (left) is Holne Chase Castle, a small Iron Age earthwork; and nearer still, the crag of Eagle Rock. Mariners' Way can be seen climbing behind Lovers' Leap and fording a stream before running through Greypark Wood to Warren Bridge, where it crosses Ruddycleave Water into Hardridge Wood and returns to the river bank.

The walker should go no further but return to the hotel. Drive westward over Holne New Bridge; at a sharp bend at the steep of the hill, branch right into the Spitchwick road. Notice the fine pile of Leigh Tor, left. Remain on the riverside road to Buckland Bridge; park near the footpath gate (left), where there is space for only one car (718719). Walk down to the meet of the rivers, right. (Should the small space at the gate be occupied, drive across Buckland Bridge and park on open ground before reaching the picturesque Buckland Lower Lodge, which is set in a charming woodland scene.) Track 1 follows Dartside from Lovers' Leap and Warren Bridge to the gateway seen below the Lodge, from where it crosses the road and enters another gateway on the opposite side. Return to the footpath gate beside Buckland Bridge. Enter; read the Nature Reserve notice. Follow the Webburn riverside path. The valley becomes a true gorge, and the path, so beguiling near the gate, gives way to steep, twisting switchback ways between the trees, demanding more scrambling than walking. A further stretch of open path is succeeded by another obstacle course. The river is very beautiful here; there are several glimpses of Track 1 also switchbacking on the opposite bank, and a cascade appears ahead. 150 feet above it the Lower Town road passes 'Bramblemoor Cottage', formerly 'The Glen'. Granite boulders seen in the river, some at least 6 to 8 feet above normal water level, show the astonishing power of floodwater in transporting them, for the granite boundary lies some way upstream. There is little point in further continuing the struggle up the valley: the character of a riverside track in the Webburn gorge (relevant to Track 1) will have been sampled, and a much more comprehensive view of both track and gorge will be seen from Blackadon Tor.

Return to Buckland Bridge; drive south-westward; take a hairpin bend (right) to Lower Town; after another hairpin bend pass Bramblemoor Cottage (right); stop at a small green where a track branches (right) from the road; park on the green or on the roadside space opposite (717720). Follow the track; it is known as Blackadon Lane and soon narrows to a footpath along the upper verge of Great Lot Wood, where the river is audible. As the path climbs above the trees, the spur of Blackadon Tor appears ahead and Mariners' Way is clearly seen on the opposite valley-side, there at a high level before beginning its descent to Lizwell Meet. On gaining higher ground, notice Buckland-in-the-Moor church above the high bend of Track 1, and the wooded spurs downstream completing a fine picture.

On reaching Blackadon Tor, go first to the east brink of the spur below the rocks to see Track 1 passing through the wonderful glen below. Next, move to the north brink of the spur at the outcrop of Logwell Rock; another delightful scene now lies below and ahead where, beyond the incoming West Webburn (left), Lizwell Bridge interrupts the silver thread of the river as it approaches East Webburn (ahead). Lizwell Meet is indicated by the junction of the two wooded valleys; Track 1 continues northward as the lower of two hillside tracks (right), and its final woodland thread is seen leading to the green fields of Cockingford; above all rises high Dartmoor, climax to a memorable view perhaps unsurpassed in the Dartmoor borderland.

Climb to the summit of Blackadon Tor, a somewhat unremarkable, flattish granite outcrop, and return through Blackadon Lane to the parked car. The next stage is chiefly a motoring one. Drive past Leusdon church (a not unpleasing Victorian chapel-of-ease to St Pancras's, Widecombe) to Ponsworthy, where a ford still serves traffic crossing a streamlet in the hamlet. Cross Ponsworthy Bridge (West Webburn approaching Lizwell Meet) and continue along the Widecombe road to the junction at Beard's Garage traditionally, but confusingly (see p.245), called 'Church Lane Head'; turn right and descend to Cockingford Mill, here are millwheel, mill bridge over East Webburn and Track 1 crossing the fields on the left bank from Buckland Woods to the road and continuing north to Chittleford. Return to the Widecombe road; turn right, and right again at the signpost to Dunstone. Drive through Dunstone Lane, over Dunstone Bridge and up to Chittleford. Park; walk along a gated lane (right) branching southward from Dunstone Lane. Beyond the second gate is the route of Track 1 crossing the four fields upstream from Cockingford Mill. Do not enter, but return to the car. Drive past Higher Venton Farm; in the adjoining Venton House, novelist Beatrice Chase once lived (also for a time, following her death, the present author). The numerous Chase books include *From a Dartmoor Window* and *The Corpse on the Moor*. The authoress, a member of the Roman Catholic Church, died in 1955. Pass the Rugglestone Inn and over Venton Bridge (East Webburn again). Park; from a gate (right) on the river's west bank observe Track 1 following the parallel hedge; there is no right of way, and the track shortly becomes impassable.

Drive up the hill to Widecombe village towards the tower of St Pancras's Church. Widecombe-in-the-Moor, ancient Dartmoor metropolis where families from the central basin met at the Sunday worship; where the emblem of the flourishing medieval tinners' guild of St Pancras, three rabbits sharing three ears, appears as a boss on the roof of the nave as a thank-offering for prosperity. The present church, with granite monolith pillars, predates the 120-foot granite tower and was built in the late fourteenth century.

Turn right at the Church House (recorded in 1608 as the village ale-house), where mariners could obtain food and shelter by turning aside from the track on the valley floor; descend (the Bovey Tracey road) to the next bridge upstream from Venton, Northway. The path is clearly seen approaching a gate (west bank) beside the bridge from the impassable ground near Venton. From the gate opposite, on the north side of the road, it continues beside the river through the area known as 'Pitts' to Stouts Bridge on the Widecombe-Heatree-Manaton road. The walker who elects to follow the vestiges of the old way through Pitts may risk a rebuke if seen. In any case the path is troublesome to trace, and it is more satisfactory to drive from Northway Bridge to Stouts Bridge, highest crossing by a public road of East Webburn and two-thirds of a mile from Widecombe Green. Park at the south end of the bridge and look through the wicket gate (west roadside) where the way vanishes in a copse: do not enter. From here the track passes through the Natsworthy estate via the farmlands of Widecombe Manor Farm (formerly Bag Park), Pitton and Lower and Higher Natsworthy. Below Bag Park it crossed to the river's left bank on a fine old clapper bridge, passed over a stone stile in the Pitton fields and, crossing a vigorous little stream rising near Hedge Barton, climbed to the Twitcheries, a piece of waste ground opposite the north slope of Honeybag Tor. This entire portion of the route, and its subsequent passage through the Higher Natsworthy fields, has been authenticated for me by Ted and Deborah Hannaford of Natsworthy, whose father, born over a century ago, worked in these fields and woodlands and always referred to the path – then used by local people – as 'Mariners' Way', a tradition he told them he had received from his grandfather, born in the eighteenth century.

At the head of the Twitcheries a gate leads into Field 1; follow the wall, right, ancient, massive and well maintained. The huge mass of Hameldon rises, left. Enter the next gateway into Field 2; continue beside the right-hand wall. A deep combe, left, channels a tributary to the river from Hameldon's flank. Continue through the next gateway into Field 3; follow the right-hand wall; beyond it, the tors of Chinkwell, Honeybag and Great Hound dominate the near distance. The first two are northernmost of a fine range of twelve tors reaching southward to Auswell Rocks; Honeybag Tor, a widespread wilderness of granite masses and bedding, is in particular worth a visit. Pass through the next gateway into Field 4; Higher Natsworthy Farm and the modern Natsworthy Manor are seen, right; left is the curve of Natsworthy Hill marked by ancient enclosures, with the river now some distance below. Pass through a cornditch gateway opening upon Natsworthy Common. NOTE: before passing through the fields listed, it is wise to seek permission from Mr John Gittings of Higher Natsworthy Farm (720800) as the walker has, of course, to enter them from the north beside the farm. Mr Gittings gladly gives this permission, and it is worth obtaining it in order to recapture the character of the Mariners' Way as it ascends from the depths of the Widecombe valley. From the cornditch gate follow the wall, right, until the track is seen to diverge from it on Natsworthy Common and run parallel with the motor road coming up the combe from the village to Heatree and Natsworthy Gate. On nearing the roadside the track passes through a gully and, on the crest of the plain, intersects Track 28 and fords the (flowing) Heatree leat. Natsworthy Gate and the road are on the right; ahead, the track descends to Hewstone Gate and a stile in the boundary wall of the Vogwell plantations. (Ignore a second gate in the wall further to the left.)

Natsworthy Gate – South Zeal
From this point onwards for a considerable distance, DNPA yellow dots (on trees and gateposts) and fingerposts indicate the way. It is not, however, always easy to see one mark from another, and the walker should find helpful the route description given here.

Enter the wood at the stile; the gate alongside was anciently known as Woodstone Gate – pronounced 'Hoodstone', now rendered 'Hewstone'. The track appears to fork but actually only loops; at the lower loop junction a short grass track leads, right, to a gateway. *Southward: do not be misled into following this branch.* Walk beside a deep tinners' channel to reach a T-junction of tracks (from which point the southbound walker sees the open moor beyond Hewstone Gate). The channel continues past a slotted gatepost, but Track 1 swings left into a lane that has lost one wall to forestry operations. The lane joins another beside a huge boulder and crosses a stream on an overgrown clapper bridge. From here the green way is unenclosed and is intersected by a vehicular track marked 'PRIVATE'. South Hethercombe (OS 'Heathercombe') is now visible through the trees, and a gate leads into an open field; the path is faintly defined in crossing this, but the next gate, beside South Hethercombe longhouse, stands ahead. Follow the short lane from this, cross the hard track in the valley and the rapid stream, the Burn, beside North Hethercombe,* another fine longhouse (Pl. 1). A gate stands near the back of the house; pass through this, climb to a second gate and immediately fork right. The track now descends through a plantation to the next gate and stile, which gives access across a stream to two fields of Kendon Farm. Continue to a further gate and enter the home

* Correct spelling used in *OS 1809*.

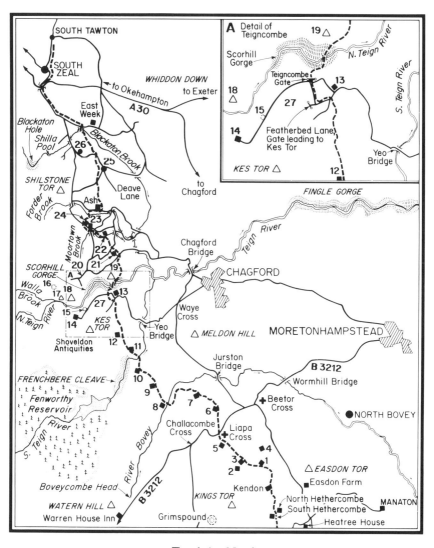

Track 1 – North

field, where DNPA signs are non-existence. Ignore a well-trodden animal track to a water-trough and follow the lower hedge of the field to a gate at the lower end of a barn. *Southward: after mounting stile beside stream into plantation, take centre of three ways and pass boles of two former huge ash trees. Note – ancient walls often reliable guide where uncertainty exists. Direct track from stile, for example, merely a forest drive across former open field, whereas true way follows old wall bounding original field.* King Down, from which 'Kendon' Farm derives its name, rises mightily above and is faced across the valley by Easdon Tor.

The entrance porch of Kendon longhouse bears the inscription NIA May the 28 1675 and a mason's mark can be seen near the top of the front wall of the house. The way continues from the barn-side gate across the farm road to another directly opposite and runs to a wooden fence and gate at the bottom of a field. It is well defined as it approaches a ford on Kendon Stream, and another gate opens upon a marshy tract. It passes beside a hedge (left) for 35 yards to a gate opening into a picturesque (but in winter muddy) sunken lane leading to the Hookner Farms; notice lying beside the way part of a double-slotted gatepost. This is a peaceful, forgotten tract overlooked by two bold Dartmoor hills. The first farm, now called Higher Hookner, was once more correctly known as South Hookner, where a twentieth-century house has been built upon longhouse foundations, and the remains of an ash-house and round-house are seen beside the track. Passing North Hookner, fork left from the farm road into a lane; pass a cottage (right) and enter a field gate (right). Turn immediately left and follow a raised way beside the hedge to a wide, open gateway. Cross the next field to a gate and a cart clapper bridge over a streamlet; this is followed by a patch of marshy ground to another open gateway with one slotted post, near which are steps in the hedge. The roofs of West Coombe are now visible, and the path curves across a pleasant, dry field under Coombe Down towards the upper side of West Coombe Farm, where another, less ruined ash-house comes into view. The farm, approached by stile and steps over West Coombe Stream, is a fine example of a medieval Dartmoor settlement: the massive masonry of the longhouse (Pl. 2) where the Mariners' Way actually passed through the central passage of what surely was a rest-house; the farmer's watermill, where a rusting iron waterwheel frame occupies a wheel-pit of far greater age; the circular ash-house (recently restored by DNPA) and great linhays and barns.

1 Track 1: North Hethercombe Longhouse. The track passes the door and winds round the side of the house. Notice the massive masonry.

2 Track 1: West Coombe Longhouse. The track passes through the central passage, emerging at the door on the right.

3 Tracks 2 and 5: Erme Pound. The united tracks pass the pound beyond the picture. The author is seated in a once-roofed moormen's shelter.

4 Track 2: Black Lane (south). Looking north, approaching the 'narrows' of the peat pass, the desolate nature of the country is appreciable.

5   Track 2: Headweir (Strane Hill) Ford. Anna Hemery stands on the ruined clapper bridge. Fox Tor and Foxtor Gulf (left) beyond. Childe's Tomb appears below the newtake wall near left.

6 Track 2: Historic Cut Lane. The peat pass runs from the right between the ancient guide-stones; from there Track 2 descends to Rush Bottom. Centre: Pinswell Hill, Black Ridge and Amicombe Hill. Right: Blacka Tor, Foresland Ledge, High Willes and Yes Tor. The track runs north at the foot of High Willes and Yes Tor.

7 Track 2: pipers celebrate Ten Tors Day, 1984. The track descends through Creber's Hole under West Mil Tor: Yes Tor on the right.

8 Track 3: The establishment of 'Jobbers' at Sheepstor village.
Evidence from 1782.

9 Track 3: Jobbers' Ford – Thrushelcombe Brook. Looking eastward
the track (at camera point) approaches the ford and makes an oblique
ascent of Thrushelcombe Hill, right. The gully (left) is a tin-working.

10   Track 4: The track, long disused, descends through Swallever
     Lane to the site of Swallow Ford on Walkham.

11   Track 3: At Erme Pits. Camping on the Jobbers' Road during field
     work, 1985.

12   Track 8: Near Parson's Cottage. From the parked car the track (in line with the highway) passes between the gorse bushes, fords Muddy Lakes and ascends to the camera point. Crockern Tor is in the background.

13   Track 8: On Hurston Ridge. From the Hurston stone row the track bears left to Deer Park Corner.

14 Track 8: Collapsed clapper bridge, Blacka Brook (HM Prison grounds).

15 Track 9: Ockery clapper bridge, Blacka Brook. The old Plymouth track crosses here: the 1792 turnpike bridge appears behind.

It is no longer a nucleated farm, and these historic features are unfortunately fast decaying.

Pass through the yard of the still working Higher Coombe Farm into a lane; enter Field 1 through a gateway of which one post has no fewer than seven slots. In Field 2 converge on West Coombe Stream (right). The path twists to reach a ford and steps and enter a copse. Here mount wall-steps above the further (left) bank, pass through the copse into the outer field of Liapa (now 'Moorgate') Farm, at the higher side of which a track leads towards the farmhouse, which stands left of the next gateway. This opens onto a tarmac drive leading past Liapa†* to the B3212 road, which here is built on the line of Track 8 (Moretonhampstead branch) below the first rise to the Moor. Cross the road; mount a stile opposite and pass through five fields. Field 1: walk along the west brink of a marsh; Field 2: descend diagonally; Field 3: walk straight to the next gate; Field 4: make for a visible open gateway; Field 5: the path is slightly sunken in descending to Lettaford – its buildings visible ahead. Of three gates at Lettaford, the first leads into a farmyard flanked by a Victorian house, the second into a very short lane, and the third onto the large green before the magnificent old longhouse of Lettaford, its massive masonry typically like that of West Coombe. Pass a third house, left, and follow the track to Jurston. An appalling car-dump lies in the green vale here, but the track soon offers scenic compensations at Jurston Ford, steps and clapper bridge on Curlicombe Brook.

Cross the bridge and Jurston Green to enter a gate beyond the higher farm and cross five fields. Field 1: go to the furthest of three gateways; Field 2: follow the hedge to the left of two gates; Field 3: follow the hedge to a stile below the looming mass of Bush Down, left; Field 4: follow the hedge to an open gateway opposite, which has one large slotted post; Field 5: mount the stile into the farm road at Lincombe (formerly known as 'Venn'). Turn left to pass through the yard before the house to a gate (right) opening into a grassy lane. Cross a clam over a stream; continue to a confluence of two more streams – each having its own clapper footbridge – a delightful glade. The way now leads to a stile beside the road to Hurston. Follow the road left, then fork right into the Lower Hurston drive; bear right between two longhouses and enter a lane. Notice a slotted post, right, and a large post with seven slots at the lane-end. Again there are five

---

* See Cross in the glossary.

fields. Field 1: follow the hedge to a gate on the right; Field 2 (very narrow): follow the hedge (left) to an open gateway; Field 3: walk to stream – ford – stile; Field 4: walk to a metal gate ahead; Field 5: a sea of mud in wet weather obscures any sign of the path, but the right of way enters Lower Shapley farmyard (the nearer of two farmhouses, left) and passes between farm buildings into the farm lane. This runs to the Chagford-Fernworthy road, but before reaching this, turn left into a gateway at a fingerpost. The path leads to another fingerpost and stile ahead. Here descend into the Fernworthy road over five granite wall-steps; cross the road (on the line of the main Track 8) and follow the Yardworthy Farm Lane. The track curves around the left side of the farmhouse and passes behind the stable to two slotted gate-posts. Enter Field 1: follow the hedge (right); Field 2: the same: Field 3: follow a cart track beside the hedge (right) to a ford on the South Teign river; the original path, however, descended the field diagonally to the lower left-hand corner and a wooden clam. Walk upstream and cross the clam. This beautiful, lonely place is at the foot of Frenchbere Cleave where the river leaves the Moor and where rocks, bracken, furze, spring flowers and birdsong are an invitation to linger; the picturesque ruggedness of the valley arises from its being on the granite – a feature unique to the north-east border-country proximate to the Moor – whereas the borderland rock elsewhere consists mostly of metamorphic shales and slates.

From the clam, ascend the steep ahead beside a fence bordering a brake and enter an ancient lane on the crest. Before this meets a tarmac road (Thornworthy-Chagford) turn left into an equally ancient lane skirting the grounds of the Teignworthy Hotel and leading into the farmyard of Little Frenchbere. Note the round-house, right; the *oblong* ash-house, left – highly unusual, and ruins of the former little Frenchbere longhouse, the yard now being used for Great Frenchbere Farm. Cross the yard and the Thornworthy road to enter a lane ahead, with the fine thatched longhouse of Great Frenchbere below (right), the working farm for two generations of the Rowe family, until the death of moorman Jack Rowe in 1984. (The bungalow, left, was built for and occupied by James Endacott (d.1974), last of a long line of Duchy reeves, or keepers.) Views from this lane extend over the entire width of the Teign border-country, bounded in the east by the Iron Age Prestonbury Fort above Fingle Gorge. A gateway with slotted posts is succeeded by a stile into a field of Boldventure Farm – on the further side of which another stile leads into a marshy tract where branches have been spread as an aid to walking. *Southward: in crossing the field north of the marshy tract take care to use the lower of two gateways.* Enter a field and pass through a gateway into a copse. Here ignore a wide track following the hedge (right), as Track 1 threads the copse diagonally and descends into a dark glade. Emerge at a stile between two streams and make for a large triangular stone, prominent in a group of boulders in the field ahead, from which Castle Drogo and the hills above Fingle Gorge are visible. Gidleigh Tor, also known as Princeps Folly, is seen rising beyond the next belt of trees. Pass to the right of the triangular stone and cross a flowing leat (to Teigncombe Farm). Step over the remains of a stile (demolished by a falling tree) and stay close beside the hedge and leat, left. Descend the sloping field to a wicket gate and enter a lane coming up from Teigncombe Farm; turn right into the lane; before reaching the farm turn left into a branch lane which joins the Chagford-Batworthy road 350 yards west of the farm. Cross the road – here on the line of Track 19 – and enter a gate on the lower side.

The track now leads into the third of the fine Dartmoor gorges threaded by the Mariners' Way – Holne Chase (Dart), Lizwell (Webburn) and, here, Scorhill (North Teign). The way below the gate is steep, and the DNPA have made a trackside drain to prevent its erosion by storm-water. Fingerposts now mark the way; this branches left from the woodland path into a steep, twisting path (unpleasant when wet) to reach the river – its sound rising constantly from below. A sturdily built clam spans the river in the gorge near Glassy Steps, but it is by no means certain that it stands over the site of the former steps, which disappeared before the span of living memory: they may have been at a fording place a short way upstream from the bridge, and the name 'Glassy Steps' is by common consent attached to the existing bridge site. A good path follows the left bank downstream from the bridge for a short way before ascending the north side. On the crest above, the path passes through a gate into an ancient lane, from where traffic may be seen crossing the Whiddon Down ridge, at 937 feet above sea level the highest point reached by the A30 road between London and Land's End. As the northbound mariner descended the lane, the huge dome of Cosdon rose above the trees to encourage him onward, for he had now accomplished the most demanding stretches of his journey and was approaching the threshold of north Devon. *Southward: in ascending lane to Princeps Folly Gate, Castle Drogo and Fingle Gorge hills appear left; notice immense slabs incorporated in wall of lane; beyond gate, enter second of three woodland paths. Large rock outcrops appear in woods, and on nearing valley floor the walker will see the river cascading around huge boulders.*

At the north foot of the lane from Princeps Folly Gate is the Gidleigh-Berrydown road, from where, through gaps in the hedge opposite, the houses and picturesque granite church (of the Holy Trinity) of Gidleigh are seen. Turn right at the road junction and left into the village. The old green, right, has long been enclosed; opposite this is the entrance to the remains of the Norman castle – really a fortified manor house built *c.*1300 – and on the left, the church gate. The praiseworthy care given to the churchyard is enhanced by tethered, grazing goats; the Gidleigh leat flows through it and is provided with a miniature clapper footbridge. Go there on a spring morning when primroses and daffodils reflect the warm April sunrays. Continue from the church past the manor pound (right) to a lane junction; directly opposite are a DNPA fingerpost and a gate opening upon the old church path from Moortown – on the route of Track 1. Field 1: follow the path on a slight ridge to the end of a partly dismantled hedge. Blackingstone Rock is now visible with the tops of Fingle Gorge; follow a wire fence, right, leading to the remaining portion of the hedge which is accompanied by the track to the next hedge ahead. Cosdon again looms ahead, and behind the walker are seen Gidleigh church tower and the signpost at the lane junction. Field 2: a small meadow; cross and enter gate into Field 3. In the left-hand corner the path is paved at a wicket gate. Enter a copse; bear left to a slotted gatepost, ford and clapper bridge on Moortown Brook. Cross; follow the track through a copse into the Moortown-Chapple lane. (When the author lived at Moortown Cot in the 1950s, he frequently followed this old path to church; there was then less decay, mud and dung!) Walk up Chapple Lane until the roofs of Moortown come into view. *Southward: 150 yards beyond Moortown Cross be certain to fork right into Chapple Lane and enter copse 200 yards further on.*

The place-name 'Chapple' springs from a ruin on the left bank of Moortown Brook near the clapper bridge, the former Chapel of La Wallen. Within its once hallowed walls murder was committed on 28 March 1328 by a 'Clerke in Holy Orders' named Robert de Middlecote, who 'maltreated a certain Agnes, daughter of Roger the Miller' and, in grave augmentation of his crime, also 'murdered the child of the Said Agnes': '*Quendam puerum vivum in corpore ejusdem*

Agnetis existentem interfecit' (Register of Bishop Grandisson of Exeter). Research into the history of this appalling act, and of the chapel itself, was carried out many years ago by the late Reverend J. Rawson, rector of Gidleigh in 1920, who wrote in his booklet, *Story of an Ancient Chapel*: 'The lonely spot by the Chapple (Moortown) Brook would be zealously avoided by all good Christians, as indeed it is by some Gidleigh folk today. Its evil repute has lived through the centuries, although the facts concerning the crime may not now be generally known.'

The ancient chapel and continuing route via a ford on Moortown Brook, and Gidleigh and Throwleigh, appear in *Donn*. From Chapple Lane, pass Moortown Farm, Cot and Gate and enter upon the open common. Cross the little Moortown leat and at once turn right at Donkeys Corner into a rough track. Pass a modern bungalow and an old house called 'Donkeys Corner'; a causeway carries the track for a short way above the prevailing mud but stops short of the sparkling little Forder Brook, and another sticky patch must be crossed before reaching a clapper footbridge and ford. Cross Ash Green diagonally to Ash Gate (cattle grid) and follow the road (a tarmac branch of the Gidleigh-Throwleigh road at Honeypool Corner) to Ash Farm. Turn left in the hamlet and pass through the lower farmyard into – (ungated) Field 1: follow the hedge, right, to a stile beside a slotted gatepost, to which formerly was hung a wicket gate; Field 2: follow the hedge, right (at right angles to the original route in mid-field because this is now cultivated); at the further corner (right) the path turns to follow a ditch and reach a renovated stile, where the original function of the slotted stile-posts has been restored by the insertion of horizontal timbers in the slots; Field 3: at the further side is another, similarly renovated stile; Field 4: as for Field 3; Field 5: as for Fields 3 and 4; the hedge is now on the left of the path, which has run from Ash across the arable plain at an even distance of about a mile from the edge of the moor, which rises in successive ridges in the west. Just as Track 1 from Gidleigh to Moortown follows a medieval church path, so does it here from Ash hamlet to Throwleigh – and, as will transpire, also beyond Throwleigh. Proof of its antiquity, if needed, lies in the succession of medieval slotted stile-posts along the route. Field 5 is bounded on its north side by Shilstone Lane, where are another stile and gateway, opposite the house named 'Little Close'. Here turn (right) down the lane until, opposite the foot of a branch lane from the right, a short flight of steps climbs the steep bank, left, from Shilstone Lane to reach a kissing-gate into Throwleigh churchyard. (The branch lane mentioned is Deave Lane, leading to Forder, which Crossing supposed the Mariners' Way to have followed – but it would have been a longer, less direct route to Moortown.)

Throwleigh church is simple, yet of great beauty. An exterior priest's door leads into the chancel beneath an arch bearing a carved, wavy stem sprouting pairs of triangular leaves. A fine fifteenth-century Easter sepulchre is built into the north wall, and the figures on the rood beam were carved in Oberammergau. Nearby is the fifteenth-century church house (now a dwelling), which must have provided comforts for many a thirsty, foot-sore mariner. In common with most church houses in the Dartmoor country, the house can be entered from the churchyard.

From the flight of steps in Shilstone Lane, the track traverses the churchyard to further steps descending to the south porch and passes around the tower to the north corner of the churchyard. Here a kissing-gate pivots within a curved wall-with-coping, the actual coping stones having been curved by the mason, such was the standard of workmanship in the 'Moorstone Age'. The way now crosses a large meadow known as 'the Balls', where it is marked by four ancient oak trees aligned in mid-field. It then passes between a clump of varied trees (left) and a small rockfield (right) before descending to a clapper bridge over South Moor Stream. The right bank approach is over an ancient stone causeway, for this is the old Clannaborough-Throwleigh church path which has been in use by the Endacott family since they arrived at the farm in 1858, to say nothing of the centuries of use it had received previously. Beyond the stream is a slotted-post stile; next cross a marshy bottom (there are traces of a causeway here in need of renewal) to a few rugged steps mounting to a kissing-gate. Follow the hedge, left, to another, similar stile, observing the fine old thatched longhouse of Clannaborough now in view. Mount the stile and continue alongside the left-hand hedge to a gateway (with one slotted post) opening onto the Throwleigh-South Zeal road.

The route of the Mariners' Way between Clannaborough and East Week is debatable. Emmie Varwell declares in her book that it enters the gate opposite the point now reached and follows the lower hedge of Clannaborough's 'Five-acre Field' which, she remarks rather vaguely, 'brings you to East Week'. Mr and Mrs Endacott declare this to be wrong because there is no sign of any path ever having passed through the further wall of the field, which is a very ancient enclosure.

According to the *OS 1904* 6-inch map, the path originally mounted to the farm and passed through the yard – a route, as the reader will by now realize, typical of the Mariners' Way – and continued as a field path to East Week Mill: this path is no longer traceable. It must be emphasized that neither of these routes is open to the public, and walkers may enter neither the Five-Acre gate nor the farmyard. The remaining alternative is the recognized DNPA-marked path; although an old footpath, I do not think this was a part of Mariners' Way, as it would have made too indirect a link between the path from South Moor Stream to East Week. The reader is warned, too, that in a wet season it is an agony to follow, threading as it does a very wide, waterlogged bottom. Those who succeed in following it will emerge triumphantly into Mill Lane, which joins the road to South Zeal in less than 100 yards, beside the rapid Blackaton Brook. This, fresh from the wild beauties of Blackaton Hole and Shilla Pool, flows through East Week to a picturesque confluence with the North Teign river above Leigh Bridge. From here, the old route of the mariners took them along the modern road into South Zeal, where refreshment and rest could be gained, by those able to afford it, in either of two hostelries – each probably older than the instigation of the track itself – the venerable 'King's Arms' and the early sixteenth-century 'Oxenham Arms'. I write 'instigation' because, of course, the Mariners' Way was never a through-track but a linking together of countless old field paths to form a satisfactory route, when first the need for one was felt. And who is to say when that was?

TRACK 2

NORTH-SOUTH TRACK
Harford Moorgate to Moorgate, Okehampton   27 miles

Route according to certain traditions known to William Crossing (1847-1928), and others received by the author from the moormen John Edmonds of South Brent, Jack Reddaway of Belston, Henry Cooper of Hartor Farm, Will Jordan of Moortown; and from the late moormen Newman Caunter of Dunnabridge, Richard Coaker of Runnage, Fernley Warne of Postbridge, John Spencer of Plymouth and Jan Waye, last warrener of Huntingdon.

An adequate topographical and historical treatment of this track – which, like the Mariners' Way, is a composite route rather than a unified track – demands a text of some length. Not only would a brief description be of little use to the walker, but in adverse weather conditions it could lead into trouble.

The need for a satisfactory route to link central Dartmoor with the border-country north and south of the great upland – as well as with Devon's North and South Hams – probably made itself felt among the Saxon moorland farmers over a thousand years ago. Increasing colonization of both the central basin and the peripheral dry heather moors, and granting of markets to rapidly growing border towns, finally brought the matter to a head, perhaps in the thirteenth century, when so many Dartmoor longhouses were built, clapper bridges erected, Ancient Tenements created, and such tracks as 2, 3, 4, 5 and 7 formed.

Natural barriers to travel north and south of the central basin are clearly shown by any good map; diversions to avoid the fen areas were costly in time, especially as animals needed for market had often to be gathered from valleys in the fen and withdrawn to points where bypass diversions could begin. The blanket bog – the fen, or 'vane' as the moormen pronounce it – forms a blanket only on hill crests and slopes, so that the valley floors offered access to the heart of each fen. This particular travel problem was solved by the removal of blanket peat lying between certain valley heads, so creating narrow, inter-valley corridors on the underlying granite, negotiable by riders and herds. It was an enterprising undertaking and resulted in the creation of two peat passes in particular which effectually opened up a north-south through-way, from Okehampton to Cornwood, Harford and South Brent. The passes, Black Lane (South) and Cut Lane, although now poorly maintained, are still usable. Other portions of the route, however, are in places obscured by subsequent peat growth and mire, the worst being a 2-mile stretch in the north Dartmoor valley of Amicombe Water – a circumstance aggravated by the abandonment of the route there, some eighty years ago, in favour of three peat passes cut in the early twentieth century by Frank Phillpotts of Okehampton to link Cut Lane with the military ring-road. The latter, built primarily for military vehicles, is based upon an ancient peat-cutters' road from Okehampton to the Hangingstone Hill peat beds, near which it is joined by Track 25. The walker who wishes to retrace as much as possible of the original route may, after using the Pinswell and Black Ridge Cuts, bypasses the bog-covered portion and proceeds to Broad Amicombe Hole, where he may regain and follow it without further deviation to Okehampton Moorgate.

The author recalls seeing herds of beasts driven through the peat passes and regrets that the increasing use of mechanized transport for animals since World War II has relegated such scenes to history. Finally it should be pointed out that the moormen's familiarity with available tracks made moorland travel, even in thick mist, a relatively straightforward business. Guide-stones were extremely rare on the moormen's routes whereas, on tracks used by travellers from distant localities – such as the monastic ways and the Chagford and Ashburton to Tavistock tracks – guide-stones were numerous and of a permanent nature.

Following the Track (northward)
The N-S Track is a trans-moorland trunk route; although composite rather than continuous, it may be walked or ridden as a through-route, to facilitate which this description has been written. The two most

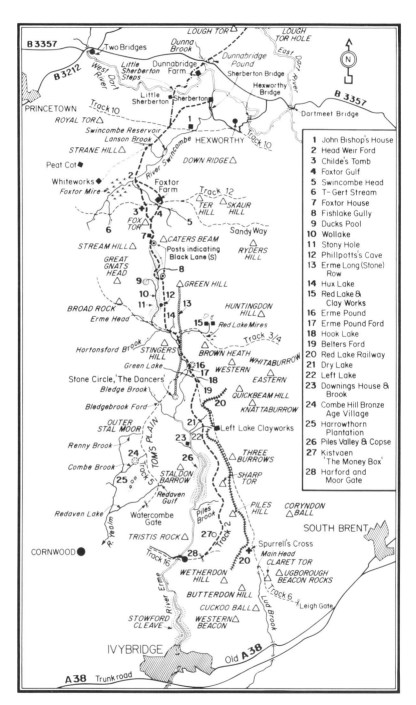

Track 2 – South

important approach- or link-tracks are listed here as 5 and 6.

Enter the Moor at Harford Moorgate (644595, also approached here from the east by Track 16). Follow the track (left) alongside the enclosure wall for 100 yards; bear right and climb the gentle slope ahead, really the foot of Piles Hill. When a false crest is reached (followed by a slight hollow) the hammer-head of Sharp Tor appears, opposed by the bulk of Staldon Barrow beyond the Erme valley, left. The outlines of Erme Plains and Quickbeam Hill also are seen, and as the hollow is crossed marks of tractor tyres and horses' hooves demonstrate a continuing use of the track. This mounts the higher slope of Piles Hill left of the crest; 200 yards below, west of the track, are visible the stones of a large kistvaen known as the 'Money Box', with a striking retaining circle. The gradient stiffens as the clearly marked track bears east to avoid the deep hollow of the Piles Brook valley; on the near, south side of this and again west of the track, is a ruined dolmen first recorded by the author and illustrated in *High Dartmoor*: one of the remaining uprights, now leaning, is 7 feet 6 inches long. Near the hill crest the walker will cross the track of a buried clay pipeline (and an inspection cover 10 yards to the left which serves as a useful checkpoint on position). Sharp Tor appears ahead backed by the huge Three Burrows as the crest of Piles Hill is reached. The track passes between two grass-grown cairns, and forks; take the left branch pointing towards Three Burrows, when the Red Lake Railway will be seen converging (right) towards it, backed by Wacka Tor.

Nearby is the Longstone, the fallen menhir terminating the Butterdon stone row which runs northward for $1\frac{1}{4}$ miles from Butterdon Hill. Its direction is continued by the Ugborough-Harford bond-stones, now close to the rail track. *Southward: beyond Sharp Tor is bend in railway and embanked straight. Track 2 (here beside stone row) forks beyond second of two pointed bond-stones. Two small cairns in sight ahead, with Wetherdon Hill and (two) cairns beyond. After pipeline, fork right towards west shoulder of Piles Hill. Beacon Rocks impressive from here and wonderful spread of in-country and estuaries of southern Dartmoor rivers.*

The row stone nearest the prominent cairn on Sharp Tor is marked with the initial letters of the commons it bounds (U and H). As the northward descent from this high col (Sharp Tor-Three Burrows) commences, the fine proportions of the moorland Erme and Yealm countries become apparent. Track 5 also is seen on the further valley-side running from Tom's Plain to Bledge Brook Ford. On the heathery ground of Erme Plains north of the col the descending track is noticeably stranded, the main strand accompanying the stone row; when some way below the railway it crosses the pipeline and a miry streamlet and runs towards a small rockfield. *Southward: fine view funnelled by hillsides of Piles Valley; prehistoric enclosures on huge concave slope below; Tristis Rock and South Hams beyond.* A village of small huts has been built on the edge of the rockfield; the track passes above it, avoiding both rocks and steep of the hill. *Southward: make for high col right of small cairn; cross clay-pipeline and join stone row en route.*

Beyond the hut circles the track remains on an even contour until reaching another hut village opposite the Erme (SWWA) water-intake, where it bears slightly uphill to reach Left Lake Ford, at the head of a picturesque hole and waterfall. A boggy patch, inconvenient to the walker, covers the right bank at the ford; therefore cross upstream. Regain the path beyond the boggy patch and make for Dry Lake Ford, which has been roughly paved and is similarly at the head of a hole. *Southward: river and track roughly parallel, latter maintaining easy level. When beyond view of Dancers' Circle (on Bledge Brook Hill beyond river) make for wide gap in prehistoric reave pointing towards river. Continue towards head of Sharp Tor; path then veers slightly left and heads for high col. Reach Dry Lake Ford by making for lower edge of mire below Left Lake – just below old clayworks.*

North of Dry Lake the track is multi-stranded and by no means easy to follow; it can be regained, however, by observing the features given here. From Dry Lake Ford, pass beside a large, green, mossy feather-bed above more prehistoric enclosures situated between large patches of rushes. An old, small mound-like clay-tip appears higher on the hill, right; by remaining on the 1,200-foot contour the walker will reach Stony Bottom, where the track crosses Hook Lake at Belters Ford, for the river and its country are, of course, constantly declining towards him. The tract ahead is vast and featureless, so that following the contour becomes the best guide among the stranded tracks. Ahead are seen two large enclosures on Brown Heath and the distant outline of Erme Pound; west of the river are the standing stones of the Dancers' Circle. The stranded way is soon joined by a more clearly defined track from the locality of the clay-mound above; this is the Blackwood Path (Track 6), well defined by reason of its once heavy peat traffic. Its passage to Belters Ford is clear, and on the right bank (of Hook Lake) the united tracks bear left and bisect the lower of the two Brown Heath enclosures seen from Erme Plains; above it, a Bronze Age stone row descends towards the higher enclosure, while the track, emerging from the lower, passes along the edge (of the higher) and shortly reaches Erme Pound.

The enclosures now passed were used by a large prehistoric community in this part of the Erme valley, as were Erme Pound and the nearby Erme Pound Rings. Plainly this locality, so attractive to today's moorland walkers by virtue of its loneliness, was in the Bronze Age a lively, almost crowded neighbourhood. From the Middle Ages, too, almost until the present day, the movement of moormen and herds of beasts along the N-S route to and from the ancient Erme Drift Pound (Pl. 3), has kept the curtain raised on this stage of traditional Dartmoor activities until its final fall in the mid-twentieth century. *Southward: in passing from Erme Pound to Belters Ford make for wide green tract on Erme Plains lying between noticeably brown upper and lower slopes of plain. Clay-mound seen high above (left); upper portions of enclosure-reaves on plain will provide sighting to guide walker after forking right from Blackwood Path into stranded way.*

From Erme Pound, Track 5 is seen descending the west river bank (opposite the upstream side of the pound) to join Track 2, which now lies beside Erme's smooth, glossy meanders – so typical of the upper reach of a Dartmoor river. Few rocks are seen on the marshy valley floor, and the remote hills close in to funnel the walker's entry into the heart of southern Dartmoor, such as epitomizes this track – one of the loneliest in all England. The north-west spur of Redlake Hill soon rises above, right, and the huge rocks and pits at Erme Head afterwards come into view (Pl. 11), the work of generations of tinners until at least the late seventeenth century. The foot of Redlake Hill is a suitable place to pause and survey the notable Erme long row; an early Bronze Age monument, it extends from the Dancers' Circle on Bledgebrook Hill to a burial cairn on Green Hill, this distance of $2\frac{1}{4}$ miles distinguishing the row as the longest of its type in the world. It 'fords' the river at Erme Pound Ford and is accompanied by the N-S track as it clings to the valley floor north of the pound. Both lines cross Red Lake at Lower Ford – the stone row mounting the spur of Redlake Hill in direct line to the ford – from which it ascends the south slope of Green Hill; the track meanwhile, here perhaps as ancient as the monument, bears left from the ford to reach the next on Hux Lake. A short way above row and track, and south of Redlake Ford, is a well-preserved kistvaen, its coverstone still partly in position and enclosed by the remains of a retaining circle. Here comes a good view of the fenlands ahead, of Erme Pits and Erme Head lying left of the Wollake valley, and the sinuous line of the Erme long row mounting Green Hill, right. The line of the N-S track is clearly seen at the foot of Green Hill, also beyond Hux Lake continuing towards the Wollake valley.

Along the right bank of Red Lake runs Track 3, fresh from its tortuous crossing of Red Lake Mires; combining with Track 2 at Hux Lake Ford, it can be seen on the valley floor approaching Wollake Ford and beyond. West of Hux Lake Ford, Track 2 bears right to follow higher ground (about 100 yards from the lower track); when equidistant from the two tributary valleys it curves away to the north, the path from which it branches descending to Wollake Ford to join the main valley track. Deep clefts seen in the hillside south of the river are, westward from Redlake Ford, Knocking Mill Combe and Horton's Combe. In curving away northward, Track 2 is stranded, but it becomes unified as it crosses the tinners' gerts mentioned below.

Wollake, Erme's first tributary, approaches its foot through a small, tin-streamed gorge known as Stony Hole. Track 2 necessarily avoids this by remaining well above the valley floor. The northbound walker will observe a wall high on the further Wollake valley-side; as he continues to ascend, this proves to be the upper wall of a small enclosure, an appendage to a small blowing house on the stream's right bank; the line of its leat channel is discernible from the track. The curve of the track continues towards some large rocks higher on the hillside; make for these until level with the head of several deep gerts coming up from the valley floor, left; the track, now well defined, re-aligns northward well below the hillside rocks to pass above the head of the gerts and make directly for an immense slab on the valley-side ahead. This is Phillpotts's Cave, a partly artificial cavern associated with Dartmoor novelist Eden Phillpotts. Below it, in the valley, is a remarkable series of parallel medieval mining burrows (spoilheaps) with carefully walled-up sides to prevent collapse, completely covering the peninsula formed by Wollake and its incoming tributary, Duckspool Stream. Below the track is the tinners' shelter known as Duckspool House, and in the near distance is seen the post marking the south end of Black Lane (South), the peat pass that formed so vital a part of the old N-S route.

Ducks Pool is an extensive swamp west of the Wollake valley; possibly once a moorland tarn drained by the tinners, it gives rise to the stream mentioned above. At its head is an explorer's 'postbox' and a memorial tablet to William Crossing, author of *Guide to Dartmoor* and many other books during the years before and immediately after World War I.

Track 2, nearing the valley floor, reaches the Black Lane (south) post where Fishlake Gully enter the Wollake valley; it indicates the crossing place (Black Lane Ford) to the west bank of Wollake to avoid Black Lane Mire. *Southward from the post: ignore paths dropping to valley floor; maintain height by making for slab of Phillpotts's Cave.* The peat pass now begins (Pl. 4). Culverts placed here and there over boggy streamlets become clogged by storm-water and peat silt and are now rarely cleaned out as they once were for the Hunt by John Spencer of Plymouth and Jack Worth, who lodged in Phillpotts's Cave while carrying out the work. The view from the scene of their labours consists of peat, peat and yet more peat, with a distant southward prospect through the funnel of Black Lane towards Three Burrows, Sharp Tor and Butterdon Hill. In a short way the path – here it can scarcely be called a track – recrosses Wollake and runs up the east bank between peat banks of considerable height. There is every reason to believe that the east side was dug away many centuries ago, for it must have been apparent to the moormen even of far-off Saxon times that this simple operation would link the adjoining (natural) passes of Wollake and Foxtor Gulf, so creating a through route from southern border-country to central basin.

At the head of the pass stands another post, marking the opening of Black Lane into Foxtor Gert. On approaching it, distant heights break upon the horizon: first are the domes of Cut and Whitehorse Hills in the northern fen; then, in the nearer, lower distance, the white splash of Parson's Cottage beside Track 8 and the humble pile of Crockern Tor central below the long cleft of the West Dart valley. From the post, the moorland vista is immense, its width extending from Cocks Tor to Bush Down and its depth to Great Links Tor, 14 direct miles away.

In the foreground beyond the post, the green trough of the Gert declines towards the rocks of Fox Tor, the path being a matter of choice on either side of the valley. On the west side, however, is a fine tinners' house known as Foxtor House, and on moving down the valley the walker will see the burrows, pits and mounds excavated by those men whose working week was spent at Foxtor House (and Duckspool House) before Elizabeth I ascended the throne. A good crossing place beside the house has long been used by moormen making for Nuns Cross Farm and Princetown. Cross to the east side and descend to the bottleneck below Foxtor Head (left) where a treacherous mire lies directly below the bluff rising to Fox Tor. The mire provides the mainspring of Foxtor Stream, which courses (east of the tor) through the deep Gulf to reach the Swincombe river.

A well-marked track fords the stream and continues past the east side of the tor; notice a fallen summit rock with twin hollows resembling eye sockets in a mammoth's skull. The continuing track from the tor descends to a hunting gate in the long wall of Foxtor Newtake. The plain lying ahead is Sand Parks, the stone structure upon it, Childe's Tomb, and the ruined buildings, right, are those of the lonely Foxtor Farm. Childe's Tomb marks the site of the death in a blizzard of fourteenth-century landowner Amyas Childe of Plymstock, and the cross surmounting it (a modern replacement of a vandalized medieval one) is one of the series of granite crosses marking the monastic route of Track 12. The next important point is Headweir Ford (Pl. 5) (sometimes called Strane or Stream Hill Ford), with two good approaches from Foxtor Head: 1, bear right from Childe's Tomb and follow Track 12 (see p. 151) to Foxtor Farm Ford on Swincombe; near the old farm leave Track 12 (here a series of grassy strands) and walk (left) round the east side of the ruin, continuing along the farm track which rounds a miry bottom, left, and runs past a pointed triangular boulder to reach the river again at Headweir Ford; 2, descend to Swincombe by following the east side of Foxtor Gulf, fording the river near the newtake corner and making for the ruined farm. Another route, more direct, is now lost on the swampy left bank plain below the farm; it was probably abandoned to encroaching mire early in the nineteenth century when Foxtor Farm was built and became a welcome staging point on the N-S route; it provided, after all, the herdsman's first sight of a roof and chimney since leaving Harford village.

At Headweir Ford the river is twice as large as at the fords upstream; it is fed within a single mile by no less than four tributaries, Foxtor Stream, Whealam Stream, Nuns Cross Brook and the Strane river, to say nothing of the water percolating through Foxtor Mire. *Southward from Headweir Ford; when path forks, go right; when it becomes stranded, Foxtor Farm comes in sight ahead. Path remains clear rounding miry bottom (right) and making for upper side of reave-enclosure, passing pointed boulder.* Beside the ford are the ruined weir and sluices of the (disused) Wheal Emma leat: Strane Hill rises above the river's left bank, with a hunting gate in the (Tor Royal) newtake wall; the buildings of the old mining settlement of Whiteworks appear left, while right, the river passes over the rapids known as 'the Boiler' and near the further bank are two ruined mining buildings, both tinners' mills, of late medieval period. Cross the river – it is sometimes necessary to wade – and enter the hunting gate. The track mounts Strane Hill diagonally (right) to be joined at a wide gateway by the Whiteworks-Sherberton track. (The river provides a beautiful scene from here, whilst southward are Childe's Tomb, Fox Tor, Foxtor Mire, the skyline chink of Black Lane and the crumbled Foxtor Farm, all overlooked by Swincombe Head, Caters Beam and the ridge of the southern fen.) Ahead is seen Dunnabridge Higher Plantation, its trees aligned with the track as it descends to a ford (on a feeder of Lanson Brook). This is followed by a ford on the main Lanson Brook, from where it climbs to a dip in a small ridge and points towards the Bellever Tor-Lough Tor col. From the dip observe the attractive little mirror of the Swincombe reservoir, and beyond it the dark cleft of Deep Swincombe. In the near distance, within Joan Ford's Newtake (right), are the remains of a Bronze Age retaining circle, while the track runs beside those of a kistvaen with cairn (left). A wall appears ahead, but its gateway its momentarily hidden by a slight rise, until on passing a large bedrock (left) the track heads towards it. The heights of West Dart country now crenellate the horizon – Longaford and Higher Whiten Tors, Rowter Rocks, Rowter, Rough Tor (three distinct points) and Wildbanks Hill.

Beyond the (iron) gate, bear slightly right; the track, now stranded, makes for another dip aligned with Corndon Tor, with Hameldon and the crinkled Honeybag Tor dominating the view; from the dip a branch path runs (right) to Swincombe Farm; ignore this and walk due north to a guide-stone marking the intersection of the way by Track 10. *Southward from dip: track seen clearly defined beyond iron gate.* Walk towards Lough Tor (directly above the conspicuous circle of Dunnabridge Pound); the walker is now approaching the central basin floor. Next, cross the well-defined Sherberton-Prince Hall track and look over a transverse wall. This newtake must not be entered, but before the land was enclosed the old way descended the hill, passed the entrance (left) to Little Sherberton and reached a ford and steps on the West Dart River – Little Sherberton Steps. From the left bank the track made a gradual ascent of the steep valley-side and followed an ancient wall to a gated lane. The lane leads to Dunnabridge Farm, in the heart of Dartmoor's Ancient Tenement land, and continues from it to cross the B3357 (Tavistock-Ashburton) road beside Dunnabridge Pound. All this can be viewed from the Sherberton newtake wall, and the reader must next follow a long diversion. Return to the Sherberton track (just crossed), walk to Sherberton and cross the farm court to the lower gate; descend to Sherberton Bridge over Swincombe. A car is now helpful, as the ancient route can be picked up only by travelling via Hexworthy and Huccaby to Dunnabridge, where a car can be parked near the great pound. The track comes up from Dunnabridge; crossing Dunna Brook, it passes by Dunnabridge Pound Farm, traditional home of the pound-keeper. *View of original route southward from B3357: lane to Dunnabridge Farm and beyond; path alongside field wall; oblique descent of rough valley-side; steps and ford; trees surrounding Little Sherberton above right bank; transverse wall of Sherberton Great Newtake above.* The great, thick-walled enclosure has a long history as a pound for beasts found illegally depastured on the Forest of Dartmoor. The care with which the pound-keepers' accounts have been kept, particularly during the seventeenth and eighteenth centuries, reveals the traditional ways of the moormen and their riding skills and ability to stay in the saddle for many hours at a time.[*] Passing between pound and pound-keeper's house, the track reaches a newtake wall near the pound's upper side and continues as a metalled road (tarmac beyond Bellever) to Postbridge. Ascending, it passes through another gateway on the crest of Loughtor Heath. Then follows an open gateway, where the old Brimpts Mine workings are seen on the right – these including a dangerous, open shaft. The valley below (right) is that of Cox Lake; fine tors rise beyond – Corndon, Yar and Sharp – and the stones of a double row and menhir (the 'Loughtor Man') on Loughtor (OS 'Laughter') Heath are visible, left. Both Bellever and Lough Tors are now near, and Hameldon, Chinkwell, Hey, Holwell and Rippen Tors form the distant horizon above the green fields of ancient Sherwell (right). As the track descends northward from Loughtor Heath, the fields of the ancient tenement of Babeny are seen, and Loughtor Gate appears ahead:

---

[*] See *High Dartmoor*.

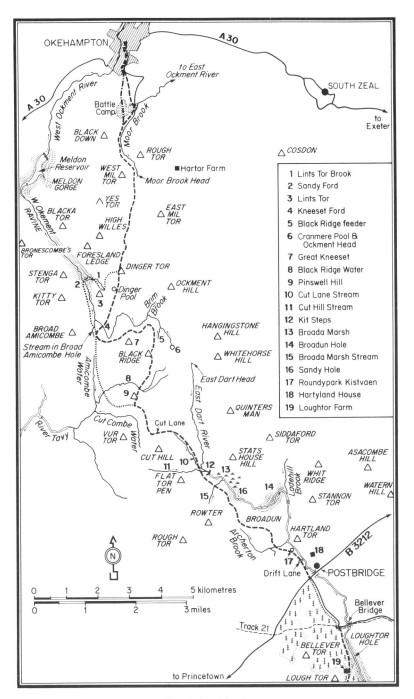

Legend:

1. Lints Tor Brook
2. Sandy Ford
3. Lints Tor
4. Kneeset Ford
5. Black Ridge feeder
6. Cranmere Pool & Ockment Head
7. Great Kneeset
8. Black Ridge Water
9. Pinswell Hill
10. Cut Lane Stream
11. Cut Hill Stream
12. Kit Steps
13. Broada Marsh
14. Broadun Hole
15. Broada Marsh Stream
16. Sandy Hole
17. Roundypark Kistvaen
18. Hartyland House
19. Loughtor Farm

Track 2 – North

Bellever Gate is a mile further through the plantation.

A short way beyond Loughtor Gate the track forks; take the right fork descending the hill past Loughtor Hole* Farm, pass through a gate and follow the track through open farm fields to a third gate, labelled 'FORESTRY COMMISSION', after which the trees again close in. The track finally emerges from the plantations near Bellever Bridge, where it intersects the Lych Way (Track 21); crossing Bellever Green as a footpath east of Bellever Youth Hostel, it continues as a narrow motor road to intersect the B3212 (Tavistock-Moretonhampstead) road at Postbridge. Hotel, guest-houses, post office and capacious public car-park make Postbridge an ideal stage for the walker on Track 2. The magnificent clapper bridge stands on the Trans-Dartmoor Track (8), the modern road largely following its line.

The walker setting out northward from here will encounter the next public road nine direct miles away at Okehampton Moorgate and will certainly walk a greater distance to reach it. The wide, grassy way opposite the foot of the Bellever road is the historic continuation of Track 2; aptly named 'Drift Lane', it was in times past a droveway formed specifically for driving herds of beasts to graze on the north moor during the summer months. DNPA have laid down a short but convenient causeway where the ground is soft, and have built a tiny footbridge over Gawle Lake. At the north end of Drift Lane, pass through the gateway and follow the stony track ahead, noticing Hartyland House (the former Ancient Tenement of Hartland) nearby. From the ascending track, known as the 'Turf Road' from the quantities of peat once carried over it by packhorses, the view opens to include Rowter Rocks (left), Broadun (ahead) with hut circles and enclosures, Siddaford Tor (distant) and Hartland Tor (above Hartyland House) backed by Asacombe and Meripit Hills. The tree belt running westward from Drift Lane Gate is known as 'Archerton Trees'; from here, the direct alignment of Drift Lane and the Bellever road is at once obvious.

Passing an iron gate in an enclosure wall, the track crests the plain ahead and affords a view of the large Roundypark kistvaen, right; this fine grave of the early Bronze Age was undoubtedly that of a person of consequence belonging to the Broadun community. Here also is seen Archerton Brook flowing at the south foot of Broadun to join

* Land Tax List 1798, 'Lofter Hole'; Tithes Apportionment 1839, 'Loughter Hole'.

East Dart under Hartland Tor. The track soon reaches a stony, picturesque ford on the brook and bears a little right to follow the wall on the Broadun slope. Walk for a short way beside the wall, then follow a reave northward alongside the sunken Turf Road; (ignore the wall-side track ascending to the crest of Broadun, right). Track 2, still for some way united with the Turf Road, ascends to a gate in Broadun Newtake wall; the country ahead now becomes wilder, and the gentle hills and woods of the central basin drop behind. Pass through the gateway; the track is sunken for a short way; here comes again that sense of remoteness experienced in crossing the Sharp Tor-Three Burrows col: ahead now is a magnificent nothingness that is somehow unique to this great English moorland. The track deftly steers one between tracts of mire on this high saddle – Rowter, marked by a grassy knoll is left, and Broadun, right – and runs directly ahead to the rugged opening of Sandy Hole. Here, East Dart rushes through a channel artificially deepened by medieval tinners for the purposes of carrying away the waste material from their workings in Broada Marsh, the dire consequences that followed included the silting-up of Dartmouth Harbour and the wrongful arrest and imprisonment in Lydford Castle of Richard Strode, MP for Plympton. The track meanwhile, maintains a high level above the river valley and rounds the head of a rush-filled gully, from where are seen river pools and meanders below. As the Hole is approached – its mouth is known as 'the Oak and the Ash' – the channel of the old Birch Tor & Vitifer Mine leat is visible on the further valley-side, whilst ahead the lonely heights of the northern fen rise to an apex at Cut and Whitehorse Hills, each only a few feet below 2,000, bordered by Quinters Man and Stats House Hill away to the right. *Southward: from brink of Sandy Hole maintain even level towards skyline below knoll of Rowter, leaving Broadun distant, left. When path ill-defined, ignore others dropping to valley; beyond knoll, path reappears well before Broadun Newtake gate. High points in central basin visible with Bellever Tor predominant. On clear day, dark mass of Fox Tor and skyline chink of Black Lane visible.*

A slight ridge rises west of the Oak and the Ash, where the well-defined, ascending track crosses the undulations on the west side of Broada Marsh. Pointing directly towards Kit Steps and the valley of Cut Lane Stream, Track 2 brings the walker to the threshold of a wild splendour. The huge basin of Broada Marsh lies spread before him, its palette of colours changing with the seasons; the fen shows a

well-defined edge under Stats House Hill in the east – below the
boat-shaped 'house' of Stat the peat-cutter on the horizon; the line of
Stats House Cut, more causeway than peat pass, ascends from the
valley in line with Flat Tor Pen; the track fords Broada Marsh Stream
and heads for the fords on Cut Hill Stream and Cut Lane Stream,
while the great domed hill of Cut overlooks the scene with magisterial
aloofness. The track intersects another, once much used, between
West Dart Head and Kit Steps; this necessitated the cutting of a
shallow peat pass known as 'Johnson's Cut', which enters the valley of
Broada Marsh Stream through Cowflop Bottom and follows the north
bank. Near the confluence of this stream with East Dart is a tinners'
cache, whilst on the further valley-side, dwarfed by the giants ahead,
rises the lowly ridge of Flat Tor Pen; even so, its height exceeds that of
the celebrated Hey Tor by 300 feet!

The 'steps' at Kit Steps are boulders close-set in the river beside a
well-used ford, providing a crossing place to link the path from Stats
House Cut with Track 2 and Johnson's Cut. A path on a firm, grassy
hard links Kit Steps with the track at Cut Hill Stream Ford; Track 2
does not actually run to the river bank but maintains a higher level to
reach Cut Hill Stream at a bend, which it fords beside a large tinners'
mound on the left bank. The ford is a short way below the
twentieth-century peat pass leading to the summit of Cut Hill, the
'Northwest Passage'. This is explorers country, remote and
untameable, its topography impossible to visualize from the most
realistic map-reading. The track is well marked to the next ford, 250
yards on, at Cut Lane Stream; near it, right, is a tinners' house of four
or five centuries ago. Follow the gravelly path up the valley along the
grassy right bank, the jagged fen close on each side, to the valley
head; here it bends left to enter the fen at the east end of Cut Lane,
perhaps Dartmoor's oldest peat pass – certainly as old as Black Lane
(South). It is likely that more of such 'cuts', as they are known, were
made in medieval times than is generally realized, but those
concerning this chapter are Black Lane (South), Cut Lane and the
modern Pinswell Cut, Black Ridge Cut and Huggaton Cut. There is a
fine easterly view from the pass over the East Dart valley to Quinters
Man, Kit Hill, Kit Rocks, Stats House Hill, Siddaford* Tor and
distant Hameldon. Ahead, the pass crests the north slope of Cut Hill
and affords a memorable vista; it remains always in my mind together

* Correct spelling; used by *Greenwood, OS 1809*, and William Crossing.

with other superlative views from the summits of Snowdon, Scafell and the Worcestershire Beacon: in the west is Tavy country, where Vur Tor, less than a mile away, is the sovereign height, and in the north are the tops of Ockment country – the highest land in southern England. Broad Amicombe rises above the Hole bearing its name, and Dinger Tor marks the position of Track 2 on the plain rising beyond to Foresland Ledge and High Willes. Far away, through the funnel of the West Ockment ravine, are the sunny fields and woods of North Devon, glimpsed also between the Belstone range and the dominant mound of Cosdon. Cut Lane, still defined and usable (Pl. 6), crosses the watershed and enters Tavy country between two set slabs at its western end, from where its descent of Cut Hill's north-west slope is marked by small granite posts. *Southward from Rush Bottom: locate posts and set slabs; it is otherwise difficult to find Cut Lane.*

Descend to Rush Bottom, watered by a stream joining Cut Combe Water. Follow the right bank of the latter until stranded paths bear right to mount Pinswell Hill towards a small granite post. The original N-S route continued along the foot of the hill, followed the 1,500-foot contour to a ford on Black Ridge Water, then clung to the left bank of Amicombe Water to reach Broad Amicombe Hole. This stretch of the route is mentioned on p. 41 as being submerged by mire, untraceable and impassable, even as it was in William Crossing's day. Therefore use the two peat passes, Pinswell and Black Ridge Cuts, which will guide you to the north spur of Black Ridge, from where good ground reaches westward to the original route, there descending northward from Broad Amicombe Hole. 'Pinswell' is the Dartmoor name for 'Little Kneeset'. The south opening to the pass is marked by the small granite post mentioned; this bears a small plaque commemorating the enterprise of Frank Phillpotts of Okehampton in cutting the modern passes in the heart of the northern fen, an area as large as Torbay.

Follow the pass; observe marker stones placed on peat hags and banks; they serve as helpful guides in this moonscape of fissures and gullies, so please replace fallen ones. From Pinswell Cut descend to a well-defined ford on Black Ridge Water and locate the Phillpotts post at the entrance to Black Ridge Cut; it can be elusive. Stranded paths ascend towards it, and a clear path leads to a small cairn and set stones at the opening of this longest of all peat passes. Follow the pass to the summit of Black Hill; climb onto the left bank of the pass and observe treacherous pools of black peat-sludge in the bog. There is a splendid view from here, too, of the West Ockment ravine and the 'roof of Devon' at High Willes. The north end of the pass guides the walker into the desolate valley of a nameless feeder of West Ockment. On reaching the north (Phillpotts) post he faces the Hangingstone-Whitehorse ridge and must turn left to follow the upper edge of the valley. Continue northward for a quarter of a mile, noticing the confluence (below, right) of the feeder stream with the infant West Ockment river. (It should here be mentioned that the much sought-after postbox at Cranmere Pool is at the head of West Ockment, less than a mile upstream from the confluence and easily reached.) *Southward: passing confluence, keep well above stream and near edge of fen until two large boulders appear in stream-bed below head-mire; several gullies open from fen into valley, longest being marked by post; turn uphill and enter Black Ridge Cut.*

Reaching good ground on the Black Ridge spur, follow the contour westward; the route is serpentine, the walking easy and the prospect of the West Ockment ravine very fine. From the head of Jackman's Bottom climb to Great Kneeset, where the small tor gives excellent views from its elevation of 1,864 feet. From here cross the crest of Kneeset Foot, well up from the river, in a north-west direction to reach the head of Broad Amicombe Hole. Here are traces of the throughway of the old N-S route; this crossed Broad Amicombe Stream, ran down the left bank and continued beside the river .to Sandy Ford. Although this ancient portion between Pinswell and West Ockment country has for long been virtually impassable, Broad Amicombe Hole is of interest as a natural pass where the walker will be in touch with a moormen's travel route perhaps over a thousand years old. From here, he can look across the river upon an English moorland scene unique in its wild grandeur. *Southward: summit of Great Kneeset easily attained from Broad Amicombe Hole. Cross spurs eastward; turn south with river to follow path to Black Ridge Cut. NOTE: to stumble across fen in direct line from Great Kneeset to Black Ridge may prove physically challenging but has little to do with retracing ancient travel routes!*

From Broad Amicombe Hole the walker has a choice: 1, ancient way via Sandy Ford; now impassable due to river erosion of long lengths of old left-bank path, it can be 'shadowed' from sheep paths above; notice two tinners' houses near the opposite, right bank. The bond-stone at Sandy Ford marks the meeting of Forest and Commons, where the river is inconveniently wide for crossing on foot; the way then leads over a plain along the right bank of the approaching Lintstor Brook to another ford. Cross; mount to the east side of Lints Tor from where Dinger Tor is seen atop the ridge, left. Cross the hollow at the head of this little valley and follow the well-defined path ascending to Dinger Tor; characteristically, it remains below the edge of the fen. 2, a more direct and better defined route (one not mentioned by Crossing) passes down the *right* bank of Broad Amicombe Stream to a ford on the river (situated a mile upstream from Sandy Ford). Cross; mount the hillside ahead. Dinger Tor will shortly come in sight; the track makes directly towards it and in under a mile from the ford reached Dinger Pool. From here can be seen, south of the river, the good ground below the edge of the fen on the Kneeset spurs, which allows walkers and riders to pass easily above the head of each re-entrant. Also noticeable is the well-defined path mounting Broad Amicombe Hole, which is likely to have been in use long before the abandonment of the Amicombe valley route; not only was it an excellent substitute for the eroded track on the river's left bank (which would ultimately have become an impracticable route for large herds of beasts) but it would provide the best access from the Okehampton area to Broad Amicombe Hill and Kitty Tor – a route still in use by moormen today.

On the plain lies Dinger Pool, a pleasant little oasis in the wilderness. Here on a recent spring day, I put up several red grouse: two were fledglings, and on going to their point of flight I discovered the nest, where tiny feathers showed that the birds had been preening. The clear path passes from the pool to Dinger Tor near a yellow military range sign; southward, it points directly towards its visible continuation in Broad Amicombe Hole, and northward, it becomes stranded on approaching Dinger Tor, where it passes a guide-stone in the form of a large set slab, now leaning out of vertical. Here it is joined (left) by the older route (1) from Sandy Ford and Lintstor Hollow. Further up the hill is another leaning slab, also, I imagine, a guide-stone. Beyond the small, shining mirror of Dinger Pool the track is well defined on nearing the tor, where it merges with the metalled military road. The small, cohesive rockpile of Dinger Tor stands over 1,800 feet above sea level and affords fine views; those of Dartmoor's northern wilderness are magnificent, the proportions of which may be judged from the fact that Lints Tor, sheltering deep in the West Ockment ravine, is some 40 feet higher than the bold Rippen Tor, loftiest of the Hey Tor group. *Southward from Dinger Tor: track first points towards Vur Tor then veers towards Dinger Pool; passes the two guide-stones. Points seen include Cut Hill, Vur Tor and, in near distance beyond Great Kneeset, Walkham Head, Great Mis Tor, Lynch Tor. Hangingstone and Whitehorse Hills rise south-east and Amicombe forms western skyline marked only by Stenga and Kitty Tors. Big country; prospect of vast and virtually trackless fen spreading southward perhaps frightening to inexperienced walkers. If mist is dropping over fen, do not attempt walk southward.*

The rough road (now the original N-S Track) passes over Dinger Plain between the 2,000-foot High Willes-Yes Tor ridge, left, and the great frontier hill of Cosdon, right, the two massifs framing a view into an infinite distance enveloping north Devon and Exmoor. A large bond-stone near the track, left, bears the initial letters of Okehampton and Belstone parishes, here the meeting point of the parish commons with the Forest of Dartmoor. The first dwelling sighted since leaving Postbridge now appears on the right, protected by its coniferous windbreak; this is the lonely Hartor Farm, scene of Eden Phillpotts's powerful novel *The Secret Woman* and today the holding of moorman Henry Cooper. The track now begins an almost uninterrupted descent of 1,400 feet to Moorgate and Okehampton, commencing with the steep initial gradient to Moor Brook Head. This stream passes from its source-mire across a ford into the brief gorge of Creaber's Hole; so heavily cluttered is the slope of the huge West Mil* Tor (left) that boulders have reached to the floor of the Hole; $1\frac{1}{4}$ miles below, Okehampton Battle Camp is spread hideously along the Moor's north escarpment.

Curving with the brook as Black Down rises ahead, and near its left bank, the ancient way reaches Moorgate twenty-six miles from Harford Gate, providing perhaps one of the most challenging moorland walks in England today (Pl. 7). Evidence exists, including *OS 1809*, to show that the track originally crossed the site of the present military compound and descended past the fringe of the Saxon village in Okehampton Park, via Saxon Gate and Park Road into the town. Below it, until its demolition in 1539, rose the massive keep and masonry of Baldwin de Brionne's great castle of the late 1070s. Henry Courtenay, Marquis of Exeter, was the last occupant of Okehampton Castle until his execution for treason in 1539 and the forfeiture of all his lands to the Crown. The Courtenays had held Okehampton Park as

---

* Correct spelling, always used by Crossing. OS give 'Mill' Tor. 'Mil' is a diminutive of 'Middle' – meaning the centre tor of group of three.

a hunting chase since *c.*1300, so that the earliest route of Track 2, leaving the wild spaces above, plunged into the realms of Saxon and Norman history to reach the ancient borough where, at the time of the compilation of the Devon Domesday, four burgesses and a market already flourished. Dr Susan Pearce of the Royal Albert Museum in Exeter, has suggested that the medieval farmers of Okehampton Park were evicted when the Courtenays adopted it as a deer preserve; this certainly leads one to infer that Track 2 was then diverted from its ancient route to follow that of the modern road past Fice's Well under East Hill, and so into the town. The subsequent growth of Okehampton's trade and military significance must have added greatly to the traffic of the moormen and their herds on Dartmoor's remarkable N-S Track.

TRACK 3

JOBBERS' ROAD or CAWSE
Sheepstor – Buckfastleigh   12 miles

Route according to a map of the Napoleonic period and actually marked 'Old Jobbers' Road from Sheepstor to Buckfastleigh'; also a plan of Huntingdon Warren dated 1809 (see Fig. 2). Route used regularly during the early present century by Jan Waye, last warrener of Huntingdon. It was his custom to call on Percy and Elizabeth Ware at Ditsworthy Warren, who told the author.

In the *Wollen Industry of South West England*, K. Ponting points out that the areas of Buckfastleigh, Ashburton, Totnes and Tavistock – all in the Dartmoor country – were of prime importance, and the years from 1350 to 1500 represent a peak period for rural industry. It was during this period (see *Historic Dart*) that the thriving cottage woollen industry of Buckfastleigh kept intact the now vanished hillside cluster of medieval houses in the 'leigh' of Buckfast below the church of the Holy Trinity. During the sixteenth century came a profitable expansion of the trade in undyed woollen cloths when more than seven mills were working in Buckfastleigh, while the great demand for worsteds during the two following centuries, which could be met only by water-powered mills, finally brought about the desertion of the old village in favour of the plain below, where the Rivers Dart, Mardle and Holy Brook sufficed to meet all demands. Ashburton, too, had seven working mills in 1605.

It may be judged from this that the trans-moorland route of the wool jobbers was contemporaneous with the formation of many other tracks of commerce over the Moor – most of them probably not later than the thirteenth century, perhaps much earlier. The travelling wool jobbers would long have continued to use the track for their fleece- and yarn-collecting and cloth-delivery journeys; local men, they knew every foot of their road, hard and well worn as it was during its peak

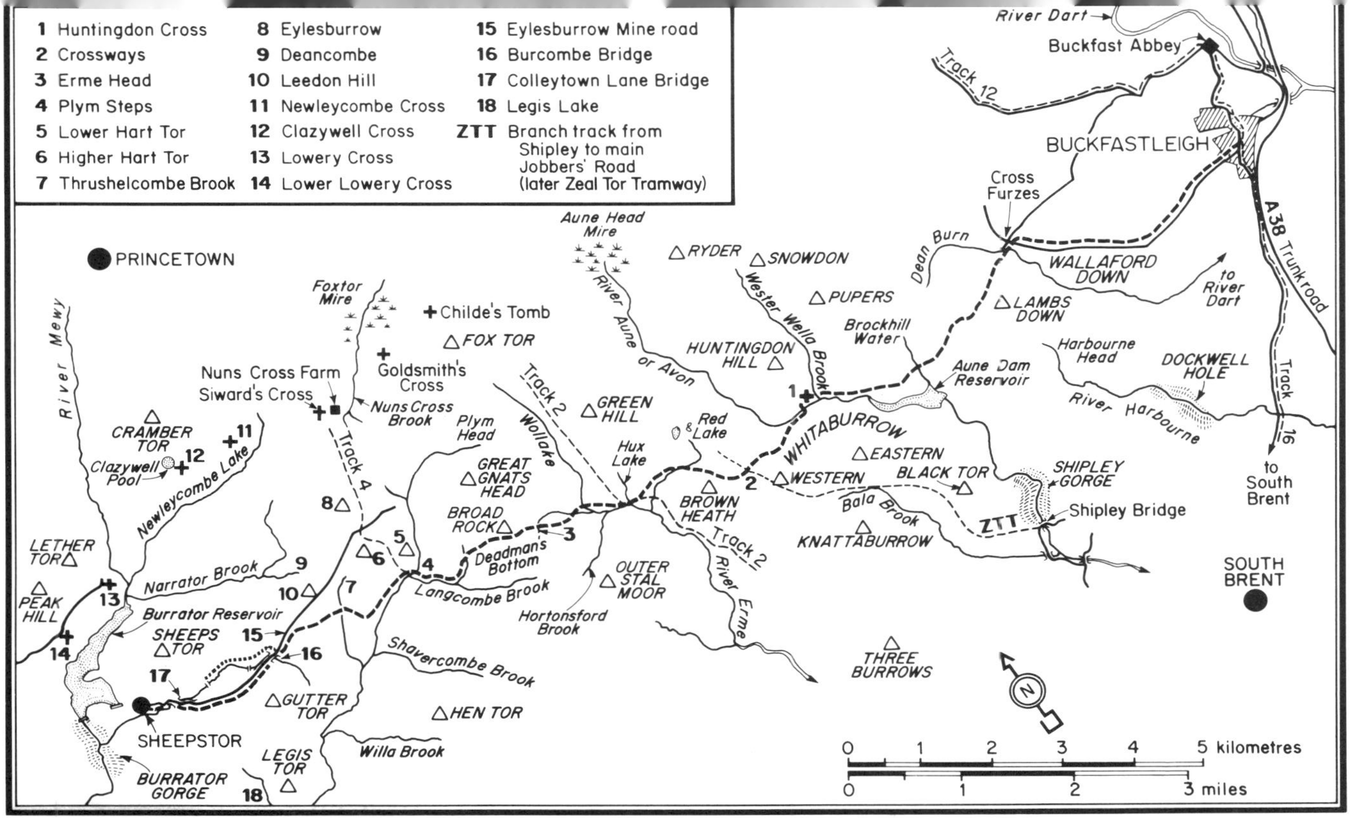

1 Huntingdon Cross
2 Crossways
3 Erme Head
4 Plym Steps
5 Lower Hart Tor
6 Higher Hart Tor
7 Thrushelcombe Brook
8 Eylesburrow
9 Deancombe
10 Leedon Hill
11 Newleycombe Cross
12 Clazywell Cross
13 Lowery Cross
14 Lower Lowery Cross
15 Eylesburrow Mine road
16 Burcombe Bridge
17 Colleytown Lane Bridge
18 Legis Lake
ZTT Branch track from Shipley to main Jobbers' Road (later Zeal Tor Tramway)
River Dart
Buckfast Abbey
Track 12
BUCKFASTLEIGH
A38 Trunkroad
Cross Furzes
Dean Burn
WALLAFORD DOWN
to River Dart
Track 16
to South Brent
PRINCETOWN
Aune Head Mire
RYDER
SNOWDON
PUPERS
LAMBS DOWN
Foxtor Mire
Childe's Tomb
FOX TOR
River Aune or Avon
Wester Wella Brook
HUNTINGDON HILL
Brockhill Water
Harbourne Head
DOCKWELL HOLE
River Harbourne
Goldsmith's Cross
Nuns Cross Farm
Siward's Cross
Nuns Cross Brook
Track 2
GREEN HILL
Aune Dam Reservoir
River Mewy
CRAMBER TOR
Clazywell Pool
Newleycombe Lake
Track 4
Plym Head
Wollake
Red Lake
WHITABURROW
EASTERN
WESTERN
BLACK TOR
SHIPLEY GORGE
Shipley Bridge
GREAT GNATS HEAD
Hux Lake
BROWN HEATH
Bala Brook
KNATTABURROW
ZTT
BROAD ROCK
Deadman's Bottom
LETHER TOR
PEAK HILL
Narrator Brook
Langcombe Brook
OUTER STAL MOOR
Hortonsford Brook
River Erme
SOUTH BRENT
Burrator Reservoir
SHEEPS TOR
Shavercombe Brook
THREE BURROWS
GUTTER TOR
HEN TOR
SHEEPSTOR
LEGIS TOR
Willa Brook
BURRATOR GORGE
N
0 1 2 3 4 5 kilometres
0 1 2 3 miles

Track 3

period of use, and needed no guide-stones. Branch tracks linked southern border-country farms with the trunk route, one from the South Brent area (Track 7) actually bearing the name 'Jobbers' Path'; others came up from Ugborough and Cornwood (Tracks 6 and 5). Where was the western terminus? Although Tavistock, approached by its own branch from Plym Steps (Track 4) might qualify as the ultimate terminus, I have submitted in *High Dartmoor* that Sheepstor was a hub of wool-trade activity on the south-west edge of the high moor. A continuing route from Sheepstor to Tavistock, where the Cistercian and later Benedictine monks of the great abbey of St Rumon were busily engaged in sheep-farming, would have crossed the River Mewy at Sheepstor Bridge and joined the Tavistock-bound monastic way (Track 12) at the site of Yannadon†.

The Jobbers' Road, having necessarily to connect with the southern farms and villages, followed a more southerly route than the monastic Track 10, and consequently breasted higher, wetter land and encountered river crossings suitable only for mounted travellers; OS maps and countless dependent publications nevertheless continue to show it as 'Abbots' Way', despite both lack of evidence and drastic unsuitability for inter-monastic travel. Only one granite cross stands beside Track 3; this, at the foot of Huntingdon Hill is a post-Reformation cross erected solely as a land boundary and irrelevant as a waymark.

West of Broad Rock the route given here is based upon field evidence, oral tradition, a map and a legal document – the latter two hundred years old and in the author's possession. The general confusion persisting over monastic ways, wool-jobbers' ways and the true function of granite crosses was unfortunately aggravated in part by William Crossing, who remarked in his *Guide* that 'Jobbers' Path is really the Abbots' Way', yet later he writes that '... it is this part of the old monks' road (i.e. on Brown Heath) that the moormen generally refer to when they speak of Jobbers' Path.' Evidence supports the moormen rather than Crossing, who does not once comment on their apparent rejection, in his day, of the label 'Abbots' Way'. It is indeed possible that Crossing did not know that it had no place in traditional Dartmoor nomenclature and that it was first used by a traveller named John Andrews writing in 1794, since which it has found its spurious way onto maps and into literature of all types. Lastly, it is hardly surprising that the physical contrast between the two tracks (3 and 12) is as marked as that existing between their respective purposes.

In the heart of the tiny moorland village of Sheepstor is the late medieval church of St Leonard, formerly attended by families from twenty-three farms and two warrens, a sad comment on the incompatibility of agriculture and an impounding reservoir (Burrator) for a great city. The medieval church house provided hospitality and refreshment until early in the present century, and several fields and at least two buildings were set aside for the packhorses of the travelling wool merchants, the location to this day being known as 'Jobbers'. The existing building is a barn of some antiquity, once a small dwelling-house, the walls raised in recent years by breeze-blocks and supporting a corrugated roof. The entrance doorway is central to the east side, and the building now contains stabling for ponies or cattle. Jobbers is now rented by a Sheepstor farmer. A hollow in the ground within the enclosure is likely to have been a pond, which was fed by a leat from Sheepstor Brook. Part of the east wall of the enclosure has the appearance of having been reinforced, perhaps for the support of a lean-to roof on vanished wooden posts. The south gate opens upon a brookside meadow.

The collecting of numberless fleeces in the valleys of Mewy and its tributaries, where was sited a large sheep-farming community like no other on Dartmoor, as well as of combed wool and homespun cloths, formed the business aim of the yarn- or wool-jobber. The only attempt to show the Jobbers' Road on *OS 1809* extends from Redlake Ford to Water Oke Corner where, for the first time in cartographics, it is marked with the celebrated fictional 'Abbots' Way'.

Following the Track (eastward)
From Sheepstor village follow the Eylesburrow mine road past Colleytown Farm and along the flank of Ringmoor Down. The jobbers could call at the valley farms by ascending Tor Lane from the village (left fork beyond St Leonard's Well) and turning into Great and Little Yellowmead, or by forking left at Colleytown to follow the valley floor track past Nattor and Little Yellowmead to Burcombe clapper bridge, Gate and Ford, where they could rejoin the track that later became the mine road. The ancient route is now largely impassable and includes strictly no right of way.

From Burcombe Ford (where the motor road ends at a car-park 579673), the mine road is seen ahead ascending Leedon Hill, a foothill of Eylesburrow.* Pass the former homestead of Ditsworthy Bungalow, last moorland home of Elizabeth Ware (d.1983) of

---

* Spelling used by *Donn* and *OS 1809*, and consistently by Crossing.

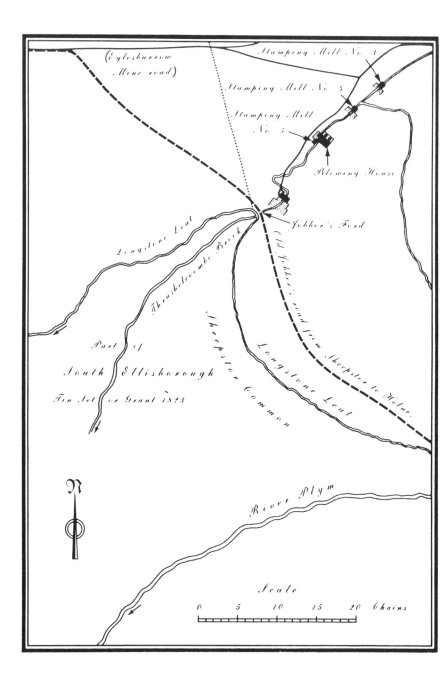

Jobbers' Road from Leedon Hill to Plym Steps. (Passages in brackets are interpolations by the author.)

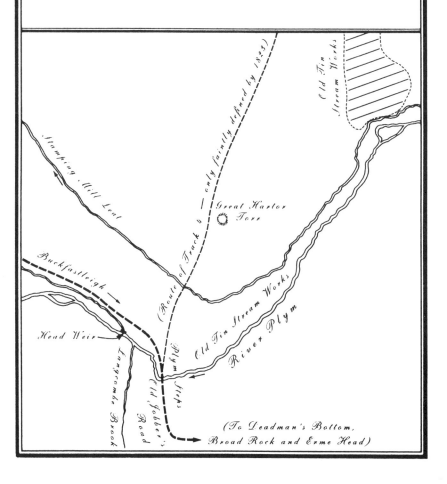

Ditsworthy Warren, and the fine pile of Gutter Tor (right); cross the Longstone leat at a wide, paved clapper bridge. Some way up the mine road and visible on its right verge is a large boulder: this marks the important junction of Jobbers' Road with the mine road. On reaching this point, notice a wide, shallow grass gully, a typical packhorse track, leading southwestward (right) and making a direct ascent of Leedon's grassy slope. Follow it to the plain of the hill, where it becomes stranded – strands lying mostly to the walker's right, some in places sunken. Continue in the same direction (towards the south slope of Thrushelcombe Hill) until a gradual descent begins towards Thrushel Combe. The strands soon unite as a sunken way, which crosses an ancient, dry leat* following the slope of Whitenknowles from NE to SW. The view from here of the Plym valley, right, is excellent, whilst visible ahead is the skyline 'chink' of the sunken way where Track 3 passes over Broad Mead (p. 68). The Longstone leat now comes in view, right, its line rounding the southern area of Whitenknowles Hill. Track and leat converge to reach the valley at Jobbers' Ford (Thrushelcombe Brook) (Pl. 9).

Here study Figure 1 carefully. Two attempts seem to have been made to show the line of the leat west of the ford, and two of the track; the dark, partial lines were abandoned in favour of the labelled lines; the walker approaching the valley will observe, however, that the upper partial line, nearer to the leat than the labelled track, is the more correct one. Cross the broad, green Ditsworthy-Eylesburrow track and descend to the ford, which has stony approaches. Notice the masonry remains – both nearby and further up the valley – of the stamping floors of the once flourishing Eylesburrow Tin Mine (see Fig. 1).

Westward from Jobbers' Ford: cross Ditsworthy-Eylesburrow track on right bank; walk towards Gutter Tor. Leat is nearby, below left; when it curves away (left), cross old leat channel and bear to right of Gutter Tor; track stranded on crest; next make towards houses and church of Yelverton; tips of Bungalow Firs appear; take strand(s) bearing to right of Firs, when sunken way will be seen leading down to mine road.

The Longstone leat headweir just below Jobbers' Ford marks the point of crossing by the former flowing leat from Plym, still in use in 1829 when the 'Ellisborough' map was drawn. The track mounts the left bank of the combe and runs for some way immediately above the (now dry) leat – and nearer to it than Figure 1 suggests; disregard a

---

* Possibly an earlier cut for the Longstone leat from Thrushelcombe Brook only.

green gully and path mounting higher from the left bank; pass a small set stone (right of track) and continue towards the giant menhir of the Thrushelcombe Bronze Age burial sanctuary. Although a bracken-field intervenes, the track survives as a clear path leading to the large, tilted cover-stone of a fine kistvaen. It is less clear in crossing a bracken-free area, but the walker should continue towards the menhir, when he will regain the path, again through bracken; it intersects the associated stone row and becomes a clear, grassy road rounding the foot of Thrushelcombe Hill towards the River Plym. The sanctuary here consists of three stone rows, each with associated menhir and ruined grave, a huge cairn known as 'Giant's Basin' and the large, almost perfect kistvaen already passed *en route*, within the remains of the cairn that once covered it. The routing of the track provides yet another example of the adoption of prehistoric monuments as way-marks (see p.93).*

Curving eastward with the contour of the hill, Track 3 offers a pleasing view of Plym in its transitional passage over step-like granite bedding between its upper and middle moorland reaches; Lower Hart Tor, Hartor Hill Pound and the lonely hills of the southern fen appear ahead. At the pound the track is joined by Track 4 and descends to the valley floor as a well-defined road, peaty and sunken near Plym Steps. Signs of steps no longer remain, but tradition firmly places them there, the crossing place being named Plym Steps to distinguish it from Plym Ford, just over a mile upstream, where small stones have been placed casually to facilitate crossing the river; this is wider at Plym Steps and awkward to cross when swollen, and reliable steps would certainly have been needed by the pack-train driver. *Westward from Plym Steps: Track 4 bears right at head of sunken road; Track*

* In the interests of the walker the author admits to having previously been mistaken in placing the Jobbers' Road crossing of Thrushelcombe Brook at Thrushelcombe Ford beside the Eylesburrow blowing-house, in giving the western approach as the wide grass track leading thereto from the summit of Leedon, which he now recognizes merely as a miners' access way to the blowing-house, and in routing the track too high on the south slope of Thrushelcombe Hill. The facts now laid before the reader are the fruits of extremely intensive field work and research on Dartmoor travel routes since mid 1982, by which time desirable amendments to *High Dartmoor: Land and People* were no longer admissible. It also should be stated that the entire western portion of Jobbers' Road is omitted from OS maps, as is the dry portion of the Longstone Leat. 'Drizzle-combe' should of course be Thrushelcombe and 'Scout Hut', Ditsworthy Bungalow (the last moorland home of the late Elizabeth Ware of Ditsworthy Warren). There are no fewer than three leats on the south slope of Thrushelcombe Hill, of which OS shows only one, and that incompletely. We know that the highest placed, New Engine Leat, was not cut until after 1823, as it does not appear on the mine plan of that date.

3 runs to left along earthen path; passes oval island; branches right to maintain contour level; passes lower edges of scree areas and below large cairn, right. The track is well defined south of the river at the foot of Calveslake Hill, where it runs quite near the Langcombe valley floor. Tin-streaming operations here are extensive, and two ruined tinners' houses lie among the pits and burrows spread everywhere. On approaching the tributary valley of Deadman's Bottom, the way again becomes a stony, narrow road: reaching a fork, the right branch fords Deadman's Stream and continues up the Langcombe valley towards Yealm Head; the left fork is Track 3, well defined as a grassy way. Following the stream's right bank, it becomes sunken near the valley head and, unrecorded by previous writers, if for me one of Dartmoor's most satisfying ancient ways. The elongated head of Deadman's valley contains two mires in hour-glass shape; the road descends below a large boulder to ford the stream on the hour-glass neck; the crossing is oblique and the continuing track runs for a short way along the further bank before ascending through a stony gully; at the gully head it is joined by another from a higher ford. The way is now clear as it passes between two areas of miry ground (rendered conspicuous in early summer by the white heads of cottongrass) and approaches an area of scattered, rather flat rocks on the south slope of a small, domed hill ahead. Walk to the right of the rocks and towards a very large, flat, whitish rock; pass to the left of this. The track remains clear and practically unstranded the whole way from Deadman's valley Ford to the hill crest just ahead, where it becomes a sunken way in crossing Broad Mead on the Plym-Erme watershed. A branch track joins it here from the west flank of Great Gnats Head (left); this is an old peat track (identified as such by Crossing – also as 'a branch of the Abbots' Way'!). From the hill crest – the Great Gnats Head-Langcombe Head col – the walker in either direction will be impressed by the dramatic scenic change before him. Eastward are the peatlands of the southern fen and the huge hollow of the Erme head basin directly below; enveloped now by the wilderness, the walker senses that he is far from civilization. Descend east from the col; the sunken way gives place to a narrow but clear track; ahead is the large, flat Broad Rock, with the name and the letters 'BB' (Blachford manor Bounds) engraved upon it, marking the boundary between the Forest and western commons. The first water of Erme glints below the background height of Brown Heath, and the dome of Three Burrows marks a skyline reaching westward to Outer Stal Moor. Track 3, consisting now of firm, grass strands, runs downhill south-east to Erme

Head Ford. *Westward from Erme Head; track stranded but clear. Ascend from ford below scattered boulders. Beyond Broad Rock, track sunken on hill-crest. View: western Dartmoor heights in order of appearance – Sharp Tor, Peak Hill, Sheeps Tor and enormous spread of Cornish in-country. Avoid branch track (right) to Great Gnats Head; large, whitish rock soon seen; pass to right, Deadman's valley next seen, cutting across view of Lower Hart and Sheeps Tors.*

The stranded track passes between a hillside rockfield, right, and the fringe of Erme Head Mire, left. Strands unite near the valley floor; under the brow of Outer Stal Moor, right, a feeder of the river passes through a gully deepened by tinners; Erme Head Ford is here, the track beyond it at once bears left – ignore the path running ahead – to follow the right bank of the infant river, its waters abundantly swollen by the large head-mire (left). Near the north-west verge of the mire, towards Great Gnats Head, is the boulder inscribed 'A', signifying the head of the river known for so many previous centures as 'Arme'. John Speede, in his map of Devonshire of 1610, names the south Dartmoor rivers (west to east) as 'Plym Flud', 'Alme Flud', 'Arme Flud' and 'Aune Flud'; he also shows border-country Ermington as 'Armington'.

The track now enters upon an extraordinary landscape of mounds, pits and craters, where tinners raised ore from the Middle Ages until the early eighteenth century, several adventurers being named in both record and tradition. The largest excavations are right of the track, but the foot of Erme Pits Hill, above the river's left bank, also evinces intensive mining activity (Pl. 11). Continue to Erme Pits Ford; cross; follow the left bank to Wollake Ford. There are clear approaches on each side; Wollake is a tributary of some volume rising on the north edge of the fen and flowing across it to join Erme on the south edge. This is big, wild country, and the absurdity of regarding Track 3 as one suitable for monastic travellers becomes obvious.

A well-trodden path along Wollake's west valley-side is a convenient, oft-used route from Erme Pits to the postbox at Ducks Pool and the William Crossing Memorial. The east side is marked, well above the valley, by a formerly much-ridden path branching from Track 3 beyond Wollake Ford; this is the North-South Track (2) – see p.46. Alternative ways, parallel and about 100 yards apart, lead eastward from the ford to Hux Lake Ford, beyond which the pattern is repeated. There is no doubt that southbound travellers on Track 2 would take the well-defined lower way to Redlake (Lower) Ford, whilst jobbers would follow the higher track over the flank of Green Hill; from here notice the fine view of the entire, lonely upper-reach valley of Erme.

The track bisects the Erme long row and makes an easy ascent over good ground to Redlake Higher Ford, from where its eastward continuation alone is marked by Greenwood – as 'Abbots' Way'! The crossing of Track 2 at Lower Ford is seen below, right. The streamside path running up the valley from Lower Ford is badly eroded in its higher portion, but it doubtless formed the original way; the walker should now follow the higher, alternative path. *Westward: path forks on flank of Green Hill; ignore right branch into Hux Lake valley.*

The complicated and often very wet crossing at Redlake Higher Ford is reached below the small clay-tip, left; Redlake Mires are widespread above the ford, and the higher, conical clay-tip of the old works appears beyond, left, while the sunken way ascending from the left bank to the Crossways is clearly seen. Cross; enter the sunken way between the last two of the long line of Harford-Ugborough bond-stones; the ultimate stone, known as the 'Outer U Stone', stands on the verge of rushes bordering the track and bears the letters 'HU'. An easy ascent leads to the Erme-Avon water-divide and is well defined on the north-east slope of Brown Heath. A quarter of a mile beyond the Outer U Stone it is intersected by the Red Lake Railway track (built 1910) beside the ruins of Sammy Thompson's Cottage, from where it makes a large, sweeping curve, again well defined, to reach the Crossways. In this remote area it comes as a surprise to encounter not one but two railroads. The Crossways signifies the intersection of Track 3 by the Zeal Tor Tramroad (built 1846-7), where the old road passes above the site of the former Red Lake peatworks peat press (below the mounds of old clay workings) and so to the brink of Avon country. The tramroad was based on an ancient track from Zeal which, joined by Track 7 at Bala Brook Head, here joins the main Jobbers' Road. Between cottage and workings, ignore several paths branching right from the main curve of Track 3. Reaching the watershed, notice (west) the hollow of the Erme head basin, (north) the lofty mound of Ryder, and (east) beyond Huntingdon Hill the escarpment cutting across the south-east in-country.

Pass below a small clayworks hut; descend Bush Meads into Avon country. The track was here described by traveller John Andrews as 'A Stony Ridge'. Below the crest it becomes sunken and nears the huge gert, right, of Piper's Beam; the view ahead now includes Avon flowing from Higher Bottom towards Huntingdon† and, on Huntingdon Hill, the rabbit buries and enclosure-outlines of the once successful Huntingdon Warren. The track approaches Buckland Ford Water at the foot of a series of bends easing the gradient; ignore a path branching left, notice the yawning mouth of Piper's Beam, right; cross the Water at the ancient ford, whence a Brent manor boundary cross erected in 1557 has long since vanished. A further stretch of sunken way leads to Avon's right bank, where, after a few more yards, it becomes almost overgrown by mire. Therefore follow the parallel sheep-path above, which gives a fine view of the sweeping tracts of surrounding moorland and leads down to the river at Huntingdon Ford. If the river is up, the walker risks a wetting, for no bridge exists or is known to have existed here, and the 'clapper bridge' dignified in Gothic lettering on OS Tourist and other maps was built half a mile upstream by warrener Michelmore of Huntingdon in 1809 for the warreners' use. Cross; follow the track (right) past Huntingdon† to the ford on Wester Wella Brook. This beautiful, clear tributary comes down from the high land between Ryder and Snowdon, and the trees and wall of Huntingdon home newtake are seen on its west valley-side. The newtake wall at Huntingdon Corner long ago sacrificed its stones to picnic-fire builders and is now derelict. (See Figure 2.)

From Wella Brook Ford eastward the track is unmistakeable and well trodden today by walkers from the Buckfastleigh area making for the Avon valley. It passes at the foot of Hickaton Hill and makes an easy ascent of Brock Hill. The Avon reservoir (1957) appears below and the ancient enclosure of Billers Pound above, while the ungrassed, stony portion of the road is clear; stone pillars standing in the river near Wella Brook Foot (right) formerly supported a barrier-fence against animals approaching the reservoir. On the opposite hillside is the leat that once conveyed water to the Brent Moor clayworks; one is refreshed on a hot day by the sight and sound of the river nearby, and the view from the flank of Brock Hill includes the dam and the southern in-country beyond. The track is a true road on the shoulder of Brock Hill where it bisects part of a Bronze Age village; beyond the next valley, Brockhill Water, its visible continuation (over Grippers Hill) leads to a skyline chink, from where it descends to the eastern in-country. Two other prehistoric enclosures appear near Brockhill Ford. On ascending Grippers Hill, the heights of Snowdon and Pupers rise, left, while to the right is the curve of the dam, an architectural concession to its environmental setting of huge, curving hills. Rockfields in the intermediate distance provided building material for the Bronze Age hut dwellers, their ruined homes submerged 3,000 years later when the reservoir was formed. Prior to the flooding of the valley, Lady (Aileen) Fox of the University of Exeter excavated the settlement, which yielded features and artefacts of considerable

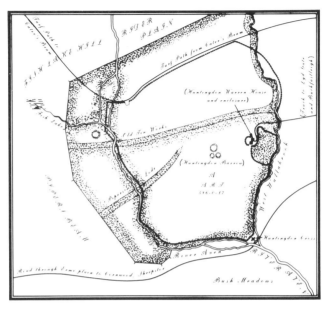

Jobbers' Road at Huntingdon. (Passages in brackets are
interpolations by the author.)

interest. Interested readers may consult Lady Fox's Report, given in
High Dartmoor.

A wooden pole stands (at the time of writing) on the summit of
Grippers Hill and forms a useful guide, as Track 3 is here completely
grassed over, and other tracks and paths on the hills could confuse the
walker. From the pole the descent to Water Oke Corner is clear; cross
the well-defined Track 26; then, also clear, that from Lyd Gate to
Skerraton Gate; follow the decayed cornditch wall at Water Oke
Corner past two iron, blue-tipped posts, to a new hunting-gate. The
big valley central to the beautiful border-country view is that of the
lowland Dart. *Westward from hunting gate: follow track diverging
from wall (ignore path ascending in line with wall). Track 3 bears
slightly right of Eastern Whitaburrow, first big height to appear;
curves at pole to approach Brockhill Ford; brings into view funnel of
Avon Valley at Higher Bottom between Whitaburrow ridge and
Huntingdon Hill. Beyond Brockhill Ford track seen as stony road.*

The track crosses Lambs Down (locally 'Lemson') to a stony ford (on a tributary of Dean Burn) helpfully marked by DNPA blue-tipped posts; for fingerposts marked 'Abbots' Way', of course, read 'Jobbers' Road'. Ancient boundary reaves on the down indicate probable medieval cultivation. The descent to Dean Burn Ford is overshadowed by huge, ancient beech trees, and the ford itself is an idyllic spot, with a clapper bridge of two openings for packhorse driver and pedestrian. *Westward: on ascending from ford, Water Oke Corner soon visible, with Pupers and Snowdon right. Follow blue-tipped posts.*

The ascent from the ford to the lane junction near Cross Furzes (700667) is short and steep; the (post-medieval) guide-stone is marked 'B' (Buckfastleigh, south-east), 'A' (Ashburton, north-east) and 'T' (Tavistock, north-west). The acute right-angle bend in the post-medieval way to Buckfastleigh was rendered unavoidable by the necessary crossing of Dean Burn at the head of the gorge where the ford and bridge are situated. The route crosses the lonely ridgeway of Wallaford Down above Larkham Wood (right) and King's Wood (left), with fine views through gateways of Dartmoor's eastern escarpment and border-country. Continue ahead at Wallaford Cross; pass Fullaford Cross, joined by Track 16, enter the town and cross the River Mardle at Market Street Bridge. The older, medieval way from Cross Furzes went via Hockmoor Head, where it joined the trans-Dartmoor monastic way (Track 12) coming down from Holne via Hawson†, and ran to Buckfast, 600 feet below Cross Furzes. Hoskins states (*Devon*) that, 'The original settlement of Buckfastleigh was at Buckfast, about a mile north beside the River Dart, where an abbey was founded and endowed by King Canute.' It is likely that weavers' cottages were situated in the higher part of the village, where also lived many of the abbey's lay employees, and the siting of the thirteenth-century church on the hill crest (above the then unsuspected limestone caves) was a typical medieval gesture in honour of the overseeing Holy Spirit. The necessary clearing of forest to build the village created the 'leigh' of Buckfast. The confusion common today between the Jobbers' Road and the monastic way, perpetuated in maps and literature of all kinds, is likely first to have arisen through the abandonment by later wool jobbers of the ancient, direct road from Cross Furzes to Buckfast and the consequent modern assumption that it was a monastic path – especially as Buckfast monks were known to have used it to reach Brock Hill, where abbey flocks grazed and lay-brother shepherds used the medieval sheep-farm mentioned on p.72.

TRACK 4

JOBBERS' ROAD (TAVISTOCK BRANCH) TAVISTOCK – PLYM STEPS 12 miles

Route according to tradition received by the author from the late Ern Cole, moorman of Long Ash Farm (Walkham).

Tavistock is mentioned in the Introduction to Chapter 3 as of importance in Devon's medieval wool trade. Although the town could easily be reached by jobbers travelling west from Sheepstor, as described on p. 62, a direct route from the main track leaving the Forest to Tavistock would obviously have been more convenient. This approached the town along Tavistock, grand trunk road from Windypost† (Tracks 8, 10, 12, 13) via Moortown and Whitchurch Down. Tradition (see above) detailed the Tavistock branch as set out below. It should be made clear that there is no public access to the following two portions of the route: 1, from the wall of Vixen Tor Newtake to the bank of the River Walkham; 2, from the right of way at Long Ash (i.e. the Merivale-Walkhampton track) through the newtake to Long Ash Hill.

Following the Track (eastward)
Whereas the post-medieval Tracks 8 and 10 ran eastward from Windypost via Merivale (549752), the medieval Jobbers' Road to Buckfastleigh went via Long Ash. Passing on the north side of Windypost†, it crossed Beckamoor Water at Feathertor Ford; from there, while Tracks 8 and 10 swung north-east to Merivale, the older way descended due east to the (present-day) funnel-opening between the newtake walls of Merivale and Vixen Tor. Here it crossed open moor since enclosed by the latter and followed the south boundary of the former (by far the older) to the River Walkham. A clapper bridge

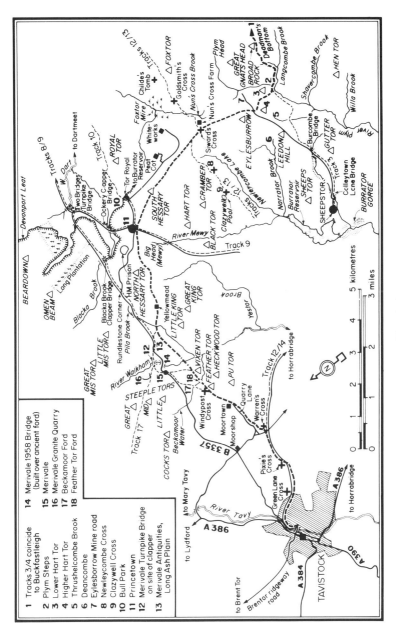

Track 4

1 Tracks 3/4 coincide
   to Buckfastleigh
2 Plym Steps
3 Lower Hart Tor
4 Higher Hart Tor
5 Thrushelcombe Brook
6 Deancombe
7 Eylesborrow Mine road
8 Newleycombe Cross
9 Clazywell Cross
10 Bull Park
11 Princetown
12 Merivale Turnpike Bridge
   on site of clapper
13 Merivale Antiquities,
   Long Ash Plain

14 Merivale 1958 Bridge
   (built over ancient ford)
15 Merivale
16 Merivale Granite Quarry
17 Beckamoor Ford
18 Feather Tor Ford

and fording place here were long ago destroyed – 'washed out' as the moormen say – by flood, but the interesting circumstantial evidence for their existence strongly supports the old tradition. Here, at the former Swallow Ford, a narrow, walled lane obliquely ascends from the east river bank and passed before the ruin of the Long Ash Longhouse; this lane was significantly known as 'Swallever' (Swallow Ford) Lane (Pl.10). Reaching the old riverside track between Merivale and Walkhampton, the way turned left for a short distance before bearing right into a green way ascending Long Ash Hill over then unenclosed land. The way (in the newtake) is marked by a 'curb' of stones similar to those on the ancient route A of Track 9 near the River Cowsic (p. 97). At the head of the newtake the way regains the open moor and runs directly (east) to the menhir of the Merivale antiquities. A prominent leaning stone further eastward marked the route towards Yellowmead Ford on Pila Brook, near where it was in later times absorbed by the post-medieval route (via Merivale Ford) marked by the T-A stones of Track 10.

From here the way coincided with Track 10 (see p. 111) as far as the Devil's Elbow inn in Princetown. At the inn, turn into the yard on the higher, west side of the building, where once was the depot (upper terminus) of Sir Thomas Tyrwhitt's tramroad of 1823, the Plymouth & Dartmoor Railway. A right of way leads ahead through a wide thoroughfare known as Ivybridge Lane, so named from the custom, in the early days of the convict prison at Princetown, of escorting discharged prisoners over the Moor by this route to Ivybridge railway station, before the opening of the GWR Princetown branch. Beyond the lane-head gate the track is clearly defined as it follows the wall (left). At the hillcrest ahead a fine view includes Peak Hill, Sharp and Lether Tors, the sweeping line of Cramber Down, the Plym ridge and, in the distance, Plymouth Sound merging with the English Channel; a standing stone inscribed 'PCWW' (Plymouth Corporation Water Works), one of several in the locality, marks the boundary of the Burrator reservoir catchment area, while direct ahead rises South Hessary (locally 'Lookout') Tor. From here is seen a detailed view of Hart Tor and upper Mewy country backed by the lower Walkham tors, and northward are North Hessary and Great Mis Tors. The track passes at the west foot of Lookout Tor, which 180 years ago was an observer's post to warn of the expected Napoleonic invasion. 500 yards beyond, the wall leaves the track and descends, left, to Peat Cot. Here beside the wall is the site of another Napoleonic lookout station, a purpose-built one named Peat Cot Castle and so marked on the Tithes Apportionment Map of 1840; hence the Princetown-Peat Cot road has ever since been known as Castle Road.

The line of the wall from Ivybridge Lane is continued southward by a reave; this, marking the Forest boundary, has come from the south-east slope of North Hessary Tor and in approaching South Hessary is in places fragmentary. It is accompanied by the track for a further mile and a half and runs directly to the summit of Eylesburrow. About a mile onward, the track is intersected by another in a slight hollow; this is 'Uncle's Road', an old packhorse road from Peat Cot to the south-west border villages. From here observe the bold outlines of Down and Sheeps Tors above the valley of Newleycombe Lake. A short way ahead appear the trees and roof of Nuns Cross Farm, now a youth adventure hostel. As the track descends towards the farm, it is joined (right) by Track 12 ascending from Newleycombe Bottom. Beyond the junction stands the ancient *Crucem Siwardi*, Siward's†, its relevance to the present track emphasized by the Forest boundary reave from South Hessary Tor, beside which it stands. Walk a further 200 yards beside the reave, until Track 4 bears left beside a PCWW stone, while the reave continues past other such stones to Eylesburrow. The track now becomes a stony road, once used by horse-drawn vehicles employed at Eylesburrow Mine. *Westward: from plain of Eylesburrow Common, reave clearly seen passing Siward's† and making for South Hessary Tor.*

Reaching the high plain of Eylesburrow Common, the track crosses its width until, beside a large fallen stone possibly once a waymark, it rises to the shoulder of Eylesburrow and branches left as a well-defined way, crossed shortly by a stony mine road leading (left) to Maynard's Valley and Plym Ford. A large, heather-covered mound appears ahead; join a grassy mine road leading to it; near the mound, Track 4 leaves the grassy way to continue southward; slightly stranded, it crosses a third mine road obliquely and becomes a wide, green way heading towards Lower Hart Tor. Pass the head of a gully (leading into Evil Combe, left); this is marked on Fig. 1 as 'Old Tin Stream Works'. Notice the small, broken pile of Higher Hart Tor a quarter of a mile to the right. A scattering of rocks appears ahead; pass along their west fringe. Beyond a second group, make for the head of a gully about 100 yards west of the outlying rocks of Lower Hart Tor. Track 3 can be seen from here crossing the foot of

Calveslake Hill south of the Plym valley. Descend the hill until a well-defined channel is seen on the lower flank of Thrushelcombe Hill (right), backed by the river. This is the Eylesburrow Mine New Engine leat (see Fig. 1), which was crossed at a ford by the track, by then receiving only sporadic use. The leat continues along the upper wall of Hartor Hill Pound (left) to reach the site of its headweir on the upper Plym. Track 4 descends towards the river as a sunken way and joins Track 3 (right), which reaches Plym Steps as a wide, sunken, stony road. *Westward from Plym Steps: fork right from main sunken way into north branch; from head of gully (west of Hart Tor) make for heathery mound beyond two areas of scattered rocks; join wide green way crossed by mine roads.*

TRACK 5

WATERCOMBE – ERME POUND   3 miles

The important link with Track 2 appears on *OS 1809, Greenwood* and *Besley.*

Following the Track (northward)
Enter the Moor at Watercombe Gate (625611) where the enclosure, Watercombe Waste, dates only from the early nineteenth century. Turn left, cross Redaven Lake in a shady dell and pass to the open

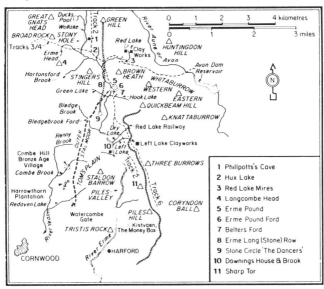

Track 5

moor through Dip-trough (New Waste) Gate. Follow the northward track mounting the Staldon-Combe Hill ridge, passing (left) Harrowthorn Plantation and a Bronze Age village. Ford Combe Brook below the headmire and ascend to the ridge, from where may be seen (right) the Staldon stone row, its tallest members cresting the hill. The track then descends towards Renny Brook Head to pass along the east verge of a mire. Away to the north-east now apears the 'Dancers' stone circle (see below).

From Renny Brook Head descend to Bledgebrook Ford, an excellent crossing place upstream from Blachford Bottom, where the view of Three Burrows and Sharp Tor is impressive. Continue north-eastward to pass near the fine retaining circle known as the 'Dancers' – sometimes as the 'Cornwood Maidens' – forming the lower terminal of the Erme long stone row on the plain of Bledgebrook Hill. The track next crosses Green Lake on a hard between the headmire and Green Bottom; away to the right appears the Erme long row, its stone removed in Green Bottom by working tinners. In only 500 yards the track reaches Erme Pound Ford on the river, its descent and crossing being visible from Track 2 (see p. 45).

TRACK 6

THE BLACKWOOD PATH
Shown on *OS 1809, Greenwood* and *Besley*   5½ miles

This ancient peat road makes a forked approach to the Moor from the southern border-country; one root runs from Ugborough village via Hillhead and Leigh Cross to Leigh Gate, the other from Wrangaton Gate; both roots join the main stem on Wrangaton golf course and climb the escarpment steeply beside Lud Brook. 'Blackwood' was a name once in common use on Dartmoor to denote peat cut for fuel.

Following the Track (northward)
Park at Wrangaton Moorgate (673582). Cross the golf course and follow Lud Brook upstream, passing between Cuckoo Ball (left) and Claret Tor (right). On the unenclosed slope of Cuckoo Ball, some large leaning slabs and traces of a barrow almost certainly denote a ruined dolmen; such identification is rendered more likely by the nearby (and similar, though larger) recorded remains, within the newtake, of another dolmen. The ascending track skirts the east side of Lud Brook's source at Main Head and remains well defined in crossing Beacon Plain, 600 yards west of Beacon Rocks, to Spurrell's†, where it intersects Track 16. Notice in this locality that cairns (of prehistoric burials) crown almost every hilltop.

Follow the ridge north of Spurrell's† to where the way unites with the Red Lake Railway track to a point half a mile north of Left Lake; bear downhill towards Stony Bottom and join Track 2 (see p. 44 – there less clearly defined than Track 6). This route is clearly marked by *Greenwood* – though the railway was not then in existence, of course. It is possible that an alternative, higher junction of these tracks occurred on the high col – though ground evidence is slight, and it is

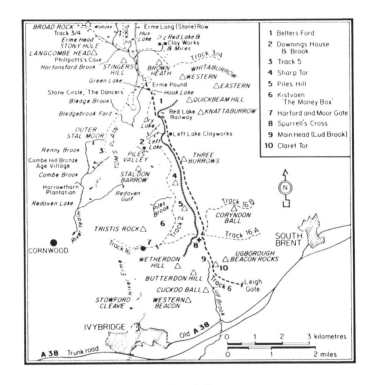

Track 6

so shown on *OS 1809*. Crossing (*Guide*) remarks that, 'This part of it is now very ill-defined. In places it is altogether lost, and where discoverable is little more than a narrow footpath.' I find it difficult to accept that a peat road in regular use until comparatively recent times would become 'altogether lost' by the late nineteenth century when Crossing was exploring the Moor, and it seems more probable that the route outlined here, and supported by *Greenwood*, is the true one. The relatively poor definition of Tracks 2 and 6 on Erme Plains would be due to the driving of beasts, and the passage of solo riders, across a wide, open plain where strands rather than a sunken way would result – Erme Pound lies a short way ahead.

TRACK 7

JOBBERS' PATH: AISH RIDGE – BALL GATE – CROSSWAYS (JUNCTION WITH TRACK 3) $3\frac{3}{4}$ miles
BRANCH FROM ZEAL AND SHIPLEY (LATER ZEAL TOR TRAMROAD) TO CROSSWAYS $2\frac{1}{2}$ miles

NOTE: the reader is referred to the Introduction to Track 3 as of particular relevance here.

The rise of the cloth industry in Devon in medieval times makes an interesting story. It concerns the spinning and weaving activities carried on in most small towns by the mid-fourteenth century and their spread into the villages and remote country cottages. It was at this time, too, that many fulling mills were constructed on the banks of the rivers pouring off Dartmoor. Totnes, Buckfastleigh, Ashburton and Tavistock had already become centres of the cloth industry, though the cloths produced in the west of the country in Tavistock, and sent to Plymouth for export, were very coarse and remained in demand only for a century or so. Hooker writes in his *Synopsis* that the industry depended mostly on locally produced wool; thus we have a picture of production and transportation involving the crossing of southern Dartmoor, which at once explains the purposes and needs of the travelling yarn-jobbers. In Tracks 3 and 4, the routes of the jobbers between the Tavy and Dart valleys are detailed; those who regularly visited villages and farms in the South Hams would have found it more convenient to use tracks which branched from the main trunk route, via Coryndon Ball Gate, Aish Ridge and Pennaton. Villages where spinners operated, served by these routes to the Moor, would have included South Brent, Diptford, Halwell, Harbertonford, Harberton (Hoskins wrote of a large woollen mill still working there in 1950), Rattery and Ugborough. Dean Milles of Exeter wrote in 1755

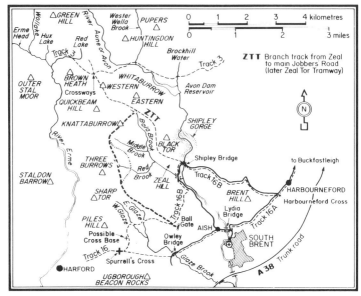

Track 7

about the decay of the cottage industries, so that it would be reasonable to regard Tracks 3, 4 and 7 as becoming disused for wool traffic, and consequently neglected, by the onset of the Napoleonic Wars, an event which finally reduced the Dartmoor cloth industry to a shadow of its former self.

It would, of course, be quite wrong to assume that the Dartmoor jobbers used only the tracks just listed, but these were named from the former regular wool traffic. It should also be remembered that branches of Track 2 – this reaches a conveniently placed junction with Track 3 at Redlake Lower Ford – which offered the jobbers easy contact with villages and farms in the west sector of the South Hams were Tracks 5 and 7; similarly, jobbers needing to call at farms in the central basin or in the Holne district could well have found it convenient to use Track 10 and 12. The route of Track 7 via Ball Gate and Red Brook Higher Ford is shown on *OS 1809* and by *Greenwood*, who, however, does not show the link to the Crossways near Western Whiteburrow. William Crossing writes (*Guide*): 'A road runs up the hill from the hamlet of Aish ... to Aish Ridge and

Coryndon Ball, terminating at Ball Gate ... From this point there is a track to the head of Bala Brook ... It crosses the head of Red Brook at Higher Ford ... As this track leads to the Zeal Tor Tramroad ... it is sometimes spoken of as Jobbers' Path.'

Finally, the reader of *High Dartmoor* may be confused by the earlier nomenclature used there for Tracks 3, 4 and 7, which are indexed respectively as 'Jobber's Path or Road' (3), 'Jobbers' Path or Road (branch)' (4) and 'Ball Gate – Bala Brook Head Track' (7).

Following the Track (northward)
NOTE: It is not possible to drive a car to Ball Gate, and parking information is given below.

Three lanes of approach to Ball Gate were used, according to where in the South Hams the jobber started his journeys: 1, Lydia Bridge – Aish – Gribblesdown Gate (684608; a car may be parked inside the gate; walk across Aish Ridge to enter the lane leading to Ball Gate); 2, from Pennaton, a medieval settlement a mile west of South Brent (a way now partially overgrown); 3, via Wrangaton – Owley Bridge – Bulhornstone – Coryndon (or the loop track from Bulhornstone bypassing Coryndon). Approach-tracks 1 and 2 converge at the west end of Aish Ridge, and 3 ascends to Ball Gate over the west flank of Coryndon Ball, a picturesque , rugged approach to the Moor above the enclosed Treelands Down and Treelands Farm in the valley, right. Approach track 2 is not only a direct link with Ugborough and other South Hams villages but, for the walker, by far the most delighted approach, where bluebells, campion and stitchwort so pleasantly enhance an early summertime walk and the old lane – aptly named Summer Lane – makes a gradual ascent over an easy surface to Aish Ridge. The lower portion of the lane one Broadymoor (south of the Owley-Aish road) is now completely overgrown but is remembered by Brent people as a pleasant walk less than forty years ago; it left the Pennaton-Cheston road and passed over Broadymoor before crossing the Owley road (where a car may be parked) and climbing Aish Ridge.

Pass through Brent Moorgate at the lane head and notice that an ancient lane once continued the way, one hedge of which has been demolished. From the west end of the ridge-crest is seen the well-defined Bulhornstone branch from the main Ball Gate track, crossing the east flank of the Ball and descending to the farm as a lane between enclosures. An arrangement of gates, walls and fencing at

Ball Gate forms a court for sorting stock. The imposing gate pillars are a relic of the old Brent Manor lands, one having lost its capital. Pass through the gates to a meeting of tracks: Track 16 follows the transverse cornditch wall between Glascombe Corner and Diamond Lane; ahead, the way forks: right, as a grass track; left (Track 7) between the great dolmen (see below) and the south-west slope of Wacka Tor; it then runs parallel to the (flowing) Coryndon leat and is well defined in passing up the East Glaze valley. The remarkable antiquities near Ball Gate are noticed in detail under Track 16 on page 187.

From East Glaze Head the track passes an extensive tinworks and crosses Vags Hills to Hickley Plain, which is the Three Burrows-Wacka Tor ridge. A backward glance shows it to be aligned with the lane beyond Ball Gate: the huge dome of Three Burrows rises west of the track, and a wonderful view extends beyond the border-country to the South Hams. The track remains near the foot of Three Burrows and brings into view ahead the parallel valleys of Red Brook and Middle Brook – the latter seen to contain a lonely ruin – and its line passing over Red Brook Ball between the valleys. The distant skyline is marked by the mound of Knattaburrow, a useful waymark for the walker, for the track approaches the Knattaburrow cairn from Middle Brook Ford, *en route* to Bala Brook Head.

Descending from the plain to the Red Brook valley, the track crosses a grass plain verging a wet area (right) of purple moorgrass and becomes a sunken way. Beside it (left) is a large boulder topped by a fine rock basin. Reaching the valley, the track follows the brook's right bank but diverges from it to avoid the headmire. (For the best walking, follow the high bank, left, for 500 yards when Red Brook Higher Ford will be seen below; lying near the head of the combe, it is a well-worn crossing with clear approaches on either bank.) *Southward from Higher Ford: valley tracks on floor and along steep bank seen merging to continue towards Hickley Plain.*

Beyond the ford, continue over Red Brook Ball in direct alignment (behind you) with Track 7 on Hickley Plain. The way ahead is clear, as the crossing of the deep upper valley of Middle Brook – Petre's Pits Bottom – is beside the ruin seen from Hickley Plain. This is Uncle Ab's House, where the horses used on the Zeal Tor Tramroad were stabled under Uncle Ab's resident care. A great deal of early and mid nineteenth-century tin-mining has taken place in the Middle Brook valley, and a large wheelpit, where a wheel once operated ore-crushing drop-stamps, is situated further downstream. *Southward from Middle Brook: track crosses high shoulder of Red Brook Ball and points initially to Wacka Tor, then swings towards Three Burrows.* The OS maps correctly shows the NW-NE elbow-bends as the track rounds Middle Brook Mires – where ground definition is good – and continues towards Ab's House. The valley floor has been deeply excavated by the latter-day miners but was less so in the days of the jobbers' pack-trains; at all events the track crosses the valley beside the ruined building and ascends the south flank of Knattaburrow Hill. Although well marked here, it can be misleading: several paths branch right, one being conspicuously clear, but the walker must keep always left. A cairn north of the path marks Knattaburrow's summit; the track does not make for this but passes below it. The large, grassy tussocks on Knattaburrow Hill make fatiguing walking, but a gradual ascent reaches a level plain only 500 yards short of Petre's Pits Bottom; the ruin of the large Knattaburrow cairn is on this plain; beyond the cairn the path becomes stranded and poorly defined. Knattaburrow cairn has a deeply marked circumference ring and offers views revealing the fine proportions of the southern commons, with Beacon Rocks and Three Burrows their impressive culmination. Coryndon Ball, Butterdon Hill, Hangershiel Rock, a portion of the Red Lake Railway track and distant Staldon Burrow are backed by the English Channel. In the mid-distance appear the lonely mounds of Old Hill and Red Brook Ball, crossed by Track 7 between Middle and Red Brooks. Northward, the immense cairn of Eastern Whitaburrow is the dominant sentinel over all. (Note the misleading OS markings for the Whitaburrow cairns – 'Petre's Cross' for Western Whitaburrow and 'White Barrows' for Eastern.)

The track, passing Knattaburrow at almost 1,500 feet above sea level, crosses peaty ground to run north-east towards the Bala Brook valley. It is marked by OS as leading towards the east (right) shoulder of Eastern Whitaburrow; this is only partially correct, and it eventually becomes necessary to change direction towards the west (left) shoulder. Excavation and the spread of mire in this part of the valley have destroyed all signs of the former ford, but it is easy to cross Bala Brook a little higher upstream and so reach the junction of the track with the ancient Zeal track – converted in 1846 into a horse-tramroad for the carriage of peat. Here it swings abruptly left and climbs towards Western Whitaburrow. The tramroad was constructed by adventurers named Davy and Wilkins, who obtained a licence from the Duchy of Cornwall to cut peat at Red Lake Mires (Erme) and transport it to a newly built works at Zeal near Shipley Bridge. Here the peat was converted into peat charcoal, and naphtha gas manufactured as a by-product. The tramroad, with wooden rails spiked to granite sets, utilized the course of the old moorland track coming up from Zeal; this would previously have been used by jobbers as a branch connecting the farms of Zeal and Shipley with Track 3, the main Jobbers' Road – indeed, the original track is shown on *OS 1809*, and the tramroad is described in detail in the author's *Walking the Dartmoor Railroads*.

Track 7 passes a $\frac{3}{4}$-mile stone (of the 1846 tramroad) and makes a gradual ascent over Bala Brook Heath towards Western Whitaburrow, the smaller of the two cairns on the lofty Whitaburrow ridge. In the midst of the cairn, the labourers of Davy and Wilkins built for themselves a tiny house. They broke the arms from Petre's†, erected here in 1557 to denote a boundary point (on the land granted to Sir William Petre following the dissolution of the monasteries) in order to use the cross-shaft as a fireplace lintel, and they succeeded in filling their peat-fired cooking-pot with rabbits poached from nearby Huntingdon Warren (Avon). From the hillcrest is seen a tremendous moorscape embracing many square miles of the southern fen, a picture of desolation and loneliness marked by the hand of man only at the conical tip, ruined buildings and railway trackbed of the old Red Lake Clay works. This early twentieth-century undertaking included a steam-haulage railway ascending from a terminus at Bittaford on the BR (ex-GWR) main line near Ivybridge.

The track ascends from the shoulder of the Whitaburrow ridge towards the converging Red Lake Railway; passing some old stone-built clay-settling pits, it meets with Track 3; this intersection of the old way by the 1846 tramroad was dubbed by the peat and clay workers 'the Crossways'. It is a true crossways, as the tramroad was continued beyond the Jobbers' Road to a point where a large peat-press had been built, for extracting moisture from the peat before loading it on the tramroad trucks. The name serves to emphasize the tradition surviving at that time regarding the former long-lasting importance of Track 3, which was recorded by a traveller only fifty years before the tramroad-builders arrived, to have been 'a Stony Line called Jobbers Cause, nearly East and West, which tis said was antiently a Road much used for travelling ...'

It goes without saying that moormen using Track 7 from Bala

Brook Head to Crossways after the building of the tramroad, had merely to follow its line through the heather, as can walker and rider today.

TRACK 8

TRANS-DARTMOOR PACKHORSE TRACK
CHAGFORD – TAVISTOCK   18¾ miles

Chagford, an attractive old border-country town, now with excellent hotel accommodation, assumed commercial importance as early as 1305, being then appointed a stannary town for the marketing of Dartmoor tin and the seat of the Stannary Court for north-east Dartmoor. The court met in a two-storey building in the square which collapsed, with some loss of life, on 6 March 1617. The wealth of the medieval tinners' Guild of St Michael contributed to the beautiful interior of the parish church, which Bishop Bronescombe had dedicated in 1261. The successful weekly market and development of the wool trade in the town led to much trans-moorland travel, and a Chagford-Tavistock route was in use in very early times, carrying local moorland as well as through traffic between Exeter and Truro. The wool road to Ashburton via Beetor†, Swallerton Gate and White Gate also received heavy use from the medieval period until at least 1848, when the Chagford woollen mill closed.

The ancient trade route listed here as Track 8 was superseded by the trans-Dartmoor turnpike road of 1792 and was the moorland portion of the Exeter-Cornwall track clearly shown by *Ogilby* as 'Exeter to Truro'. It left Exeter via Cowick Street, climbed Longdown, descended to Dunsford and crossed the River Teign at Clifford Bridge, from where it followed the ridgeway past the Iron Age forts of Wooston and Cranbrook and ran south-westward from Easton to Chagford. An alternative route from Exeter crossed Teign at Steps Bridge and ran via Doccombe to Moretonhampstead. Crossing the River Bovey at Wormhill Bridge and approaching the Moor, it intersected the wool road at Beetor† and Mariners' Way at Moorgate,

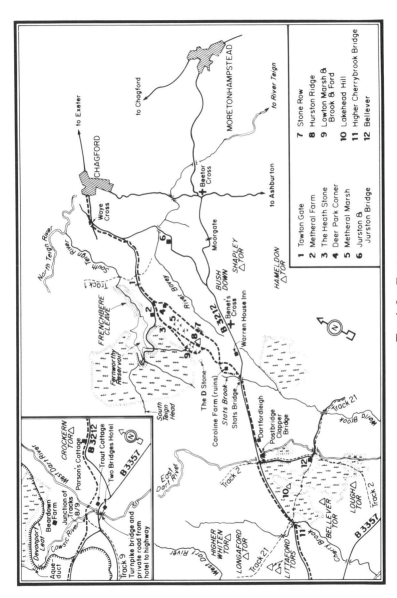

Track 8 – East

1 Towton Gate
2 Metheral Farm
3 The Heath Stone
4 Deer Park Corner
5 Metheral Marsh
6 Jurston & Jurston Bridge
7 Stone Row
8 Hurston Ridge
9 Lowton Marsh & Brook & Ford
10 Lakehead Hill
11 Higher Cherrybrook Bridge
12 Bellever

before climbing the escarpment. From here it crossed the upper Curlicombe Brook under Bush Down, passed Benet's† and New House (now the Warren House Inn) and reached the junction with the Chagford track at Stats Bridge. This route from Moretonhampstead, although not shown by *Ogilby*, is given by *Vancouver* and became the basis of the turnpike road and is represented today by the B3212 highway; no further description is therefore given here of the Moretonhampstead branch.

From Tavistock westward into Cornwall the old Truro track is the basis of the modern, serpentine road to Gunnislake across the Devon border, where it crosses Tamar on the fine old Greystone Bridge. Callington and Liskeard lie on the route as it continues via either Bodmin or St Austell to Truro.

A moorland branch of Track 8 led to the coast at modern Plymouth in medieval times; leaving the main track at Two Bridges, it crossed Blacka Brook at the Ockery clapper bridge and ran south-westward to Sutton Pool (Plymouth) near the line of the B3212 and A386 roads, via modern Yelverton and Roborough. It is today motorable except at its point of departure from the Tavistock track on Cowsic-side and on Roborough Down south of Yelverton Rock. An historically important branch, it is described and numbered here as Track 9.

Following the Track (westward)
Leave Chagford Square by Mill Street. Fork left below the Moorlands Hotel and drive to Waye Cross, site of a vanished guide-stone. Turn left and ascend the hill to another guide-stone site near Tunnaford, where now a signpost points to Fernworthy. Take this road; pass a turning (left) to Corndon, notice wall-steps (left) and a farm drive (right) to Yardworthy, where Track 1 intersects the route. Cattle-grid and moorgate ahead indicated Tawton Gate (682851), from where an alternative route led to the junction with the Moretonhampstead branch at Stats Bridge.

Route A, as shown by *Besley* and outlined in *High Dartmoor*, is given here only in skeletal form; in the light of more recent investigations (1983-5) I prefer to regard route B as the main track. It should be noted that wide, green ways climbing Hurston Ridge, visible from the Fernworthy road, are mostly misleading; they link Hurston and Lakeland with Higher Meripit via Stannon Newtake.

Route A (west side of Tawton Common): just beyond entrance to

Metheral Farm, branch left from Fernworthy road into grassy, sunken way. Heath Stone stands in angle of roads. Make for dip in small hill ahead 300 yards east of the plantations boundary wall; track here joined by branch from Metheral Ford; pass west side of Metheral Marsh and ford feeder stream; track sunken and stony for short way, then poorly defined in approaching Lowton Marsh; loops – west to ford Lowton Brook, east to pass further side of marsh; traceable in heather as it veers left to join green way mounting ridge. Hurston stone row (on route B) 350 yards east of track; inscribed 'D' Stone (Forest boundary mark, D=Duchy) 200 yards north of track on crest of Asacombe* Hill: large set slab, left; stranded, heathery track leaves green way and passes near slab; descend westward in line with lower Caroline corner; join main route B near ruined hut circles.

Route B (east side of Tawton Common). Shown by *Ogilbys Greenwood* and *Donn* (see below). 350 yards above Tawton Gate branch left from the Fernworthy road into a stony track approaching the Willandhead cornditch wall. Follow this to the south-west corner (Deerpark Corner), from where the road is grassed over but clear for a considerable way as it runs above the Metheral Brook valley (right). It flanks a small hill ahead, passing well above Metheral Marsh which lies at the foot of the hill. Route A is clearly seen from here on the further side of the marsh. Route B, wide, sunken and roadlike, crosses a substantially built reave and ascends towards the now visible blocking stone of the Hurston stone row (Pl.13). Other instances of ancient tracks utilizing prehistoric monuments and eaves as guidelines are found in this book, on pp. 68, 77, 111, 146 and 258, whilst the Peter Tavy peat track, mentioned on p. 231 as branching from Track 21, goes on to pass the Langstone Moor menhir. The fine double row on Hurston Ridge, 150 yards long, is perfectly preserved, its tallest member at the grave standing 6 feet high and 4 feet 10 inches wide at base. Reaching the row, the track becomes stranded; remain near the row; just beyond the higher end, curve round a small but prominent bed of rushes, right, and converge with a parallel reave ascending southward from Metheral Marsh. A second, transverse reave crosses both track and row; relevant distances just above this point are, left to right, 12 yards from row to track and 48 yards from track to parallel reave.

---

* So spelt in the Lydford Tithes Map of 1840 and pronounced by the Moor people Asacombe.

Beyond the rushes follow a grassy gully beside a parallel reave and observe a skyline chink marking the passage of the track on the crest ahead, whilst in the gully is a group of boulders, of which at least one could once have been a vertical guide-stone. *Eastward from crest: way clear, descending beside reave to rushes, bearing right to upper end of stone row, following row, continuing as sunken, grassy road above Metheral Marsh and running to Deerpark Corner.* The D Stone appears a third of a mile north as track and reave, mutually entwined in two places, together cross the crest. There is much to see from here: the central basin rimmed by the southern and western hills, with Bellever Tor monopolizing the near distance; left is the cairn-topped dome of Watern (OS 'Water') Hill: ahead are features to guide the walker to Stats Bridge, the entire route here being clearly confirmed by *Donn. Ogilby* gives the names 'Turn about Brooke' to Stats Brook. I suggest the logical reason for this to be certain trading arrangements made during the plague epidemic of 1625. The moorland people had then established a 'plague market' for their wares among the Merivale hut circles on Long Ash Plain* where Tavistockians could buy and barter, but they were not permitted to go further into the Moor. Burials of plague victims at Tavistock for that year were very numerous, and I find that a total of twenty for Chagford was much above the annual average for what was then a very small village. Thus the plague struck at each end of Track 8. The valley of Stats Brook would have offered comparative shelter at the south-west foot of Hurston Ridge where the moor people also could trade with Chagfordians – who, reaching the valley and concluding their business had then, like the Tavistockians at Merivale, to turn about for home.

Eastward: track and reave seen descending to stone row – temporarily concealed by hill shoulder; track clearly reappears running to Deerpark Corner. Fine views of Cosdon, Shoveldon, tors of Kes, Middle and Frenchbere, and sides of Frenchbere Cleave; road beyond Tawton Gate disappears towards Chagford.

On the commencing westward descent the reave terminates at a transverse path; the track continues along the south verge of a narrow

---

* *Mrs Bray* (Vol. I, p. 160) writes: '... they are stated by tradition to be the enclosures in which, during the plague at Tavistock (that they might have no intercourse with its inhabitants), the country-people deposited the necessary supply of provisions, for which, within the same, the towns-people left their money.'

heather patch and, slightly sunken, is joined by route A near some ruined hut circles see p. 93. Below these, turn left into a well-defined transverse track; three ways branch from the junction (near which is a solitary boulder:) 1, a disused way descending to a ford on a feeder of Stats Brook and running to the lower corner of the Caroline enclosure: its continuation appears to have been appropriated by the eighteenth-century Wheal Caroline leat-builders as occupying the contour they needed. Branches 2 and 3 lead to the Caroline enclosure: 2, slightly more direct, turns downhill to the lower corner; 3, the upper, follows the contour of the Caroline farm leat (which carried springwater from the head of the mire), shows the greater wear and leads to the higher corner. I would interpret these as – 1, ancient way, original route of Track 8 pre-dating the Caroline enclosure and dictating the trackside position of the western cornditch; 2, first diversion of track after construction of Wheal Caroline leat; 3, later diversion of track on level beside Caroline farm leat to higher corner.

I have been unable to determine the date of Caroline Farm (later the minehouse of Wheal Caroline), but the cornditch construction of the enclosure certainly shows it to have been before 1780, and its general appearance possibly earlier. An experienced mine-manager, John Paull of Tavistock, worked the mines in the 1830s, and it is shown as 'Mine' on the Lydford Tithes Map of 1840. The stony road verging the higher cornditch bends left after crossing the Wheal Caroline leat channel and runs beside Caroline Bog and the infant Stats Brook to join the B3212 road on the line of the Moretonhampstead branch* of Track 8. South of the road the leat clings to the 1,250-foot contour at the foot of Watern Hill, while the way turns right to reach the unsightly Stats Bridge (spanning Stats Brook). The angular approach of Track 8 (from Chagford) to its junction with the Moreton-hampstead branch resulted from the need to avoid Caroline Bog and utilize the (modernized clapper) bridge. *Donn* clearly shows the angularity. The wide modern road climbs Meripit Hill, sweeps down into Postbridge and crosses East Dart on a graceful turnpike bridge. Beside it is the justly celebrated clapper bridge of three openings, over 42 feet in length, which carried Track 8 in pre-turnpike days. *Ogilby* marks this as 'Stone bridge 3. Arches', his method of indicating three

---

* Here descending from the Warren House Inn, at that time standing on the south side of the road at Cape Horn and styled 'New House'. *Donn* shows guide-stones between the inn and Moorgate at Liapa † (see p. 33).

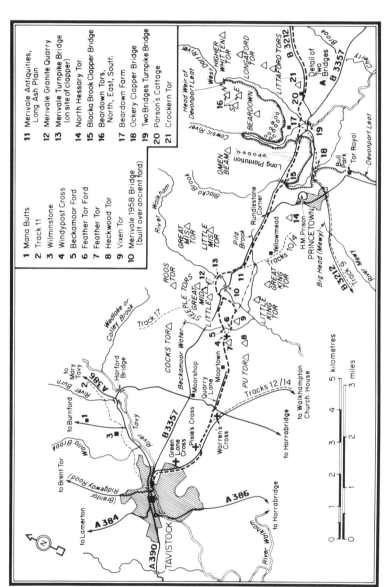

1 Mana Butts	11 Merivale Antiquities, Long Ash Plain
2 Track 11	12 Merivale Granite Quarry
3 Wilminstone	13 Merivale Turnpike Bridge (on site of clapper)
4 Windypost Cross	14 North Hessary Tor
5 Beckamoor Ford	15 Blacka Brook Clapper Bridge
6 Feather Tor Ford	16 Beardown Tors, North, East, South.
7 Feather Tor	17 Beardown Farm
8 Heckwood Tor	18 Ockery Clapper Bridge
9 Vixen Tor	19 Two Bridges Turnpike Bridge
10 Merivale 1958 Bridge (built over ancient ford)	20 Parson's Cottage
	21 Crockern Tor

Track 8 – West

clapper openings. The original way passed where Dartfordleigh House now stands – the 'leigh' by the Dart ford – to the clapper bridge; the wall built alongside the track on the west bank remains to show the line of the track where it converges with the modern road; this continues on the line of Track 8 for a further mile and a half to Parson's Cottage, last of three houses on the right, west of Higher Cherry Brook Bridge (*Ogilby* – 'Cherrey Brooke A stone Bridge') and Powder Mills before reaching Two Bridges. Track 8 has for some way onward been declared lost, but I am now pleased to place it before the reader.

Under Crockern Tor (*Ogilby* – 'A Hill of Rock called Crokka Tor') the modern road bends left from Parson's Cottage to round the small hill ahead and drop beyond it to Two Bridges; Track 8 passes onto the moor, right, just before the bend (Pl. 12). To follow it, climb a timber stile over the wall; the track is well defined to a ford on Muddy Lakes Brook (here an infant stream) and ascends the hill ahead. Here occurs another parting of ways: A, a very ancient route via Beardown Farm and clapper bridge; B, the route in use until superseded by the turnpike road, via Cowsic End and Beardown Lodge, each route throwing off a branch to the Plymouth track (9). There is space now only briefly to sketch route A; but a detailed itinerary is given for Route B.

Route A: Muddy Lakes Ford – pass ruined hut circle – through gap in transverse wall – oblique descent past flat rock to West Dart – through enclosure gate beside Crockern farm track to riverside – site of ford (washed out) and probable clapper bridge – up water-worn gully on Beardown onto sunken way on plain – across green behind Beardown Farm – sunken way points to Cowsic – join farm road – enter meadow at bend; clapper bridge of five openings seen upstream; follow raised way to river; ford; right-bank track junction: right, via gully (also water-worn) to head of Beardown Newtake – gateway – junction with B3357 road; left at junction, Plymouth branch marked by row of large stones. Continuation is through the HM Prison farmlands (no public access). It is emphasized that the express permission of Mr and Mrs A. Forbes of Beardown Farm is needed to follow the track through the farmlands.

Route B: Muddy Lakes Ford. The well-defined track bears left and is sunken in reaching a gap in an east-west wall (modern, but crumbling); pass the south foot of a flat rock outcrop. It continues as a wide, shallow, grassed-over road aligned with an old barn beside the

West Dart river. West of the rock outcrop bear left towards the modern Two Bridges and diagonally descend the valley-side, where the track is much overgrown by gorse; pass two conspicuous bedrocks and cross an old leat channel. Join the Crockern farm track 12 yards from the gate at Two Bridges. The track passes through this and descends as a green way, right, through a lower gateway behind Trout Cottage and crosses the valley floor to the river. This excellent piece of routing avoids both the steep bank below the Crockern farm track and, reaching the valley floor, the marshy tract near the embanked main road. Do not attempt to enter the lower gateway, but descend to the riverside over steps from the (modern) roadside opposite the façade of the Two Bridges Hotel. Walk to the gateway behind the cottage; turn left and follow the visible, shallow way to the river, making for the north end of an artificial row of boulders along the bank; here turn downstream. The purpose of the row, 48 yards long, was apparently to guide travellers between the river crossing and the green way behind the cottage, for a firm, wide track runs between row and river to the ford-approach 50 yards upstream from the confluence of West Dart and Cowsic. That the river was forded obliquely upstream is plain from the position on the further bank of a sunken way across the peninsula; the site of the former (recorded) clapper bridge (*Ogilby* – 'A Stone bridge') is just upstream from the ford. Excessive river-bank erosion has taken place, and no visible approach from ford (or clapper) to the right bank sunken way now remains. The late moorman Jim Mortimore of Crockern Farm was told by his grandfather that the clapper bridge was utterly destroyed by a great spate of the river during his father's time (in the very early years of last century) 'after the turnpike road was opened'. Such a spate would similarly have affected Cowsic – the two rivers rising in the same area of the northern fen – and destroyed the bridge that spanned it (*Ogilby* – 'A brooke and bridge').

It is normally possible to cross West Dart on the boulders at the bridge site; from the west bank follow the sunken way across the river to a junction of walls on the right bank and, unless the river is swollen, boulders facilitate crossing. The V-pattern of walls leading away from the right bank* is interesting; *Ogilby* and the later, more accurate maps of *Vancouver*, *Donn* and *Cary* show the branching of the

---

* This, and the route as described west of Parson's Cottage, is shown on the 1839 Lydford Tithes Map.

Tavistock and Plymouth tracks immediately west of Cowsic; assuming the V-walls delineate the branching tracks, it transpires that Track 9 follows the south side of the south wall and Track 8 the north. The rutted Track 8 leads to a gate; it is not a right of way; the gate is kept locked and the walker must approach it from the lane branching right from the highroad west of the bridge. The lane is a DNPA yellow-spot route, and stiles are marked accordingly: the gate on Track 8 is beyond the second stile. View the track's approach from the Cowsic ford and its continuation, left, in a gully. The field gradient here, although not steep, is sufficient to have induced erosion by storm-drainage. The gully is seen ascending to the upper side of the field entered by the lane, but no right of way exists (except the DNPA route, which is irrelevant to Track 8). The gully reaches the Beardown farm drive at a point where the old field hedge terminates at a carefully rounded end, its line being continued by a modern wall to the highroad. On the further side of the drive an overgrown, sunken way runs between the garden of Beardown Lodge and another ancient hedge. It emerges at the private entrance-gate of the Lodge where the curving wall shows its line, and becomes a grassy, sunken road below the north verge of the high road on Beardown Hill. The actual position of the Lodge is interesting: whilst ineffectively situated to overlook the modern entrance to the Beardown drive, it was purpose-built to overlook the pre-1792 drive branching from Track 8, being part of the establishment including Beardown Farm created by Mr Edward Bray in 1780. Follow the sunken way between highroad and wall (right); the actual point of its convergence with the road has been destroyed in the embanking of the latter near the Devonport leat bridge.

The B3357 high road (based on Track 8) now makes a direct line to the crossing of Blacka Brook, the next stream westward, by ford and clapper footbridge; the existence of the latter is not generally known and should not be confused with the fine structure upstream near Fice's Well, which some writers have suggested was on the route of the old way. There can be no doubt, however, that Track 8 was served by the now ruined bridge (Pl.14) within the prison grounds on the downstream side of the modern road bridge. Visible from the latter, it has three openings, but only one impost remains in place, there being another lying on the bank alongside. West of the brook, the B3357 is again based on Track 8; passing Pascoe's Well (left roadside) it ascends to Rundlestone Corner, where it crosses the high North Hessary-Great Mis Tor col – here forming the west rim of the central basin – before commencing its long descent (with one short intermediate climb to cross the western escarpment) into the border-country and Tavistock. The view from Rundlestone is magnificent – especially of the distant Cornish landscape broken in the near distance by the jagged tors of Walkham country. Still united, Track 8 and B3357 descend past Over Tor (right) and cross the plain of Long Ash Hill amid the relics of a Bronze Age settlement and sanctuary, to the valley 550 feet below. Here, at Merivale, the River Walkham was crossed on a large clapper bridge replaced by the turnpike bridge of 1792 – the clapper being demolished in the process but the adjacent ford remaining unaffected. The turnpike successor to the clapper is now the 'old bridge', for another structure arose in 1958 directly over the ancient ford.

It is interesting that *Ogilby* should actually show the former clapper as 'Stone bridge 2. Arches' (cf Postbridge p. 97), and *Donn* as 'Mariville Bridge' as well as giving a solid line, denoting a wall or hedge, to the right-hand track-verge at Merivale and to a lengthy portion of the left-hand verge beyond the hamlet. The building accurately marked within the lower enclosure is Merivale Farm: from this point the way continues as a well-defined track alongside the finely built boundary wall of Merivale Newtake, to a point where this curves inward opposite Vixen Tor – again, a feature accurately shown by *Donn*. The track, with deep strands, now bears westward and become increasingly sunken, passes (right) a Sampford Spiney bond-stone and reaches Feathertor Ford on Beckamoor Water – historic, wide and deeply worn. The gentle climb ahead from the ford, constant use having preserved its appearance as a green way, takes the track past the clitter of Feather Tor to where Windypost† stands on the escarpment. I believe this track via Feathertor Ford must be regarded as the main route, and the path branching from the B3357 three-quarters of a mile west of Merivale to Beckamoor Ford as an alternative; it is perhaps significant that *Donn* does not mark the latter at all. Both ways meet at Windypost† beside the Grimstone & Sortridge leat, where a bull's-eye (perforated stone) admits water into a branch leat. From here, the Tavy valley, Tavistock town, distant Tamar and Bodmin Moor comprise an absorbing study. *Eastward: pass † on north side. Green way towards Feathertor Ford clear, also continuation passing small 'SS' bond-stone to reach Merivale wall.*

At Windypost † begins the final stage of Track 8. It is sunken in descending from the escarpment and crosses the leat on a granite conduit built, apparently, especially to carry packhorse traffic.

Directly aligned with it is its distant, macadamized continuation on the flank of Whitchurch Down beyond Moortown and leading to Tavistock Town. It become stranded and crosses a plain; walk towards the trees within the southernmost corner of Moortown Newtake from where the track passes the entrance to Moortown Farm and merges with Quarry Lane. *Eastward: pass entrance to Moortown Farm and sheltered enclosure (left), noticing fine construction of newtake wall. Pu Tor is right as walker ascends, Prowtytown Rocks left. Leaving south corner, stay well out from in-curving wall and follow strands to saddle ahead; when leat reached, way becomes sunken and Windypost † seen – though of little help to eastbound traveller because invisible until within 100 yards. Extensive torscape seen from † embraces Little and Mid Steeple (left), Great and Little Mis, Hollow and North Hessary, Vixen (below), King and Little King, Swell (mid-distance), Leedon, Ingra and Peak Hill (right). Traffic seen on B3357 (Long Ash Hill); high col beyond forms bold, sweeping line concealing all signs of central basin.*

Quarry Lane, where two large quarries once worked, meets the Peter Tavy-Horrabridge road (the ancient Plymouth-Okehampton highway) ascending from Pennycomequick and continues beyond it over Whitchurch Down – in the first 60 yards or so retaining its original appearance as a stony road. The character of the down, once rough pastureland, has greatly changed during the present century, a large part having been laid out as Tavistock golf course, where it is wise for walkers to beware of projectiles; traces of the old road, however, can still be faintly seen beyond the initial stony portion, and shallow strands lead to the south (left) side of the only hill on Whitchurch Down (point 200 on the 1984 OS 2½-inch map). On crossing the slope of the knoll the walker sees the west end of the down spread before him, with the Sampford Spiney-Whitchurch road (left) running parallel with Track 8. In descending from the knoll, Pixies'† appears ahead near a group of golfing bunkers, and to the right of the small but conspicuous building on the west edge of the down known as the 'Pimple'. This houses a pumping plant for an adjoining underground reservoir and provides the best of views over Tavistock town, border-country, high moor and Cornwall. Built of Hurdwick stone quarried near Tavistock, the little building is triangular with a conical, slated roof.* Beyond Pixies' † track and road converge to run directly to Green Lane†, where its descent through

---

* For cross reference from p. 157.

Green Lane into Tavistock begins. Although *Donn* shows neither of the crosses, the road is based on the Tavistock branch of the Buckfast monastic way from Walkhampton church; thus five historically important routes, Tracks 4, 8, 10, 12 and 14 pursue their united and well-worn way through Green Lane into the town, the enclosing walls on either side appearing in *Donn. Eastward; unchecked growth of gorse prevents sighting from Green Lane† of Pixies †, but follow road, then diverge left to Pixies †. On passing over south flank of point 656, make towards Pu Tor. Stranded path veers slightly towards settlement of Moortown; beyond, actual track seen mounting escarpment north side of Feather Tor; sunken way prominent near Windypost†.*

At the foot of Green Lane the ancient way joins the 1792 turnpike road, now the B3357, within sight and sound of the swift River Tavy, which was crossed by Track 4, 8 and 10 at Tavistock Great Bridge to enter the town. A deed of *c.*1275 refers to the 'Royal Way leading to the Great Bridge' (*Calendar of Tavistock Parish Records*, translated by R.N. Worth). Tracks 12 and 14 made a more direct entry to the abbey precincts.

Few towns in England are more pleasant than Tavistock and none more pleasantly situated. Lying in a shallow basin watered by Tavy, it is overlooked in the east by the wild Dartmoor hills; northward is the border-country landmark of the volcanic Brent Tor; southward the River Walkham flows to join Tavy at the beautiful Double Waters; while in the west beyond the watershed is Tamar, backed by the lumpy undulations of Cornwall's Kit Hill and Bodmin Moor. This is plainly England's golden west, with Tavistock its gateway. The earliest settlement near the site, of which evidence remains, was a hillside village of the Iron Age now known as the 'Trendle', situated on the upper west valley-side of Tavy a mile north of the town. In historic times, possibly early in the eighth century, the Saxon settlers adopted a lower, valley-floor site for their village – their Tavy 'stock'. The founding of the Saxon abbey in 974 gave great impetus to the growth of the village which, within 200 years under the administrative influence of Norman rule, became a compact township raised to borough status, with a weekly market held on a Friday – as it is even now, in the late twentieth century – granted in a charter of 1105, and a three-day fair. Dartmoor tin-streaming had by then become an established industry, and Tavistock, as a stannary town, was recognized as a natural collecting and forwarding centre for tin and copper ore, which was transported by packhorse to the 'ham' or port of Morwell on Tamar, for onward shipment.

From the Middle Ages to the dissolution of the monasteries, the town's history is inextricably bound up with that of the great Benedictine abbey, its progress further enhanced by growing importance as a stannary town, and a wool and cloth centre. The last two industries went some way toward compensating for the post-dissolution loss of profitable monastic activities, all of which accounted for the importance of Tracks 4, 8, 10, 12 and 14. Tavistock was a parliamentary borough from 1295 to 1868, represented by two Members. The Russell family (later dukes of Bedford) acquired the borough and extensive estates of the dissolved abbey in 1539, since when the town has benefited greatly from their protective care, patronage and live interest. That great son of Devon, Sir Francis Drake, was born at Crowndale Farm, only a mile from the centre of the town.

TRACK 9

TRANS-DARTMOOR PACKHORSE TRACK: CHAGFORD – PLYMOUTH (BRANCH OF TRACK 8 FROM TWO BRIDGES TO SUTTON HARBOUR)
$16\frac{1}{4}$ miles)

Although 'Plymouth' will serve here as a convenient place-name, it should be borne in mind that the township of Plymouth scarcely existed in the early days of medieval commerce on Tracks 8 and 9. The growing mercantile importance of Sutton Pool, however, a sheltered inlet where merchant ships could anchor – and Plymouth's first and ancient harbour, brought about an expansion of the waterside village of Sutton Valletort. This was influenced in no small way by the weekly market established in 1254 by the prior of Plympton, resulting in the granting of a charter in 1439 to the new town, Plymouth, at the mouth of the River Plym. So the name may be regarded as relatively correct.

From Ockery Bridge on Blacka Brook (west of Two Bridges) to Yelverton, the track is the basis of the modern B3212 road. *Donn* shows it passing above 'Stean Lake', 'Elvertown' (Yelverton), 'Hurlstone Rock' (Roborough Rock) and over Roborough Down. As that part of the route from Cowsic to the B3212 has not previously been researched, I have sought to retrace and set it out here.

Following the Track (south-westward)
From the right bank of Cowsic at the crossing of Track 8 (p. 98), Track 9 branches from the Tavistock route and crosses the foot of Beardown Hill to become the B3212 road. Between river and road the route is indicated by the south V-wall. The way crosses the field near the modern road embankment to a laneside gateway (park near here

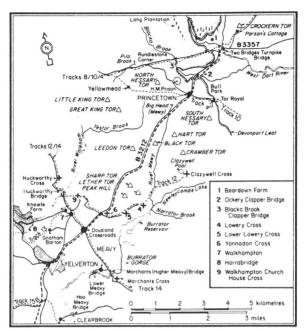

Track 9 – North

at 609750), passing the ruins of a cott in the upper right-hand corner.
Route and V-walls are shown on the Lydford Tithes Map of 1839.
The walls of the lane are not ancient and, opposite the gate, the way
diagonally crosses the field above – here the foot of Beardown Hill
where all signs have long disappeared under the plough – to the lower
boundary fence of Moor Lodge. Do not enter the field, but follow the
main road to the roadside boundary wall of Moor Lodge; look over
the wall at a visible sunken way between wall and tennis court level;
this is exactly aligned on the Princetown road at the modern junction,
and the Moor Lodge wall blocking it was, of course, built long after
the abandonment of the track. Drive along the Princetown road and
park (left) just beyond the bridge in the Blacka Brook valley. The old
road diverged from the modern highway to pass over Lower Watern
Newtake through a gateway near a riverside barn to reach Blacka
Brook, where the splendid clapper bridge of two openings (Pl. 15) has
imposts raised on high piers to maintain the original track level. The
way then ascended the west bank through a narrow lane and made a
hairpin bend to follow a track leading back to the east-west line of

Track 9 at a (padlocked) roadside gate. The lay-by space here results from the recessed south wall which points towards the clapper bridge. In the concealed hollow between the clapper and its turnpike successor once stood a strange old house with a verandah called 'The Ockery', but a tragedy within its walls during the early years of the present century led to its demolition.

If, continuing westward, we exclude nineteenth century Princetown (where the intersection of the way by Tracks 4 and 10 occurs) and pass the twin lodges on Plymouth Hill, we can experience much of the unspoilt splendour of the great expanse of Dartmoor's southwest commons, across which even now, as in Trans-Dartmoor Track days, the Plymouth-bound traveller saw only the lonely hills and the thin line of the undulating road before him. *Donn* shows no fewer than fifteen guide-stones between Beardown and Stenlake. If those bore the initial letters of Chagford and Plymouth in the style of the T-A stones of Track 10, it is remarkable that not one is known to exist, and I would like to hear from any reader who discovers a stone marked, presumably, 'C' and 'P'.

From Stenlake to Yelverton the modern road follows the line of its predecessor, intersecting Track 12 at Yannadon crossroads and Track 14 at Dousland crossroads. Practically no house existed at Yelverton until the nineteenth century, when Elford Town, the *tun* or farm of the Elford family gave its name to the locality. The track crossed Yelverton Green directly towards Udal Tor, or Roborough Rock, its line the basis of the road along the east fringe of the World War II airfield. When this road curves to pass to the west of Udal tor, the direct line of Track 9 continues beside a wooden fence, left, as a stony road along the east side of, and some 20 yards from, the tor.* Reaching a disused drinking fountain and a small obelisk commemorating Queen Victoria's Diamond Jubilee of 1897, the track crosses a road (branching from the A386 highway to Crapstone) beside a cattle grid. It is well defined on the down as it reaches a drinking trough, right; here occurs a fork, marked by *Donn*, and less clearly by *Cary*, where a straight, green way leads, right, to join a road (branching south from the Crapstone road) to Yeoland Lane, whilst Track 9 bears slightly left from the drinking trough to maintain its stony character in running between bushes to the crest of the rise near, and to the right of, a seat. On the plain of the down the left-hand line

---

* This is clearly shown by *Donn*, who marks Udal Tor as 'Hurlestone Rock'.

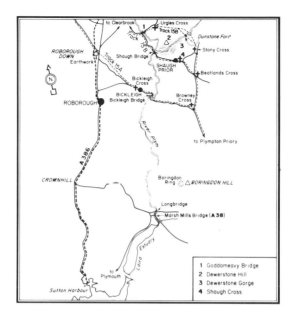

Track 9 – South

of bushes recedes and the track runs close beside the right-hand line. Houses seen beyond the bushes, right – they include the Yelverton Golf Clubhouse – verge the road to Yeoland Lane, parallel to which runs Track 9 at a distance of less than 100 yards.

A slight descent now occurs over the open ground of the golf course, but still with bushes verging the right-hand side. A large golfing bunker appears ahead and a wide area of bushes beyond it. Follow the track into these, where it passes through a series of pits of the former Yeoland Consuls Mine.* In places a grass-earthen track, in others clearly revealing its overall stone foundation, Track 9 continues beyond the mining pits at between 50 and 100 yards west of the A386 highway, intersects Track 15 and reaches a branch road (from the highway to Buckland Monachorum) at a point between a cattle-grid sign and the junction of Yeoland Down Lane (north end) and slightly

---

* That the pits belong to the earliest workings of the mine on this area of Roborough Down is suggested by their obviously having been excavated in such way as to avoid interfering with the old Plymouth road.

nearer the former. Beyond the banked up south road verge the stony line of the track is again apparent. Passing within 20 yards of another drinking trough (right), it bears slightly to the right; its continuation on the southern, higher part of Roborough Down can now be seen ahead in direct alignment. The track reaches another branch road (from the highway to the Moorland Links Hotel and Sowton) some 50 yards east of the south junction of Yeoland Down Lane. (The lane follows an ancient cornditch wall bordering land sold before World War II for house-building.)

South of the Sowton road the track curves slightly to the right, then left, and is joined by a grassy, southward continuation of Yeoland Down Lane. The true way, however, is again definable by means of its stone foundation; ascending the gradual slope of a hillock ahead it becomes a worn, stony road passing over the crest of the hillock and bringing into view an ascent, southward, to its highest point on Roborough Down beside Roborough Down earthwork. *Northward from hillock south of Sowton road: ignore grassy branch track (left) to Yeoland Common Lane and, a short way ahead, another wide, grassy branch (right) reaching the Sowton road near junction with highway. Follow always central, stony way and observe continuation beyond Sowton road.* Next, descending to cross another branch road (a link road from the highway to the main Bere Alston road), it is well defined in running to the latter which, excepting its actual junction with the highway – see p. 178 – is on the line of Track 15 (Bickleigh branch). Track 9 then crosses the road diagonally beside the Devonport leat bridge and ascends the common as a well defined road 200 yards west of Roborough Down earthwork. Its final moorland undulation carries it down to a crossing of an entrance drive to Maristow House and, 200 yards further, that of yet another by-road branching from the highway. A compensating rise now lifts its clear, wide line to the top of Roborough Hill, where it converges with the highway and joins it where Jump Gate once stood. There are two gates here today, for animals passing between the open common and the (fenced) main road, a café, and DNPA boundary sign. The descent of Track 9 into Roborough hamlet is confirmed by the line of the Maristow estate wall and the pre-turnpike cottages fronting it in the hamlet. From here its line disappears into the environs of Plymouth city and can no longer be determined on the ground.

TRACK 10

TAVISTOCK – ASHBURTON PACKHORSE TRACK (T-A TRACK)   19½ miles

The importance of this trading route, at least from the Middle Ages onward until it was superseded by the turnpike road of 1792, cannot be doubted. It was, excepting its passage on the flank of North Hessary Tor, a comparatively sheltered route, without difficult gradients or dangerous river crossings, in which it resembled the trans-moorland monastic way further south. Would one route not have served everyone's needs? Plainly, no. The monks needed as direct a route as possible from Buckfast – without having to descend into the central basin – to Walkhampton, where they could quit the high moor. Packhorse drivers, on the other hand, and other travellers on the T-A Track – often strangers to the Moor – faced what was then a lonely stretch of moorland across the central basin (south) and, more often than not, a challenge from the weather on the 1,500 foot shoulder of North Hessary Tor, the highest and most exposed land crossed by Track 10; the need for shelter and refreshment for drivers and packhorses alike could be met only at Hexworthy in the central basin.

Guide-posts were erected along the route, initially perhaps many centuries ago. An improved series of granite posts, bearing the initial letters 'T' and 'A' appropriately facing the terminal towns, was sponsored in 1669 by Plymouth Corporation, who paid £2 for the erecting of 'Moorestones on Dartmoor in the way leading from Plymouth towards Exon for guidance of Travellers passing that way'. In the event, this was a public-spirited action by the corporation, for none of the surviving stones shows the Plymouth-Exeter route (Track 8 and 9) but only the one now being described. R. Hansford Worth,

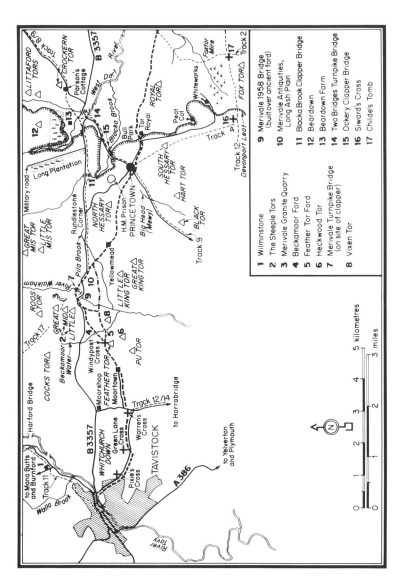

1 Wilminstone
2 The Steeple Tors
3 Merivale Granite Quarry
4 Beckamoor Ford
5 Feather Tor Ford
6 Heckwood Tor
7 Merivale Turnpike Bridge (on site of clapper)
8 Vixen Tor

9 Merivale 1958 Bridge (built over ancient ford)
10 Merivale Antiquities, Long Ash Plain
11 Blacka Brook Clapper Bridge
12 Beardown
13 Beardown Farm
14 Two Bridges Turnpike Bridge
15 Ockery Clapper Bridge
16 Siward's Cross
17 Childe's Tomb

Track 10 – West

however, writes in his *Dartmoor*: 'It is evident that, prior to 1765, the principal tracks in this neighbourhood, including both the Tavistock-Ashburton and the Plymouth-Ashburton ways [to which the present author would add the Tavistock-Chagford] had been marked with guide-stones.'

Several of the 1669 incised stones have been removed for use as gateposts and lintels, and none remain east of Hexworthy, but I have been able to discover two others not previously recorded, one being at Knowle Farm, Walkhampton. The T-A Track is easy to follow, scenically satisfying and, against the background of history, so recently in use as to enable one to imagine the days of the great wool and cloth packhorse trains winding down to Swincombe Ford, or beginning the long westward haul to North Hessary's explosed flank. Shelter on the west portion of the route was at a premium, for no trees are likely to have existed – after the depredations of the medieval tinners – on the Tor Royal site prior to Sir Thomas Tyrwhitt's planting and building activities in 1785. Even the last westward lap across Whitchurch Down, border-country though it was, could bring a lashing by an Atlantic wind unhindered since tearing across the tops of Bodmin Moor.

Following the Track (eastward)
Tracks 8 and 10 are united between Tavistock and Merivale, excepting, that is, the medieval route from Windypost† over the River Walkham at Long Ash. This will be considered first; though not passable in its entirety, it can be seen near Long Ash Farm and should certainly be visited by the historically-minded walker; details of features and permissible access appear on p. 74, as the medieval route applies to Tracks 4 and 10. I make no apology for commending the value of oral tradition. In the present case (and that of Track 4) I would have known nothing of the ancient Long Ash ford and clapper had it not been for Ern Cole of Long Ash Farm (d.1959). Ern's mother went to Long Ash in 1897 and as a young woman had known the previous tenant, John Friend, who occupied the farm in 1871 – only eighty years after the main T-A Track fell into comparative disuse.

Park in the space on the south roadside east of Merivale Bridge (552749). Follow the newtake wall on Long Ash Hill running parallel to the valley. Look over a gate in the wall approached by the ancient way ascending from Swallow Ford and the ruined longhouse, the line of stones marking it on one side being the relic of a medieval wall – the outer boundary, that is, of the Long Ash newtake of pre-Tudor times. Now follow the angle wall jutting eastward onto the common, where a still visible track reaches a menhir and stone circle, part of the Merivale Bronze Age sanctuary. Nearby are the remains of kistvaen and associated set stones. Here the track aligns with two set stones east of the menhir; there is little doubt that the first of these was erected, perhaps in medieval times, to serve as a guide-stone; it is stumpy and massive, quite unlike the type of stone normally chosen in the Bronze Age for monumental purposes. The second stone, of different appearance – it leans out of vertical and perhaps should be re-set – taller and more slender, bears the letters 'T' and 'A' appropriate to direction. It is at this stone, therefore, that I would place the junction of the medieval and later routes of the T-A Track. *Westward; view alternative routes west of river from newtake gate on Long Ash Hill.* Donn's *clearly marked route appears the better, as Beckamoor Ford alternative seen to climb some way westward before leading to Beckamoor, while* Donn's *route, more level and easy terrain, already old enough to dictate boundary of Merivale Newtake. Ancient route via Long Ash long abandoned, no longer visible. Ascent to Windypost† clear. Note that leaning guide-stone, large unmarked stone and menhir align with Windypost†.*

To reach the later T-A route marked by the 1669 guide-stones, follow in reverse the directions for Track 8 on pp. 100-103, from Tavistock to Merivale Bridge. South-east of the turnpike bridge (on the site of the former clapper) the track again appears on *Donn.* As the ascent of Long Ash Hill begins, a roadside fence (right) is seen to terminate at a tall standing stone, the most westerly *in situ* of the T-A series. It marks the parting of the eastward ways – Track 8, left; Track 10, right. The latter clings to the road-verge for a short way beyond the stone, then becomes a grassy gully behind a small car-park and mounts to Long Ash Plain; Track 8, meanwhile, is united with the modern road passing Over Tor. Track 10, with an easy gradient, avoids a rockfield lying on its north verge. On reaching Long Ash Plain, notice that the track leads towards two large set stones, terminals of a prehistoric row – also a part of the Merivale antiquities; from the row, go to a ford on the nearby leat (which certainly was flowing when the T-A Track was in use) and the next T-A stone in line with Yellowmead Newtake. Beyond it, yet another – the leaning stone – will appear. *Westward; in descending from stone row, make for*

Dartmoor Inn, when turnpike bridge and line of track round Merivale Newtake become visible.

From the leaning stone to Yellowmead Ford on Pila Brook is but a short distance. Notice beside the track a huge worked stone with a flat upper surface; a flaw on one edge doubtless caused its abandonment, and the rock from which it was cut is beside it. Another large mass lies on the verge of the track as it drops to the valley floor; work on this also was discontinued and, although drilled, it has not actually been split. On reaching the brook the walker may be confused by several animal fords, but the T-A ford has a slightly sunken approach on the cast bank, where one side of the track has been roughly banked up with large stones. Stone-pits and tinners' gullies abound here, but the track points towards stone 5 below a small Bronze Age pound and continues past stone 6 near the lower corner of Yellowmead Newtake (and in line with the rear of the house). Continuing from Yellowmead Ford, the track dips into the largest of the gullies, where intriguing evidence of its antiquity remains: the gully, like so many driven by tinners from four to six centuries ago, channelled water for tin-streaming operations; at the track crossing, stepping-stones have been laid for the passage of the packhorse-train driver; these, large and well above even the modern ground level, are hoary with age. The track is sunken in ascending from the gully and passes stones 5 and 6 to reach the Yellowmead newtake corner. *Westward; from gully, way sunken in approaching Pila Brook (passing banked-up side, left). Ford slightly out of alignment with gully and leaning T-A stone, so bear slightly left. Way appears to pass between set stones – illusion created by leaning stone and unmarked stone (ancient route), these actually over 100 yards apart. From leaning stone, next T-A stone placed to help travellers avoid rockfield.* Walk to the stone near Yellowmead corner. *Westward: track stranded; make for Great Steeple Tor.*

Yellowmead Newtake is comparatively modern; like Vixen Tor Newtake, when built it enclosed a part of the T-A Track. Of two guide-stones next eastward, the first was removed and built into a wall and the second serves as a gatepost. (This can be seen, bearing 'A' towards the unmade Fogginter road at the south-east side of the newtake.) The track, clearly defined, emerges to cross the road obliquely and reach the next stone near a small, ruined rockpile known as 'Billy's Tor'. From here, Track 10 climbs to its highest point and crosses the south slope of North Hessary Tor, 1,500 feet above the distant estuarine waters of Tavy, Tamar and Plymouth Sound.

Westward: alternative routes beyond Walkham seen converging on Windypost – main track ascending behind rocks of Vixen Tor. A scattered group of boulders, strangely shaped, appears on the hilltop, providing useful waymarks for the walker near sunken strands of the track. *Westward: in descending from boulder group, walk towards Vixen Tor and ignore paths branching to Yellowmead Farmhouse, right.*

The track now crosses a plain towards a midway point on North Hessary's flank, which temporarily blocks the eastward view, though the Mewy valley and the B3212 Princetown-Plymouth highway are visible. Two parallel, transverse gullies appear ahead, where the track curves to skirt the headmire of Yestor Brook. Before reaching the gullies, the track passes stone 12; this is mentioned in *High Dartmoor* as then lying 'A'-side down by the track, and it is pleasing now to find it re-erected on this wide, featureless plain. The two gullies, chanelling hillside drainage into the mire below, have been provided with crudely paved crossing places for travellers. A Plymouth Corporation Waterworks stone (marked 'PCWW 1917' and rendered unmistakable from the near-distance by its carefully worked, pyramidical top), bounding the Burrator reservoir catchment area, appears ahead, the track bearing right to pass 50 yards below it and reach the next T-A stone. This, still well erect, is the last but one remaining *in situ*, and it is unfortunate that, from the early turnpike era onwards, so many of these historic waymarks were uprooted and taken away by farmers for use elsewhere. The stone is below the skyline and difficult to see at a distance, being one of a succession of three or four since removed from the Hessary slope.* *Westward: on approaching erect stone near Yestor Brook Head, wonderful view opens up of south-west Dartmoor border-country centred on Yelverton and Horrabridge, backed by moors of St Austell and Bodmin, while in near distance Great Western Railway track snaking round south foot of Foggin Tor.*

On cresting the ridge beyond the erect stone, pause to study the moorland panorama: from right to left this includes Ingra Tor, Fur and Yes Tors (Walkham), the tors of Leedon, Sharp, Lether and Sheeps, the Lee Moor clay-pits, Gutter Tor and the two Trowlesworthy tors, Down Tor, Hingston Hill and Combeshead Tor, Shiel Top, Hen Tor, Shavercombe, the Plym ridge, Hart and Cramber

---

* One of these has been brought to my notice by Mr George Eggins of Knowle Farm, Walkhampton, where it is built into the hedge of a field known as 'Irish's Meadow'.

Tors, the upper reach of Hartor Brook, the summit of Eylesburrow above Cramber Down, and the distant ridge of the southern fen. Make now for a large, rounded boulder, when South Hessary Tor will rise ahead; beyond the boulder, the track is stranded on crossing a plain. Soon, Princetown will be seen, the pinnacles of the church tower beyond the next hill resembling a group of people standing in conversation. Next visible are the highroad entering the village at the lodges, the converging GWR track and Princetown-Foggintor Quarry footpath (below, right) and the trees at Tor Royal marking the direction of Track 10 east of Princetown. It was the capaciousness of the level plain between North and South Hessary Tors that persuaded Sir Thomas Tyrwhitt, exactly 201 years before the publication of this book, that the time was ripe for commercial granite quarrying, tree planting, agricultural development and, subsequently, prison building and railroad construction (Plymouth & Dartmoor Railway).

The hollow, below right, is Big Head, source of the River Mewy (OS 'Meavy'); the conifer plantation ahead occupies part of the site of Princetown railway station, and the T-A Track, now joined by the quarry path, makes for the lower corner. Seen from quarter of a mile west of the plantation are five parallel lines of communication – the B3212 road (on the line of Track 9), the River Mewy, the GWR trackbed, the Foggintor Quarry track and Track 10 – all converging on Princetown. *Westward: on rounding south-west corner of plantation take upper of two tracks, running below high bank (right); lower, more stony way is Quarry track – better defined because, whilst regular use of T-A Track ceased after 1792, quarrymen walked from Princetown to work at Foggintor until early twentieth century.*

Track 10 enters the plantation 40 yards above the corner and, inaccessible until emerging from the east side, crosses the railway track diagonally and becomes a gravelly road followed by a wire fence aligned with lodges. At the lower corner of the nearer lodge is a PCWW stone dated 1932. *Westward: from nearer lodge, Track 10 points to plantation; ascends hill beyond as green path above Quarry track.*

Donn clearly marks the east and west junctions of Track 9 and 10, the ground plan having since remained unaltered. At the lodges, turn left into Princetown village; pass the square and turn right at the Devil's Elbow Inn into the Peat Cot road. This passes over a cattle-grid and mounts to Tor Gate before descending towards Tor Royal. At the east foot of the hill the motor road swings right to Peat

Cot and Whiteworks, while the direct continuation of Track 10 is the rough road down to Sir Thomas Tyrwhitt's small mansion, Tor Royal House. A car must not be taken along this road, so park near the junction with the Peat Cot road. Now walk past Tor Royal Lodge and the drive-entrance to the house, right, pass through a gateway, cross the (flowing) Devonport leat and descend to the sheltered, wooded valley of Bachelor's Hall Brook. here comes the sensation, after the high, wild country west of Princetown, of entering an oasis; the scenic contrast, sheltered combes, fields, woodland patches, even rhododendrons to brighten the old T-A Track as it passes Bull Park Farm: somehow, Ashburton no longer seems so far away. A sturdy clapper bridge was built over the little Bachelor's Hall Brook by Tyrwhitt, where formerly a ford had served all traffic. The hill ahead is Bull Park, the enclosed portion being on the north side of the track; fork left at a track junction and ascend the hill: there is a striking view of the eastern highlands – Rippen and Corndon Tors are first to raise their heads, followed by the major height of Hameldon and the tors of Honeybag, Chinkwell, Bel, Hey (Rippen, Corndon), Buckland Beacon and, to encourage the eastbound traveller, Auswell Rocks above Ashburton; the long sweep of south Dartmoor from Down Ridge to Eylesburrow is away to the right, whilst the oasis of the central basin lies left. *Westward: pleasing surprise for walker reaching head of Bull Park is flourishing variety of trees enhancing valley below, planted 1785-90 by Tyrwhitt.*

On following the rough road eastward from Bull Park, notice several mounds on the right, spoil from tinners' trial pits. Between pits and track (30 yards from latter) is a perfect kistvaen of the Bronze Age, known as the 'Crock of Gold'. The coverstone has been pushed to one side, and about half of the retaining circle remains. Track 10 continues as a wide, stony road for some considerable way. Piles of stones along its surface show the involuntary labour undertaken by Conscientious Objectors during World War I, when the old track was to have been upgraded to metalled-road status; the work remained unfinished and the track was consequently dubbed 'the Conchies' Road'. Roadside trenches seen in places were dug to drain the road prior to laying the intended surface. Long before the 'Conchies' got to work here, however, Tyrwhitt had already taken steps to improve the old road for his own convenience and had built imposing gate-pillars at its entrance to his estate settlement at Swincombe.

Beyond the hollow of Cholake Head and the shallower Ruelake

Head, the track reaches a gate in a wire fence, from where is visible (left) the old engine-bed of the aerial ropeway plant used for transporting timber from Brimpts to Princetown station during World War I; beyond it are seen the tors of West Dart country and Track 2 passing Dunnabridge Pound. The track now descends to the Swincombe valley, with the beautiful little river on the walker's right, and the continuing way clearly seen beyond it near the ruin of Dolly Trebble's House. Roughly 100 yards beyond a large, flat slab beside the track is its intersection by Track 2, here well defined as it rounds the hill (right) and approaches an iron gate, left. Swincombe Gate appears ahead, where the right-hand post is a T-A stone pressed into duty as a gate-hanger – easternmost of the guide-stones still *in situ*. A short way below, two opposing walls form a lane; at the foot of this, near the ruins of Higher Swincombe, stand Tyrwhitt's gate-pillars. Track 10, now a wide, stony road, passes near Lower Swincombe (the ruin known as 'John Bishop's House') to approach the river at the picturesque Swincombe Ford, surely a welcome watering place in T-A Track days for the westbound 'through-train' horses and drivers who elected to bypass Hexworthy. Steps, ford and timber clam are still usable, but the latter ('Fairy Bridge') trembles unnervingly when trodden by several persons simultaneously. Follow the sunken way on the east bank and pause to inspect the little domestic ruin (left) of Dolly Trebble's House, where the fine uprights of the fireplace still stand. *Westward; notice clear definition of track throughout to head of Bull Park.*

The track now crosses Gobbet Plain under Down Ridge and passes through a gateway into a wide opening between newtake walls above the ancient tenement of Hexworthy, known as Moor Tongue. Here again occurred a choice of way. 1, directly ahead (there is today no right of way) along a grass track, through two further gateways to a wide opening (probably purpose-made) in an ancient wall and into a short, grassy lane; water drains from a well (in a circular enclosure, right) into the lane and so into the Sherberton road below, where the former junction of lane and road has been crudely but effectively blocked by boulders. 2, via Hexworthy (which the walker should take); descend through Moor Tongue and pass through Hexworthy moorgate (652727); cross the Sherberton road into a driftway and follow a stony lane into the hamlet, where two or three ways branch to the farms. It is a fascinating old way – but one the pack-train drivers must have been happy to bypass, if only because of the longer route

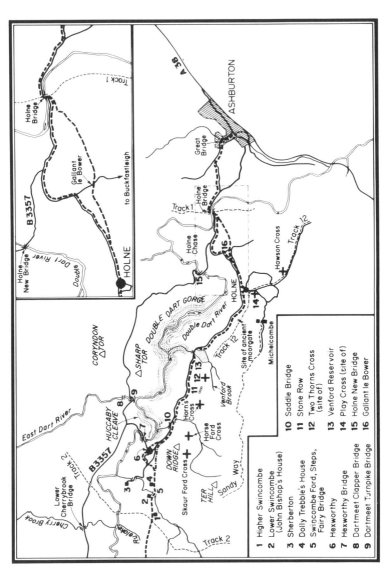

Track 10 – East

1   Higher Swincombe
2   Lower Swincombe
    (John Bishop's House)
3   Sherberton
4   Dolly Trebble's House
5   Swincombe Ford, Steps,
    Fairy Bridge
6   Hexworthy
7   Hexworthy Bridge
8   Dartmeet Clapper Bridge
9   Dartmeet Turnpike Bridge
10 Saddle Bridge
11 Stone Row
12 Two Thorns Cross
    (site of)
13 Play Cross (site of)
14 Holne New Bridge
15 Venford Reservoir
16 Gallant le Bower

and extra hill-climb involved. It is not without interest that *Donn* and *OS 1809* show only the bypass route (1 above), whereas *Greenwood* gives the alternative (2) through the hamlet. *Westward: arriving in Hexworthy, take any lane branching from road, left; all join Track 10 ascending to driftway and moorgate.*

From the hamlet, the track is the route of the present road across Hexworthy Stream and clapper bridge, past the Forest Inn (a small thatched ale-house a century ago) and, here not followed by the snaking road, obliquely up the hill beside the newtake wall, left. Track junctions 1 and 2 above met at the present road junction at Slade, from where the road is based on the track (and therefore motorable) as far as Waterworks Hill (above the west side of Venford reservoir). At Saddle Bridge the way crosses O Brook, an often turbulent stream unfordable by laden pack-animals, so that a bridge must have been existed here many centuries ago; indeed, slabs from a previous clapper have been used as foundation stones for the modern bridge. Some way upstream is, or was until a cloudburst destroyed it in 1965, a paved ford on the line of Track 12, but no tradition of a bridge. Thus the name of each crossing is explained: the ford suitable for riders – 'Horse Ford', and the bridge for pack-saddle ponies – 'Saddle Bridge'. Ascend the long, steep Cumston Tor Hill and drive into the car-park beside Cumston Tor, left. View the Double Dart valley, the spread of the central basin, the well-defined green way of Track 26 climbing Horn's Hill and, south-westward, the clear sight of Horse Ford† (above the ford so named) on Track 12. This makes clear the separate and distinct routes of Tracks 10 and 12 and why the packhorse drivers needed a bridge on the lower O Brook to obviate having to take their trains up to Horse Ford.

Track 10 (and modern road united) now contours Hangman's Hollow – so named from a tragic event related on page 260 – and rises to Waterworks Hill. The track converging with the road, left, is that from Dartmeet and Cumston Farm to Holne via Aller Brook Ford. Descend the hill to a parking space near Venford dam. Return on foot to two PUDC stones,* one on each road-verge; at this point a wide, grassy, sunken way (right) leaves the modern road and drops towards the reservoir, where its overgrown continuation can be seen inside the plantation fringing the water on the west side; this, the

---

* Catchment area boundary marks of the Paignton Urban District Council reservoir at Venford.

original course of Track 10, was adopted eventually by later road-builders, until the impounding reservoir for Paignton (built 1902-7) necessitated a diversion across the new dam. Next drive across the dam, and ascend the hill. Pause to look westward. *Westward: at road-bend on hill, observe line of original road descending over moor, left, to water's edge: exactly aligned with area of sandy shore on further side, where overplanted sunken way emerges from trees; thus only submerged portion of track and original crossing are lost to sight. Strongly built arch-bridge still stands about 70 feet below water, beside which was a wide ford. Interesting glimpse of monastic way (Track 12) beyond reservoir – Venford reave running towards Horn's†.*

The T-A Track now makes its final moorland climb before commencing a 700-foot descent to Ashburton. The traveller, passing above the Stoke farms (left), sees ahead the bluff of Sholedon and a typical South Devon landscape patched by small fields, woodlands and lumpy little hills; Holne Chase and the Dart valley are to the left, while Auswell Rocks are backed by the eastern moor beyond. The canopy of Hembury Woods rises to the apex of Hembury Fort (a tree-concealed Iron Age earthwork) and guides the eye to a point midway between those promontories where the country opens to reveal a wide vale melting into distance miniature hills; there lies Ashburton. *Donn* shows the roadside wall of the Stoke enclosures and 'Holne Gate', where now is a cattle-grid. From here drive into Holne village; pass church, post office and Church House Inn; turn left. A bypass track (now the road) probably existed in early times, but, whereas *Donn* shows only the Hexworthy bypass, here he shows only the route through the village; and this one the traveller should take, for he should not omit to visit Holne. The church of St Mary the Virgin was built probably in the thirteenth century. A window in the north transept is a memorial to Charles Kingsley, who was born in Holne vicarage in 1819 – only a few years after the new turnpike road via Dartmeet superseded the ancient T-A Track. Also in the north transept is an altar made from the oak of the ancient roof of Dartington Hall, which was demolished in 1813; it is modelled on the High Altar of Cologne Cathedral.

A tarmac road from Holne represents Track 10 over the remainder of the route given by *Donn* and *OS 1809* into the terminal town. A glance at the map, however, will show the large, indirect curve traced by this route between Holne and the bridge. R. Hansford Worth once remarked in this context to Edward Masson Phillips, who later told the author, that a more direct route existed via Gallant Le Bower* and North Park Wood. It is indeed more direct, and its absence from *Donn* and *OS 1809* is in no way proof that the North Wood track was never used by the pack-trains – a similar situation obtaining in the case of the Hexworthy bypass route (p. 117) which, ignored by *Donn*, is charted by *OS 1809*. Not only is the directness of the North Park Wood track obvious, but the descent to the bridge is better graded; the track possesses notable scenic qualitites and is far more rewarding to follow than the Chase Gate road.

Take the Holne Bridge road from the village and fork right to reach Gallant Le Bower (719700); this pleasant, leafy green is at the junction of the road from Holne with the Holne Bridge-Buckfastleigh road. Park off the roadway and follow the rough track commencing on the further side of the green. A delightful view is seen between the trees across Holne Chase to the south-east edge of the Moor. A DNP fingerpost indicates the descending track along the edge of the Bower to stile 1 and an open field, where the path follows a hedge, right. The view from here of Buckland Beacon and Auswell Rocks (unfortunately overplanted) is particularly fine. Stile 2 then leads into the next field, where grazing cattle sometimes include a red Devon bull; in such case, it is advisable to turn about. The walk from the Bower is very worthwhile, however, and the link with Holne Bridge can be made in the reverse, westward direction.

Drive to the bridge and park in a roadside space. Walk towards the entrance gate of Holne Park (it now functions as the exit of the park's one-way traffic circuit); turn right before the gate (and the Lodge) and ascend the rough track. In a short distance the way swings left to pass between two granite gateposts before making a corrective right bend. Continuing the ascent, it eventually crosses a track coming up from Holne Park House (headquarters of the River Dart Country Park) which runs into the centre of North Park Wood; the beautiful Dart valley woodlands are now seen in every direction, with a striking view of Cleft Rock towering above the Holne Chase gorge and the picturesque, white, Victorian façade of the Holne Chase Hotel in its idyllic setting. Stile 3 (in eastward order) now occurs, the gate beside it bearing the notice 'Beware of the Bull'; the walker for whom discretion

---

* The meaning of this elegant name, like Dartmouth's Gallants Bower, is the bower where the gallant may escort his lady in peace and privacy.

takes precedence over valour may now consider the visual link between stiles 2 and 3 to be adequate to the occasion.

To follow the *Donn* and *OS 1809* route from the village, take the Holne Bridge road and fork *left* to pass Chase Gate (a large cottage, right, where possibly a gate once controlled access to Holne Chase); join the ancient way from central Dartmoor to Ashburton (which ran via the Dartmeet clapper bridge, past the Coffin Stone on Dartmeet Hill, Poundsgate and Holne New Bridge – now the B3357); cross the River Dart at Holne Bridge (with four refuge bays for avoidance of laden packhorses and marked on John Spede's Map of 1610); ascend Lent Hill; fork left past Hele Farm; at Hele Cross go to the anciently named Holne Turn Cross, there joining the old Chagford Wool Road (p. 90) over Houndtor Down and Cold East Cross, turn right and descend to the town, crossing the River Ashburn at Great Bridge and arriving in North Street. Mills, cottage industries, a thriving wool market and status as a stannary town meant the passing to and fro, until the late eighteenth century, of large quantities of merchandise along the old T-A Track, its terrain well suited to packhorses but impassable by the new-fangled wheeled carts and wagons then coming into use in lowland Devon. The traveller to Ashburton on Track 10 should certainly visit the town's beautifully kept little museum (to do so he will walk from the central car-park through Kingsbridge Lane) and will be interested to see among the museum's exhibits two from T-A Track days – wool-combs from a former wool-sorting shop in Kingsbridge Lane. This provides the perfect finishing touch to a journey along Track 10 from Tavistock.

TRACK 11

THE KING WAY: TAVISTOCK – OKEHAMPTON
15½ miles

William Crossing (*Guide*) observes that the old road between Mary Tavy and Sourton is known as 'the King Way'. The origin of the name appeared to be lost in the mists of time until I was encouraged by the results of research to apply the title to the entire route. It should be noted, too, that the old way was useful in linking together several important settlements missed by the alternative ridgeway route from Tavistock to Lydford via Brent Tor.

Previous writers have been content to describe the King Way as an 'old road'; this indeed it is, but the author's search for the origin of the name was scarcely assisted by the omission, from every early map he consulted, of its northern portion between Noddon Gate and Vellake Gate – this despite its plain physical existence on the face of the Moor. From Noddon Gate northward to Crandford Brook Head it is accompanied by the regally styled 'King Wall': this ancient wall of orthostats and boulders backed by an earthen bank marks the eastern boundary of Bridestowe parish and obviously owes its name here to the proximity of the King Way. This, however, deserts the wall on Southerly Down and climbs to 1,400 feet in order to avoid valley-head mires, until it begins its long descent over Higher Prewley Moor to Okehampton via Vellake Gate and Meldon Lane – also to this day known as 'King Lane'. Such old ways are worthy of preservation, and it has been satisfying, during my field work for the present book, to have traced its entire line in detail. Two lengths of the old way – one near Tavistock, the other near Lydford – are closed to the public, but each may be traced visually from nearby, enabling the reader to view the overall course of the track; three other portions (south of Lydford) may be followed with permission, which in each case is well worth obtaining.

It is evident that the road originated in medieval times as links connecting local lanes and tracks. I see it principally as a riding track where gradients and routing would in general have been unsuited to coaching traffic; indeed, it could well have become deserted even by wagon traffic in the late eighteenth century in favour of the North Brentor ridgeway route; this in turn had declining use after the new valley road (now the A386) was opened in 1817 from Tavistock along Parkwood Road, which portion obviously was based on the ancient way from Tavistock to Peter Tavy via Harford Bridge, as shown by *Donn*. In the relevant Tithes Map of 1845 all signs of the King Way through Wilminstone and Wringworthy have vanished and only the new Tavy valley road appears. In view of the intricacies and rapid fading of the old way south of the River Lyd, I have thought it worthwhile to retrace it in some detail.

Place- and track-names on Dartmoor tend not to be fanciful, being rooted in the history of people and events. Although we have our 'Uncle's Road' and 'Joey's Lane' (Mewy) and 'Sammy Arnold's Lane' (East Ockment), it does not follow that we should interpret 'King Way' as the track of a Mr King. The directness of the track over open moorland points to its antiquity, its origins certainly many centuries older than the attachment of the name 'King Way'. The *Bedford Map* (*c*.1760) shows the southern half of the route from Tavistock as detailed here via Exeter Lane and Wringworthy; reaching Downtown (at the Dartmoor Inn), however, it follows the west side of Vale Down and continues to 'Sowton' (Sourton) on the line of the present A386 road. *Donn* shows the road – though without naming it – from Tavistock northward as far as the termination of the King Wall at the southern extremity of Southerly Down; 2 miles beyond this point, its final lap from the Moor to Okehampton is shown from Vellake Gate through Fowley, Estrayer Park and Meldon Lane, and along the ridge called 'High Street' into the town. *OS 1809, Greenwood* and the Tithes Map of 1841 follow *Donn*. Not long afterwards, *Besley* shows neither track nor wall; but *Spencer*, on his annotated map of the OS 1883 survey (price one shilling!) shows the track diverging north-east from the King Wall (which is not named) and accompanying the Rattlebrook Peat Railway for half a mile south of Points, after which it runs to Iron Catch Gate. Before World War I *Spencer* had marked in the margin of his map: ' "Iron Gates" Row of Granite Posts. Wider gap between two of them marks spot of King Way'; and later: 'all gone 6/3/21'. I had previously overlooked this annotation and now withdraw my remark in *High Dartmoor* that Crossing was wrong in referring to 'a row of granite posts' here. The track is plainly marked (but unnamed) between the King Wall and Vellake Gate on all subsequent editions of OS maps, for it must have received constant use by moormen and quarrymen during the nineteenth-century development of quarrying, ice-storage, peat-cutting and RBPR construction.

In an attempt to account for the name-origin of the track, we must rely on both documented history and tradition concerning 'the King's Posts'. Although a regular postal service between the smaller towns of West Devon and east Cornwall was not inaugurated until 1722, a petition of 1630 addressed to King Charles I, concerning 'the King's Posts', specified the need to provide posthorses 'on the Western Stages of His Majesty's Posts ... from London to Plymouth'. This resulted in a proclamation dated 31 July 1635 about arrangements subsequently undertaken for post-boys riding the 'Plymouth Road' – that is, the route from Exeter south of the Moor via Ashburton. It was not until 1720, however, that a regular mounted postboy service was established between Okehampton (then on the London-Launceston postal routes) and Tavistock. In the meantime, the King's Messengers had carried officials posts on horseback between the two towns when needed. The open moorland traversed by Track 11 would surely have been preferred by the riders to the villages and enclosed, muddy lanes of the border-country. This assumption is supported by an interesting tradition communicated to the author by Mr Norman Fry of Lydford. Norman received the tradition from his father (b.1874) who had received it from *his* eighteenth-century grandfather; it stated quite firmly that the King Way is so named 'because the King's Mail was always taken that way (between the two towns) before the regular postal service began'. There seems little cause to repudiate this tradition, which, as I have shown, is well founded upon documentation (see Bibliography) and provides an entirely logical reason for the name 'King Way'.

In Tavistock town centre, in an ancient, narrow way coincidentally (?) named 'King Street', the premises of the British Legion Club was once the Exeter Inn. This seventeenth-century house, a local historian told me, was traditionally a wagon and packhorse depot for loads between Tavistock and Okehampton before the days of fast

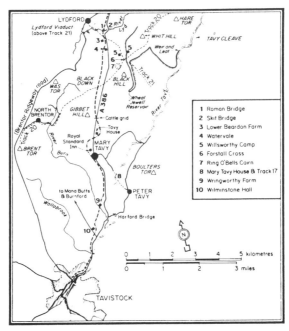

Track 11 – South

stage-coach and mail services in the early nineteenth century. The building, possessing a distinct character, once had capacious stabling, though the wagon- or coach-arch that led to the stables is now partly blocked by modern developments. Standing literally at the commencement of the ancient way from Tavistock to Exeter via Okehampton, the building has the high arch typical of such inns and certainly could have provided a satisfactory terminus for the postboy mail service between the two towns inaugurated in 1720.

NOTE: for permission to follow the old road from Lower Beardon Farm, Lydford, down to the River Lyd to view Roman Bridge, apply to Mr E.J. Friend at the farm (beside the A386 road).

Following the Track (northward)

From Bedford Square in Tavistock turn left into West Street and pass the parish church. Take the second turning right into King Street. The former Exeter Inn stands on the left before reaching Owen's Book Centre. Set out from the coach-arch by crossing the small car-park opposite; cross Market Street, continue directly ahead through Pym

Street and cross Kilworthy Hill into Old Exeter Road. On the right-hand side here is an eighteenth-century milestone bearing these distances: London 215, Okehampton 15, Callington 9, Truro 50. It is interesting on looking back to note that this route points with arrow-like directness to the coach-yard arch. Continue up Old Exeter Road between the terrace of eighteenth-century houses on the left and a steep drop to the town, right. Pass under the bridge (carrying the former Southern Railway) and follow the road (Exeter Lane, but still locally 'Old Exeter Road') above the Kelly College grounds and down to a road junction beside Wilminstone Quarry and Wallabrook Viaduct, left. Continue to a T-junction at Lower Haseldon Bridge (span removed: 501763). The major road leads, left, to Manna Butts and, right, to the main A386 Tavy valley road. Opposite the junction is a wide gateway into a small field (1) bounded on the right by the old rail track and on the left by a hedge below the garden of Wilminstone Hall. A grass track leads from the gateway to a cottage, right, beside the railway and is separated from the field by a wire fence. Go no further but walk up the Wilminstone Hall drive, call at the house, show your copy of this book and request permission to enter the field. The line of the King Way passed on the higher side of a large oak tree and now disappears in an abyss: it was destroyed almost a century ago when a pit was excavated here to provide earth for banking up the Wilminstone tennis court. From the further edge of the pit an ancient wall emerges from the undergrowth, marking the remainder of the way in this field (1) to a gateway ahead. Look over the gate into Field 2, but do not enter. A shallow depression crosses it diagonally to a slightly sunken portion of the wall at the top of the field; this shows the line of the way entering Field 3, where the former opening in the wall has long since been in-filled.

Return to the road junction; drive up the Manna Butts road past the entrance to the modern Wilminstone Farm, and stop just beyond it at a junction with a farm lane, right. Park tight to the hedge; walk along the lane. A hedge borders the left side, and a wire fence the right side on the fringe of Field 3. Look over this; the track can be seen entering from Field 2 into 3, from where it follows a sunken way to a gateway in the north-east corner. It passes through this into the 6-acre field (4), which it crosses diagonally to the wall bordering the farm lane – the site of its entry also having been in-filled. Mr and Mrs G. Medland of Wilminstone Hall have kindly enabled me to retrace the old way across their land, and in Field 4, where no visible trace now remains, a previous Wilminstone farmer, Mr Frank Downing, has supplied the missing piece in the jigsaw. Accompanying me to the farm fields, Mr Downing confirmed the route as detailed above and indicated the precise line of the way across Field 4 and its junction with the farm lane; this he was able to do by virtue of having actually exposed the stone surface of the road many years ago when ploughing in Field 4. His evidence is therefore conclusive.

Follow the farm lane to a gateway; another lane enters here from the left, the point being known at Wilminstone as 'the Junction'. The gateway affords a beautiful view of Peter Tavy church and village backed by the western range of tors. In the mid-distance traffic is seen on the A386 entering the beech avenue at the head of Wringworthy Hill. Follow the lane, which beyond the gate is enclosed by two hedges. Notice the more recent portion of in-filled hedge where Track 11 once joined the lane. Below here, the old way appears as though in a time-capsule; steep and rutted, it descends into a copse between a high bank (left) and a craftsman-built wall (right). Reaching a point where the wall diverges (right) and a green track (left), the lane runs ahead into the formidable obstacle thrown up in 1874 in the shape of the London & South Western (later Southern) Railway embankment. Beyond this the River Burn flows past the fields of Wringworthy Farm. To make the necessary visual link, follow the diverging wall to the foot of the embankment, ascend the latter and walk up-line (left) for 130 yards; push through rhododendrons (right) and look down on the river, where the old road can be seen emerging from beneath the embankment beside a short length of wall and running to a wide, shallow ford on the river directly opposite Wringworthy farmhouse.

Even though the river may be low enough to cross without difficulty, the Wringworthy lands must not be entered this way. Return to the car; drive along the A386 for almost a mile and take the first turning left on Wringworthy Hill (beyond the Tate & Lyle depot) down to the farm. Park in the car space, left; go to the farmhouse and request permission to follow the King Way through the farm lands: Mr and Mrs Maurice Anning have kindly agreed to grant this to personal callers carrying a copy of this book. Proceed as follows: walk up the farm drive beyond the car space and pass through a gateway into the riverside meadow; a slightly raised way leads to the bank, where masonry suggests the former existence of a bridge, though no corresponding signs appear on the further, right bank. The Devon historian R.N. Worth, however, confirms in *TDA* 75 of 1943 that, 'A

16 Track 10: T-A guide-stone, Swincombe Gate.
Down Ridge is beyond.

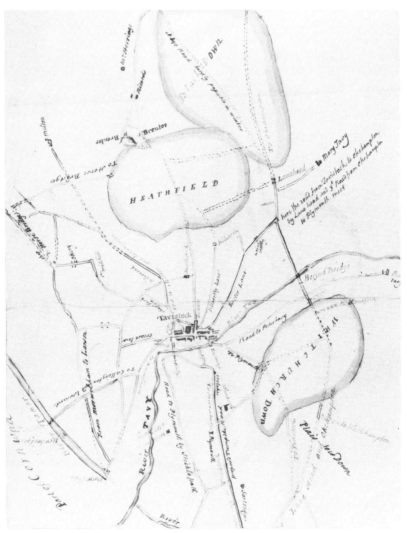

17 Track 11: The Bedford Map, *c.*1760, showing the southern portion of the King Way. (*The Marquess of Tavistock and the Trustees of the Bedford Estate.*)

18 Track 12: Horse Ford, O Brook. Notice stones deposited by flood of 1965.

19 Track 15: Urgles. The Buckland monastic way joins the road to Goodameavy Bridge. Roborough Down beyond.

20 Track 12: Approach to Skuar Ford. Ter Hill beyond.

21 Track 12: The stone surround at the site of Two Thorns†. Dr Andrew Fleming, co-discoverer with Nicholas Ralph, walks eastward towards Venford Bottom. Holne Lee is beyond, crossed by Track 12 from centre to right near horizon.

22 Track 10: Swincombe Ford and Fairy Bridge. Track 10 continues beyond as a sunken way and the ruined Dolly Trebble's House appears (left).

23 Track 11: Vellake Gate. Riders descend King Lane. Meldon Down on the extreme right.

24 Track 17: Quarrymen's Path –
looking east. Kerb-stones lead to the
Steeple Tors ridge. Right – Mid
Steeple Tor.

25 Track 17: Quarrymen's Path –
looking west. The overgrown paving
leads to the Iron Age hut circles
(above walkers' heads). Horizon –
Gibbet Hill.

26 Track 12: Raddick Lane. The Tavistock monastic way descends to
Riddipit Steps on the River Mewy.

27   Track 18: Black Lane (north). Crossing the Meads before descending to Brook's Head. Horizon: left, Black Ridge; right, Vur Tor.

28   Track 19: Peat carts on the Teignhead Road below Kes Tor,
c.1903. (Crossing's Dartmoor Worker *by courtesy of Brian Le Mes-
surier.*)

29 Track 19: Approach to Teignhead Farm. The Teignhead Road crosses Great Mire Stream (one impost of clapper bridge seen near bottom, right); behind the ruined farm the track passes through the open gateway and ascends through the newtake, keeping left of Teignhead Great Mire.

30 Extension of Track 19 to Whitehorse Hill: the badly broken causeway, the Sand Path.

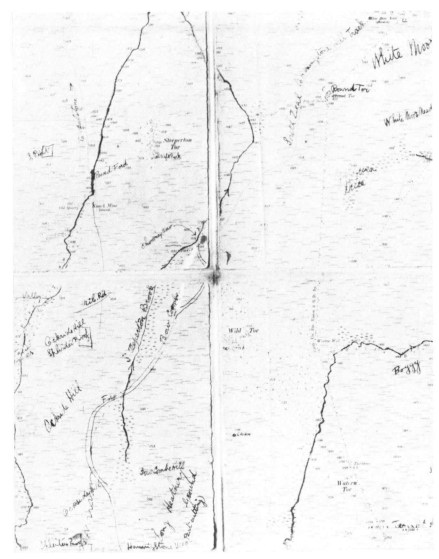

31   Track 20: John Spencer's marking of the original route showing
the descent from Ockside Hill and the crossing of the hour-glass neck
linking the two mires.

bridge about 2 miles NE of Tavistock carried an ancient road over the River Burn', this point doubtless being its site. From it runs a shallow, sunken way to the farmyard, which I would identify as Track 11 in preference to the raised way mentioned above. Return to the yard. A barn directly ahead (beyond the farmhouse) was built, Mr Anning informs me, about a century ago on the course of the track. Pass through an iron gate, 1 (right), and immediately turn left to reach the foot of a well-defined sunken way mounting the hillside, right; this also was an enclosed lane, but the south hedge has been removed to facilitate cultivation of the field. At the head of the steep, pass through Gate 2 into a field where the north hedge has been removed; notice tree-boles remaining in the south hedge at regular intervals. From Gate 3, observe traffic on the A386 road passing the further side of the field. Here, all semblance of a track has been entirely erased, but the road certainly crossed the field and, at a sharp bend shown clearly on early maps, joined the line of the Harford Bridge road where an avenue of beeches now commences. I believe this avenue once to have extended down to Gate 2, for the age of the beeches suggests it could have been planted before the old way gradually went out of use early in the nineteenth century. It is obvious that much work was carried out by Wringworthy farmers, following the road's total abandonment, in order to increase arable acreage by removing unwanted hedges and ploughing; indeed, Mr Anning has found the soil in the corner of the field to be much thinner than elsewhere. *Donn* and *OS 1809* show not only the junction of Track 11 with the Harford Bridge road but also its crossing of the River Burn and course through the fields listed here as an enclosed lane, so supporting the route evidence I have given.

Return to Wringworthy Farm; drive up Wringworthy Hill and park on the west roadside opposite a cottage (right 505777). Examine the eccentric hedge pattern on the east roadside near the lower end of the beech avenue, where a false verge has been created opposite the point of emergence of the old way from the highest Wringworthy field, to join the Harford Bridge road; the false verge continues to the cottage, beyond which it recurs with, this time, the original road enclosed between an ancient Devon hedge (furthest from the road) and the modern hedge (verging the road). It is apparent from this that the line of the old road was abandoned when the Parkwood road was made in 1817 in favour of the new (present) line now in use and that, whereas the King Way once passed at the east end of the cottage, the A386 now passes at the west end along what is locally called Burntown Straight.

Next drive to the car-park of the Royal Standard inn in Blackdown hamlet. The oldest part of the inn, containing the public bar, is at least four centuries old. The name of the inn, a point of pride to both former and present landlords, is traditionally attributed to its overnight use, some three centuries ago, by a royal personage; could it be that the Royal Standard of a Stuart was raised at Blackdown during at least one night in the seventeenth century?

Walk from the car park down to the chapel; turn right into the lane beside it. Crossing mentions a tradition placing the old road 'quite near to the site of the present Black Down Wesleyan Chapel'. Although the route of the King Way has been obliterated by development at Down's Garage, it reappears as the drive (right) to 'Moorview'. Beyond the wood fence adjoining the house it enters a field which is scheduled for building development – though at the time of publication an overgrown gully is still traceable. It then crosses the drive to Blackdown Nursing Home (notice the in-filled gap in the drive-side wall, left) and appears as a sunken gully ascending towards the north end of the nursing home garden, where the corner of an old hedge was carefully rounded to admit the way – but a stone shed has since been built across its width. Passing beyond the shed through the garden of 'The Bungalow' Standard Court, it enters Moorside Lane (which leads from the Royal Standard Inn past the cottages of Standard Court); a short way up the lane it passes into the private grounds of 'Prince Arthur' – a house named from a notable event of over a century ago, when, Duke and Prince Arthur of Connaught was entertained there – is visible in the grounds as a sunken way.

So far, the walker is able to view the Blackdown stretches of Track 11 from the lanes and gates detailed. Return now to the main road and walk uphill to a short lane, left, beyond the inn. Here the way emerges from the garden of 'Broomassie' into the lane and at 'the Arches' crosses a stream that has deeply excavated its valley below the east side of the high road; this feature would have dictated the site of the bridge (as well as of its King Way predecessor) built for the 1817 road. East of the road it enters the garden of Tavy House, where it can be seen from the drive gate as a sunken gully on the further verge of the garden. (This gully may be inspected by asking permission at the house and showing a copy of this book.)

Beyond the Tavy House garden the way runs into Holditch Lane, where it is seen ascending through the former. Walk into the lane (last turning right below hilltop) and observe the sunken way passing into the garden of 'Crossing', the cottage on the left. Beautifully situated, with views over western Dartmoor, the cottage bears a plaque on its roadside wall, reading: 'In this house William Crossing (1847-1928) lived for many years and wrote his *Guide to Dartmoor* and other works. Dartmoor Preservation Association 1952.' Crossing has written of the King Way in his *Guide*: 'I have been able by careful examination to trace it from the village of Black Down to Higher Bowden, near Meldon, a distance of between eight and nine miles. There are now no remains of it in the village named, nor, with the exception of a few faint traces at its northern end, can it be seen on Black Down itself, but the line it took can nevertheless be determined.' In the light of the detail provided in this chapter, it comes as a surprise to read in the *Guide* that, 'There are now no remains of it in the village named'; even more surprising is that highly respected author's failure to recognize a portion of it in his own garden, despite the indisputable character and continuity of the route through Black Down hamlet as described here; indeed, several of the sunken gullies occupied by the track still appear on the 1904 OS 6-inch map.

From the garden of 'Crossing',* the way follows a field hedge into an old lane known as 'the Ashburys'; this reaches the main road just above the cattle-grid, where a gate allows a glimpse between two road-signs into the overgrown lane. The time and assistance so readily given me by Bill and Mary Warne of Standard Court demand special acknowledgement here; they enabled me to record with certainty the old way on its passage through Black Down, which apparently proved so elusive for Crossing. As former host and hostess of the Royal Standard Inn for twenty-five years, Bill and Mary possess a rich store of Black Down history and tradition.

The route of the old way from the roadside gate at the Ashburys has been obliterated in the construction and subsequent maintenance of the A386, but it can be picked up again above the west roadside in a short way, where it runs parallel and very near the highroad for almost a mile before diverging from it near the milestone (left) marked 'Tavistock 7 Okehampton 8 Truro 57'. *Southward: notice route near verge of high road (on plain of Black Down under Gibbet Hill) avoids higher ground before reaching gate at the Ashburys.*

The track is clearly marked and on nearing Barrett's Bridge

---

* I have been requested by the owners of 'Crossing' to ask readers *not* to enter their garden or call at the house.

intersects several narrow, rutted moorland tracks. Crossing the Blackdown Mine leat (disused), it reaches, in three quarters of a mile, the broken relic of an ancient reave-bank lying (left) at right angles to the highway and connecting with the Henscott cornditch wall; before reaching the reave-bank the King Way intersects Track 20, 100 yards west of the road. Beyond the reave-bank it descends to twin fords on a feeder of the River Burn – the higher one a good riding ford, the lower, slightly less direct, more suitable for wheeled traffic. Brent Tor is predominant in the west from here, whilst the way ahead could only have appeared to riders, on a wet, cold day as forbidding. The range of heights visible (left to right) are Sourton Tors, Corn Ridge (between which lofty points the traveller needed to pass). Brai Tor, Great Links and Lydford Sharp Tors. Beyond the twin fords the tracks unite and the well-defined sunken, grass road crosses a track descending from the main road cattle-grid (right) to pass through a wide (iron) gateway (1) into the fields of Watervale Farm, where its sunken passage may be seen running through an intermediate gateway (2) to that of a lower field (3). Do not enter the fields. From Gate 1 is seen a fine view of Lydford village, castle and church; also clear is the line of the old way joining the modern road beyond the Lyd valley. Watervale Farm was once – at least until 1845 – the Waterfield Inn, and appears as 'Waterfield' on both *OS 1809* and *Greenwood*. The Waterfield Inn, like the Royal Standard at Black Down, occupied a site equally convenient for travellers on the King Way and the new turnpike road. A car may be parked on the east roadside near Higher Beardon. Walk up the road and turn into the lane beside Watervale; look over Gate 3 at the way descending from Gate 1 through the intermediate Gate 2. It continued across the lane into a field of Prestcott Farm; little sign of it now remains, however, until it nears the highway, where it becomes sunken on approaching the roadside gate above Beardon Bridge over Sounscombe Brook (Lyd). The bridge is a sturdy clapper, reinforced to carry modern traffic, and the brook passes from it into a deep hole (in the Higher Beardon fields) where no track could pass. Opposite the entrance to Lower Beardon Farm, the Lych Way approaches the highway through Down Lane. As the highway bends right to reach Skit or Kitts Bridge (built between 1832 and 1835), the two ancient ways (Tracks 11 and 22) are united for 350 yards. The milestone – 'Tavistock 7 Okehampton 8' – beside the road here is shaped like a tombstone. Beyond it is the 'Take-off' stone, being the point where a third horse, taken on at the last turnpike without toll charge to assist

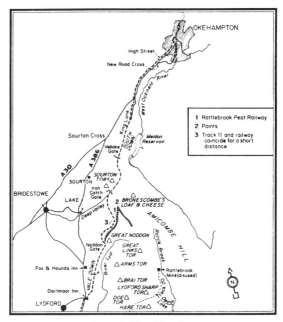

Track 11 – North

in haulage on hills, had to be unhitched, or 'taken off'.

As Track 22 bears left below Lower Beardon Farm, Track 11 enters a farm field (right), where Mr E.J. Friend's permission is necessary to enter. It leads to the fine structure bridging the River Lyd, known as 'Roman Bridge'. The ancient ford on the downstream side is a good place from which to admire the bridge, and the roadway from its north end is seen to enter a private garden, in which the owner of Skit Cottage is the fortunate possessor of a well-defined length of historic highway where the King's post-boys were wont to gallop across the brawling River Lyd.

The very narrow Skit (Kitts) Lane branches left from the highway of Skit (Kitts) Bridge and leads to Lydford village. It is unsuitable for a car, so continue north from the bridge to a bend in the road, where space exists for one car in a gateway (left). Park briefly; walk down Skit Lane for the entrance to Skit Cottage; Track 11, emerging from the owner's garden, is crossed by the lane and enters a sunken way, right. Return to the car and look over the gate at the approaching sunken way. From this point the highway follows its line to the

Dartmoor Inn, 630 yards north; beyond the entrance to the inn the track branches right from the highway and passes through Moor Gate. A car may be parked inside the gate and away from the entrances to hotel, left.

Follow the wall (left) for a further 420 yards; enter a gateway into an enclosed area – actually a part of Vale Down enclosed during the nineteenth century – and follow the wall left (the original outer cornditch) to a transverse wall half a mile ahead. Here pass through a hunting-gate, left, and regain the track within a few yards by turning right through a moorgate at the head of a lane (530863); this is Noddon* Gate at the head of Shortacombe Lane, which branches from the highway beside the Fox & Hounds Inn, Bridestowe; the continuing moorland track from Shortacombe Lane leads to Noddon Ford (Lyd), with a branch (left) to Lyd Head. Embedded in the track at the gateway is a bond-stone inscribed 'BS', one of a series marking the outer (shared) boundary of Bridestowe and Sourton parishes. Notice that the wall (right) inside the gateway – it now blocks the passage of the old track – is more modern than the original Vale Down cornditch; the latter is used on large, vertical slabs, and its original cornditch function is continued northward from Noddon Gate, where it is known as the 'King Wall'. *Southward: on descending Down towards Noddon Gate track seen alongside Vale Down wall and aligned with distant shoulder of Black Down.*

The walker retracing the old road will see that big country lies ahead, for the bold summits of Dartmoor's north-west escarpment continually overlook his path. The King Wall consists of large, vertically set slabs backed by an earthen bank; for half a mile it has been adopted as the base of a cornditch wall; 140 yards north of Noddon Gate, a track is seen to emerge from a cutting, right and enter the newtake, left, where its curving line may be followed by the eye towards the site of Bridestowe railway station (on the former Plymouth-Tavistock-Okehampton-Waterloo Southern Railway line), below and beyond the A386 highway. This is the track of the former Rattle Brook Peat Railway (RBPR), connecting the peatworks at Rattle Brook Head with the main line at Bridestowe – a skilfully planned, true mountain railway ascending to over 1,800 feet above sea level. Like many other West Country mineral lines, it was closed when the works ceased to operate in the early 1930s.

---

* Correct spelling; used by *Greenwood, OS 1809* and William Crossing.

Beyond the intersection by the railway of Track 11, the latter gains sufficient height to round the heads of Crandford Brook and of the steeply falling streams on Coombe and Lake Down. Do not, however, follow the stony track (leading to Lyd Head) that diverges (right) from the wall, but the clear, grassy way ahead. Track 11 later diverges from the King Wall on Southerly Down and bears right towards the railway bridge; for a short way it accompanies the railway, here approaching its shunting loop known as 'Points'. Near this the track leaves the railway and passes 150 yards below Points. Well defined, it continues northward to cross Lake Down at a high level and an even contour above the head of Deep Valley. Through this great cleft, formerly called Withycombe Bottom, courses the stream known as Lake, its name bestowed also on the hamlet below. The Southern Railway was carried across the valley by the splendid Lake Viaduct, a beautiful piece of Victorian railway architecture of slender piers and arches embossed upon the distant borderland backcloth of lanes, fields, woodlands and cottages. To see the viaduct, leave the track and descend to the head of Deep Valley, where views west into Cornwall and south along the moorland escarpment are very fine. In a deep boundary ditch, right, stands a bond-stone marked with the initial letters of Okehampton, Bridestowe and Sourton parishes and where formerly – according to Crossing and a local informant I have myself questioned – was a gateway known as Iron Catch Gate. *Spencer*, however, has written 'Iron Gates' at the point where the King Way crosses the boundary ditch a short way above the bond-stone, at a height of 1,400 feet where the broad, gravelly character of the road certainly leaves no room for doubt that a much-trodden way passed here; the approach from the south, too, is seen from Lake Down as a wide, grassy road. But, how dispel the confusion? It is clear that a lower loop tracks runs past the bond-stone before rejoining the higher, main track on Sourton Down; it could therefore be maintained as a half-truth that the King Way passes by the stone. I now have no doubt, however, that Spencer's placing of Iron Catch Gate at the higher crossing of the boundary ditch is the correct one. Beyond the ditch, the way is stranded; follow the right-hand, clearest strand, when distant Meldon reservoir and a standing stone near ahead soon come in view.

Sourton Tors, numerous masses of craggy basalt rock, are well worth a diversion to visit and easily reached from either crossing of the boundary ditch. The upper crossing will provide the walker with a base for discovering two features of particular interest nearby. 30 yards north of the (upper) crossing, and in line with distant Yes Tor, is the remaining half of an apple-crusher, a fine relic of the moorstone age, abandoned, apparently, due to fracture in the working. A further 30 yards brings one to the remains of a large stone circle; the stones, all of which are fallen, trace a diameter of 110 feet. Views from this lofty point of the wild country eastward are very good; notice especially the great hollow of Corn Hole beneath Corn Ridge. Other features appearing are Meldon reservoir, the British Rail quarry at Meldon, Prewley waterworks, mounds and pits near the standing stone, and two more stones, one on either side of the track, lower down the hill. Shelstone Tor and Corn Ridge (right) are backed by the 2,000-feet High Willes-Yes Tor ridge; the crags of Blacka Tor (West Ockment) are overlooked by Foresland Ledge on the south shoulder of the ridge and, in smooth contrast, the slate hills of the Moor's northwest fringe rise steeply from the valleys below. The track, now unified and clear, runs towards the waterworks (where numerous glass skylights gleam in sunshine like a host of parked cars). It is then seen to pass between the twin standing stones towards an enclosure wall at the foot of the hill.

Turn aside to inspect the pits and mounds, relics of a nineteenth-century industrial enterprise. A number of shallow, oblong pits were terraced on the hillside and a leat was cut to bring water from a spring; the pits were confluent, each overflowing into the pit below. The controlled water supply entered the pits when winter began, and Nature, on this bleak, exposed north-west slope responded over the next few months by freezing solid the water in the pits. Workmen from nearby Sourton village then cut the ice into cubes and stacked them in a specially built store near the lowest pit. With horse-drawn carts in late spring and early summer they would load the ice for transport to Okehampton, Tavistock and Plymouth hotels and fishmongers. Thus – Sourton Ice Works! It seems a pity that such a venture should have endured for only a decade (1875-85), a circumstance perhaps due to a succession of mild winters.

The terrain on Sourton Common (locally 'Higher Prewley Moor') is seen to consist of a multitude of small, earthen humps; these do not cover rocks, nor are they the work of moles – although the moormen call them 'molehills'! They are, one botanist has suggested, possibly the remains of arctic vegetation. It is noticeable that they occur only on the border-rock, never on the granite, on the west and north-west commons of Dartmoor. The track, rutted on each side and in the centre showing long usage by horse-drawn carts, passes between the twin guide-stones to reach a reave-bank joining with the Vellake newtake wall; it intersects this at a point where a gateway once stood, of which one post alone remains; drillings for gatehangers show that the now crumbled reave-bank was once of sufficient height to enclose stock. The track now converges with the newtake wall and reaches Vellake Gate (Pl. 23), marking the end of the King Way's course over high Dartmoor. *Southward from Vellake Gate: follow wall; pass through reave-bank; ignore wide track to old quarry (left); ascend ahead between twin guide-stones; Ice Works pits and mounds and rocks of Sourton Tors appears right of track below hill-crest; single guide-stones near crest.*

A 'court' has been formed at Vellake Gate for sorting stock (*cf* Ball Gate, p. 86), from where the way crosses the west flank of South Down through the rough, enclosed King Lane; descending into West Ockment country, it reaches Higher Bowden and acquires a tarmac surface; half a mile onward is the overbridge that once carried such Southern Railway star trains as the Atlantic Coast Express, the Brighton Express and the Waterloo-Plymouth Express. The branch lane (right) leads to Meldon reservoir car-park, a convenient rendezvous for the walker if transport awaits him after his trek from the Dartmoor Inn, Lydford. The King Way slips beneath the bridge and reaches the few houses of Meldon hamlet. Pass the Methodist chapel and entrance to Meldon Farm, right, then fork right at a lane junction. Descend to a clapper bridge over a stream, pass through a beech avenue and notice the lane's direct alignment with the main A386 road ahead, which it joins at Graddon Cross.

A mile further north, the old way again retain its direct line when the A386 curves away, right, to follow a series of bends into Okehampton. The junction, New Road Cross, is marked by a large 'OKEHAMPTON' town sign, adorned by the borough's coat of arms, from where the King Way runs north-east along the old coach-road known as High Street into the town centre. The final descent into the town is steep; at its head a branch road leads, left, to the fine parish church of All Saints, with an 80-foot, granite tower built in the fifteenth century; the position of the church high above the town is due to the gradual abandonment, in Norman times, of the ancient village of Saxon origin, which, with its wooden church, occupied the hill-shelf surrounding the church. High Street reaches the town at the first of two bridges spanning the converging East and West Ockment rivers; the peninsula dividing them was regarded by William the Conqueror as a site of strategic significance, especially as it was crossed by the ancient trunk road into Cornwall from counties to the east of Devon and he approved the building here of a castle by his newly appointed Sheriff of Devon, Baldwin de Brionne. The castle was completed in the 1070s and recorded in the Devon Domesday in 1088. The reader might expect to learn of its occupation and garrisoning during the English Civil War by troops of either allegiance, but the building had, in fact, been demolished over a century before, when its last occupant, the Marquis of Exeter, was executed for treason in 1539 – that year of sacrilegious violence when the glorious abbeys of England were plundered and their communities dissolved by a greedy, rapacious monarch.

A brief historical note on Okehampton appears on page 58. Its situation at the immediate north foot of the Moor had the natural effect, through centuries of prehistory and history, of confining east-west traffic from Devon to Cornwall to the ancient route (now the A30 road) across the plain of the twin Ockments flowing below the castle.

A NOTE ON DARTMOOR MONASTIC WAYS AND THE FOUR BORDER-COUNTRY MONASTERIES

It must be stated at the outset that no documentation is known to exist relating to trans-moorland monastic travel routes. Although tradition survives, it is slender in the extreme, consequently the whole subject rests upon a framework of intelligent deduction and conjecture. Field evidence shows that ancient routes have in places altered from time to time, chiefly due to developing land-use. The monastic ways described here are rendered probable, both in routing and inter-monastic purpose, by the existence of waymark Christian crosses of a common type and period. At best they will enable the walker to retrace the actual ways of pedestrian and mounted religious, while at least they will afford some highly satisfying moorland walking.

Frequent travel was necessitated by the business of administering monastic estates; in the case of all four Dartmoor houses the estate lands included large tracts of common land on the Moor as well as border-country manors. Those of Buckfast extended to the manor of Holne and lands bordered by the River Avon; Plympton administered Shaugh Prior, Meavy and Sampford Spiney manors and parish churches, and Tavistock's responsibilities included Walkhampton, Denbury, Hatherleigh, Werrington, North Petherwin, Burrington, Ottery, Ogbear, Morwell (where the 'ham' or settlement of Morwellham had been the port for Tavistock from the twelfth century onwards), Parswell, Peter Tavy, Holyeat, Week, Foghanger, West Liddaton, Lamerton, Monk Okehampton, Milton Abbot, Abbotsham and North Brentor with the hilltop church of St Michael de Rupe, while the abbey flocks grazed Whitchurch Down and Cudlipptown Down on western Dartmoor.

D.L. Edwards, in *Christian England*, writes that the *conversi*, illiterate lay brothers, worked 'in the fields and among the sheep' and that the Cistercian Order became a major force in the international wool trade. In the wool 'boom' years' of the thirteenth century, Buckfast Abbey, then a Cistercian house, exported large quantities of wool to Flanders from the ports of Totnes, Dartmouth and Kingsbridge, J.C. Dickinson writes in *Monastic Life in Medieval England* that manual labour essential to the establishing of Cistercian monasteries 'was rapidly and effectively undertaken by the thousands of lay brethren who flocked to Cistercian cloisters'. Also that, 'In England by the late 15th century the Cistercians had done not a little to develop the wool trade on which so much of England's wealth in later medieval times was to depend.' We learn from *English Monasticism Yesterday and Today* (E.K. Milliken) that the abbot would often 'have to be absent from his monastery ... to administer the monastic estates, which would involve lengthy journeys from manor to manor', and that, 'The bursar was responsible for collecting the rents of monastic property in the surrounding district ... There were also laymen, such as bailiffs and stewards, employed in the administration of monastic estates ... The head of a monastery had also to preside over certain of his manor courts ... The Cellarer, on account of his duties ... ought frequently to visit the manors ... He had often to be away on business but ought to be prompt at the canonical hours whenever he can find leisure.' The Cellarer had also to give 'special priority to the needs of pilgrims'. The Cellarer of Tavistock, for example, was responsible for the abbey fisheries (see also p. 166) and for collecting corn ground at Pomphlett Mill (Plymstock), which was grown by abbey tenants. Certainly important guests were from time to time escorted from one monastery to another. A recorded instance of this* occurred when King Edward I, who with his retinue rested overnight at Buckfast Abbey on 31 March 1297, was escorted by monks to Plympton Priory. From all this it may be understood that the evidence for the existence of trans-moorland monastic routes is irrefutable. To it I would add the essence of my many conversations with Dom Leo Smith OSB, present Abbot of Buckfast. It follows that reliable routes may be regarded as a *sine qua non* of moorland monastic travel where the monks' needs were for a waymarked route of moderate gradients, easy river-crossings, an avoidance of major hill crests and to reach shelter, food and facilities for saying Mass without undue delay.

* *Buckfast Abbey*, Stéphan.

TRACK 12

MONASTIC WAY: BUCKFAST ABBEY – TAVISTOCK ABBEY   20 miles

In direct contrast to the needs of the travelling monk, as set out in the foregoing Note, were the simple ones that sufficed the wool-jobbers and the moormen – those whose frequent task it was to ride Track 3 and 4 and relevant branches in all weathers over the exposed southern heights of the Moor; those who were, so to speak, born to it. There were no guide-stones to give reassurance in mist, gradients were steep, crossings at times dangerous and intricate and the only shelter to be met with would have been a lonely tinners' house: certainly the average monk, a great part of whose life was sedentary, was not born to such conditions of travel. The records of Buckfast Abbey show that the monks in general came from homes distant from Dartmoor; they would therefore not have possessed either the geographical knowledge or the intuitive topographical sense of the native. Chapter 3 perhaps amply demonstrates that the route marked 'Abbots' Way' on Ordnance maps, and consequently adopted by many writers and dependent bodies, was drastically unsuited to monastic travel, and that convincing evidence now exists to show that Track 12 was the authentic route. To avoid the confusion surrounding the subject of moorland monastic routes, I have dispensed altogether with the term 'Abbots' Way' – which is, in any case, unhistoric – and substituted the simple title given here.

Buckfast Abbey

On a beautiful Dartside plain within the *Buckfestre*, the 'fastness or stronghold of the deer', King Canute in 1018 founded a house for a Benedictine community. Their pastoral activities involved the use of a

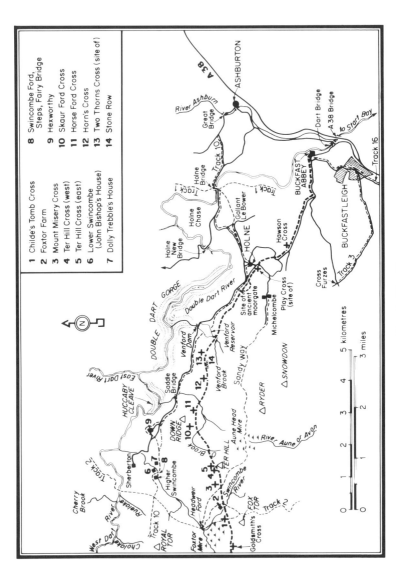

Track 12 – East

Legend:

1 Childe's Tomb Cross
2 Foxtor Farm
3 Mount Misery Cross
4 Ter Hill Cross (west)
5 Ter Hill Cross (east)
6 Lower Swincombe (John Bishop's House)
7 Dolly Trebble's House
8 Swincombe Ford, Steps, Fairy Bridge
9 Hexworthy
10 Skaur Ford Cross
11 Horse Ford Cross
12 Horn's Cross
13 Two Thorns Cross (site of)
14 Stone Row

large area of south-east Dartmoor for grazing sheep (according to the *Devon Domesday*, Buckfast Abbey owned 670 sheep in 1088). The need must soon have arisen for a satisfactory communicating route with Tavistock, at that time the only other pre-Conquest monastery in the Dartmoor country; two very remarkable men held the abbacies, Livingus of Tavistock and Alwin of Buckfast, and their characters and energies were such as to call for frequent interchange and communication between their two houses. Livingus, as a confidant of and adviser to King Canute, is likely to have taken an active part in the planning of the new royal foundation beside the River Dart; such an inter-monastic route, to be direct, had to cross Dartmoor. Circumstantial evidence suggests that a route was purposely surveyed and marked out by rough-hewn granite crosses – despite a lack of documentary record. A convenient branch of the route, crossing the edge of the south moor (Track 16) and similarly marked by crosses, eventually came into use to connect Buckfast with the thirteenth-century foundation of Plympton Priory.

The administration of abbey manors and use of Dartmoor commons for stock-grazing involved the monks and lay-brothers of Buckfast in much travel over Dean, Buckfastleigh and Holne Moors, and the manorial parish of Holne, where monks served the church, lay on the route of Track 22. In 1315 the abbey was shipping wool to Flanders from Teignmouth, Dartmouth and Kingsbridge. Holdings in 1447, a list of which was found by Stéphan to have been copied in 1607 from the abbey ledger book, proved the 'right of the said monastery to their three Moors adjoining to the south part of the King's Forest of Dartmoor in Devon, parcel of the Duchy of Cornwall ... One of them is called Southolne Moor, parcel of the manor of Southolne; the second is called Buckfastleigh Moor, parcel of the manor of Buckfastleigh, and the third Moor is parcel of the manor of Southbrent.'

Crosses on the Buckfast-Tavistock route are numbered in a westerly direction and referred to in the text by the symbol † and a number; road junctions in Devon, with or without standing crosses and often of only three roads, frequently bear the name 'Cross', and my purpose in using the symbol here is to prevent confusion between road junctions and actual stone crosses, cross bases or cross sites. The Buckfast-Tavistock series is:

1 Hawson†	2 Play†	3 Two Thorns (Holne Moor)†
4 Horn's†	5 Horse Ford†	6 Skaur Ford†
7 Ter Hill (east)†	8 Ter Hill (west)†	9 Mount Misery†
10 Childe's Tomb†	11 Goldsmith's†	12 Siward's†
13 Newleycombe†	14 Clazywell†	15 Lowery†
16 Lower Lowery†	17 Yannadon†	18 Walkhampton Church House†
19 Huckworthy†	20 Warren's†	21 Pixie's†
22 Green Lane†		

Stone crosses on other monastic and ancient, secular routes, also symbolized, are referred to always by name.

Following the Track (westward)
In the grounds of the magnificent modern Benedictine abbey of St Mary at Buckfast stand two ancient crosses. One, discovered during World War II at Great Palston Farm, South Brent, was removed to the abbey and set up by the monks; the other is included here in the trans-moorland monastic series as † 20 and accounted for on page 156.

From the abbey buildings the trans-Dartmoor monastic way to Tavistock ran via Hockmoor Head – where the abbey tower is visible from the high roadside bank – to Hawson† (1) (710682) – the head of which was discovered in a nearby wall. Here fork right and descend to the valley of Holy Brook; cross at Langaford Bridge. The tarmac road swings to the right but the original way ascends the narrow lane ahead known as Langaford Hill. At Play†, (2, site of), William Crossing has suggested formerly stood the restored granite cross now in Holne churchyard; monks making directly for Dartmoor could here bypass the village and ascend to a junction with the Hexworthy-Holne Bridge road, where the track leaves the trodden ways of modern man for many miles to come. The medieval cross, standing over 4 feet above a modern three-tier base, now surmounts the churchyard grave of a former vicar of Holne and members of his family, the Reverend John Gill (1827-1917) whose incumbency lasted from 1858 to 1917! It is seen near the war memorial cross at the head of the churchyard steps. The fragment of a broken column, which may be a relic of the original shaft of the cross, stands in a ditch under the wall of the Church House Inn near the steps.

Preserving its alignment with † 2, the way becomes a short lane (to which the lower approach is blocked) behind the house named 'Bear Wood'. An ancient wall may be glimpsed through the wild profusion of undergrowth in this lower approach and is seen to curve into the road approaching from Play†. A gate stands at the lane-head; do not enter this field, but observe the well-defined sunken way ascending beside its south hedge (left); that this was formerly a lane is shown by the foundations of the since removed north hedge. It is regrettable that this direct, graded approach to the high moor should have fallen into complete disuse, and it is now a no-access route to Sholedon Gate (where notices prohibit entry) near the house named 'Stoke Shallows'. The gate is easily reached, however, by a hard track (left) from the cattle-grid at the modern Holne Moorgate. Park in the disused quarry here at 698699.

The way, accessible to all on the open moor above Sholedon Gate, but in early medieval times threading a network of enclosures extending westward to a moorgate beyond Venford Bottom,* passes the wall (left) of 'Stoke Shallows' (formerly called 'The Shanty' and so marked on maps) and mounts to the crest of Sholedon, where it crosses the Holne Moor leat (known locally as Hamlyn's leat). Beyond the leat, the stranded track points directly ahead while the leat (right) describes a curve along the upper edge of a gorse and bracken field. Track and leat again converge as the Ringleshutes Mine road appears (right); this crosses the leat on a cart clapper bridge of six imposts, intersects the monastic way and bears left to the old mine in Ringle shutes gert. Re-crossing the leat, Track 12 is clear (but stranded) beyond the bridge; follow it to a thorn tree occupying a green patch in a slight hollow, at the base of three diverging lines – two tinners' gullies and a bracken-covered reave ascending the hillside ahead (Holne Lee). (An old dry leat channel also transversely crosses the hollow, and each of the gullies, left, is marked by a thorn tree.) Follow the furthest right of the three lines (the reave) to the north spur of Holne Lee where, bisected by the Holne Town Gutter (leat), they pass beside a ruined prehistoric cairn and a reservoir catchment boundary stone – 'RDH' means Rural District of Holne and 'PUDC', Paignton Urban District Council. Cross the curving leat (Holne Town Gutter) and, in a few yards, recross it. Pass a set slab and a thorn tree; observe now that the reave is in absolutely direct line with a sunken

---

* Sholedon Gate is likely to have been established in later medieval times after the desertion of the Holne Moor settlements and enclosures.

lane ascending west of Venford Bottom.

It will be understood that a track, whose main functional use ceased 450 years ago, will only now be visible on the ground through its use in later centuries. Such use may almost have dwindled to nothing during the second half of the twentieth century, but signs nevertheless remain on this and other Dartmoor monastic ways, where portions of tracks have continued in use until a new generation of mechanized moormen took to wheels in place of boots and saddle. Thus Track 12, passing the tree and the set slab beyond the leat, follows the continuing reave to its hillside termination on the edge of a gully beside a double-trunked thorn tree, beyond which no signs remain of the former link with Workman's Ford in Venford Bottom and the sunken lane beyond it. The way ahead is nevertheless short and direct. Simply descend to the bottom and pick up the path leading to access stiles in the reservoir perimeter fence. At the fence corner, notice the overgrown outline of a medieval longhouse, left; there are signs that the occupants used a ford on Venford Brook (it may indeed have been they who named the brook) upstream from Workman's Ford and that the longhouse was the main lower terminal of the hedged, sunken lane ahead. Opposite the ruin, outside the fenced area, are the outlines of an ancillary building. Follow the lane, which certainly pushes back the centuries, to a point where a clapper bridge of two openings carries the continuing track uphill; built in 1859 to bridge the Wheal Emma leat, it could well represent continuing use of Track 12 by the moormen until the leat ceased to flow in the early years of the present century. The site of the moorgate that once headed the lane ascending from the longhouse is here, in the midst of a breached prehistoric reave. All the foregoing features, excepting the Wheal Emma leat and clapper bridge, appear in Fig. 3.

The Venford reave, ascending beside the lane, continues towards two thorn trees; 12 yards north of the reave and beside the trees is the stone setting discovered in 1982 by Dr Andrew Fleming of the University of Sheffield and listed here as † 3 (Pl. 21). Fleming and his co-researcher Nicholas Ralph have suggested in their *Report on Medieval Settlement and Land Use on Holne Moor, Dartmoor: the Landscape Evidence* that, 'This stone setting was the site of the most easterly cross on the route across Dartmoor, and that this route must have been established before 1239 ...'* Thus in this area of busy

---

* I have twice visited the stone setting of † 3 with Dr Fleming.

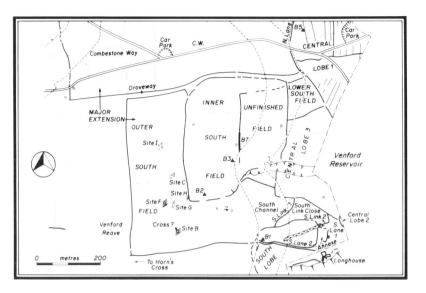

Area of Holne Moor studied and mapped by Andrew Fleming and
Nicholas Ralph, and crossed by the monastic way (Track 12).

medieval activity between Holne Lee and Horn's Hill there lies a field
system including cornditches, reaves, ruined longhouses, a droveway,
the hedged lane and moorgate site now described. See Fig. 3.

From † 3 continue beside the Venford reave until † 4 is seen ahead;
the tip of the cross would have been visible to a rider at † 3, and to a
walker 50 yards beyond. The poor remnant of a triple stone row
appears on the south side of the reave, with a fallen menhir and a
grave hollow at the upper end containing one large stone. This
monument could well have been regarded by the religious as a
waymark, as the route from it to † 4 is a good one. Pass a PUDC
stone and notice, left, the great hollow of Brockley Bottom below
Holne Ridge; the tors above the Double Dart valley appears, right,
and the central basin lies spread below. Near the crest the way is
stranded and sunken; Down Ridge is ahead, and Skaur and Ter Hills
rise to the left as Track 12 crosses the plain of Horn's Hill on the
south side of † 4, intersecting Track 26.

† 4 stands 7 feet 6 inches above its 12-inch high granite base, a

venerable relic; rustic in form, it has more than once been broken, repaired and re-set and has been provided in modern times with a replacement shaft. The cross stands central to the plain of Horn's Hill. Track 12 is well defined on each side of the cross and becomes slightly sunken to the west, where it passes a ruined cache (right), perhaps once a tinner's beehive hut, and descends the west slope of the hill to two set stones and the ruins of a kistvaen with one each of end- and side-stones.

From the hillside is seen the green trackbed of the Hexworthy Mine tramroad; beyond it, to the right, are † 5 and † 6 on the south flank of Down Ridge. The stranded way descends from Horn's Hill through heather, past two adjacent thorn trees and a prominent boulder, to reach the valley floor over a layer of crude stone paving. It fords a streamlet descending from the deep gully, left, beyond which it becomes a level grass track approaching Horse Ford on O Brook (Pl. 18). Immediately below it is the dry channel of the mid nineteenth-century Wheal Emma leat, and beyond that the silver thread of the small-capacity Hamlyn's leat, here taken in from the brook. *Eastward from Horse Ford: green track leads to streamlet ford and ascends from paving to pass thorn trees.* The crossing-place at Horse Ford on O Brook (Pl. 18) was destroyed by a flood in 1965 but is enhanced by waterslides, cascades and rowan trees. It is at this point that Track 12 leaves Holne Moor to enter the Forest of Dartmoor. From the site of the ford it swings left, then becomes sunken in curving to ease gradient on the ascent of Down Ridge. The large wheelpit of Hexworthy Mine appears left, and † 5 is seen ahead as the sunken way levels out. The cross is likely to have stood originally lower on the hillside, so accounting for its name (Horse Ford†); it was erected in its present position by a Hexworthy moorman at the instigation of William Crossing, after being found fallen. Track 12 intersects the Hexworthy mine road near the miners' barracks (hostel) and ascends the gentle slope ahead within sight of † 6 (Pl. 20). From the cross, † 7 and † 8 are seen on Ter Hill; † 6 is some distance from Skaur Ford, but its site is strategic in informing the traveller that he is about to join the Hexworthy-Aune Head Track in order to reach Skaur Ford (left). Had the cross been sited at the ford, it would have been invisible from both † 5 and † 7 on Ter Hill – whereas here it can be seen from both points.

Skaur Ford (O Brook) is deeply marked. A glance at the map will show the horseshoe bend of the brook, west of which lies an extensive tract of unpleasant, miry ground; the need to avoid this left one alternative open – a double crossing of O Brook. This portion of the route, together with the westward continuation to the crest of Ter Hill, is remarkable for good ground and easy gradient, yet seems to be little known to walkers in general. *Eastward from Skaur Ford: follow the Hexworthy track until way branches right and visibly leads to † 6.* Cross O Brook at Skaur Ford and turn right along the brook's right bank to reach Sandy Ford; here re-cross the brook; remain on the Aune Head track as far as a pointed triangular slab, possibly once set as a waymark.

Leave the Aune Head track and follow a path (right) to a ruined tinners' house. Ascend the bank and pass a round-topped stone which, perhaps once erect, also served as a waymark. Track 12 now passes a group of small boulders and a tinners' mound, then brings into view † 7. It keeps well above the low ground, right, and climbs over good terrain to approach † 7 along a level contour. Here, on Ter Hill, the way mounts to its only true hill crest and reaches its highest point at 1,550 feet. It runs clearly from † 7 to † 8 which, together with † 9, the next westward, were found fallen and re-erected in 1885. A fine view is seen from the Ter Hill crosses of the central basin and distant northern heights. *Eastward from † 7:* be careful initially to follow level contour path: it remains clear on gradual descent to features near O Brook – in eastward order, tinners' mound, boulder-group, round-topped stone, tinners' house. Swing right to triangular set slab; join Aune Head-Hexworthy track. Turn left; cross brook at Sandy Ford; remain on track. Two animal fords ahead; ignore both; remain on track until stony, sunken approach to Skaur Ford; cross. From † 8, take a clear green path, the right fork of two such paths; in less than 100 yards † 9 will come in view.

This fine cross stands at the highest corner of the Foxtor Farm newtake, a wind-beaten spot known graphically as Mount Misery. The provision of a gateway here by the newtake builders in 1809 was to provide access for two ancient ways: Track 12, which doubtless continued to receive sporadic use by moormen long after the dissolution of the monasteries, and the Sandy Way from Michelcombe, which descends from Aune Head to Mount Misery *en route* for Headweir Ford on Swincombe. Track 12 bears away left from the cross, descends through the newtake and crosses Swincombe at Foxtor Farm Ford; it can be seen from † 9 bisecting two parallel reaves to reach † 10. Pass some flat rocks; when the track becomes

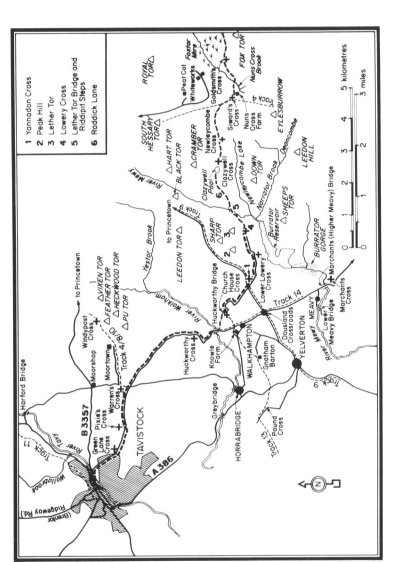

Track 12 — West

Key (numbered locations):

1 Yannadon Cross
2 Peak Hill
3 Lether Tor
4 Lowery Cross
5 Lether Tor Bridge and Riddipit Steps
6 Raddick Lane

Harford Bridge
to Princetown
Windypost Cross
Moorshop
Moortown
Track 4/8
△VIXEN TOR
△FEATHER TOR
△HECKWOOD TOR
△PU TOR
Yestor Brook
River Walkham
LEEDON TOR △
to Princetown
Track 9
SHARP TOR △
River Meavy
BLACK TOR △
△HART TOR
△CRAMBER TOR
Clazywell Pool
Clazywell Cross
Newleycombe Cross
Newleycombe Lake
Narrator Brook
SOUTH HESSARY TOR△
ROYAL TOR△
FOX TOR △
Nuns Cross Brook
Fortor Mire
Peat Cot
Whiteworks
Goldsmith's Cross
Siward's Cross
Nuns Cross Farm
EYLESBURROW
Deancombe
LEEDON HILL
△DOWN TOR
△SHEEPS TOR
Burrator Reservoir
BURRATOR GORGE
Marchants (Higher Meavy) Bridge
Huckworthy Bridge
Church House Cross
Lower Lowery Cross
Track 14
Dousland Crossroads
MEAVY
Lower Meavy Bridge
Marchants Cross
YELVERTON
River Meavy
Track 9
Gnatham Barton
WALKHAMPTON
Knowle Farm
Huckworthy Cross
Greybridge
HORRABRIDGE
Track 13
Pound Cross
Warren's Cross
Green Lane Cross
Pixie's Cross
B 3357
TAVISTOCK
A 386
River Tavy
Track 11
Wallabrook
(Brentor Ridgeway Rd.)

N

0 1 2 3 4 5 kilometres
0 1 2 3 miles

stranded, head towards Childe's tomb († 10); it then rounds an area of broken ground (left) by bearing towards the lonely house at Whiteworks, bringing in sight the ruined Foxtor Farm. *Eastward from farm: path ascending from river (right) is Track 2. Track 12 bears left from it to ascend diagonally through newtake. Stranded but well marked. In very short way head of† 9 appears.* Pass to the left (south) of the ruin and follow a sunken way past a well preserved tinners' house (left) to the river. Cross; the ground on the left bank has been so torn apart by tinners – they would have had no cause to preserve the old way after the 1539 dissolution – that it is no longer traceable. Strands cross the valley floor, however, and lead to the path, seen from Mount Misery, bisecting the parallel reaves: † 10, Childe's Tomb, is now directly ahead. Although this has undergone a hotchpotch restoration, it has at least helped to preserve the monument in substance. The cross, a modern replacement of its broken medieval forerunner, surmounts the kistvaen in which, according to tradition, the remains of the dead hunter Amyas Childe were temporarily laid on discover.

Pass a small, isolated boulder (visible from † 10) and several tinners' mounds; ford T Gert Stream in a wet gully and ascend a low hill ahead. From the crest, † 11 is visible, and a backward glance reveals the directness of the route via † 8, † 9 and † 10. On nearing † 11, the path passes several tinners' pits, a large split boulder, a set stone and a fallen stone showing signs of preliminary working as a cross, but perhaps abandoned due to flaw. Goldsmith's Cross († 11), named after its discoverer and restorer (Lieutenant Goldsmith RN in 1903), overlooks the well-defined crossing of Whealam Stream, with a sunken approach on the west bank, and the continuing path towards Nuns Cross Hill, where the former farmhouse, treetops and newtake wall are visible. Cross Whealam Stream; follow the path rounding the spur of Whealam Hill: there are two main strands, one on the grassy plain of the valley floor just above Foxtor Mire, the other a few yards higher passing through a tract of heather covering the hill spur. As the paths continue to curve, eventually to unite, heather-covered tinners' burrows appear below; right, a steep gully is seen on the east slope of Nuns Cross Hill and, just beyond it, a transverse wall crosses the valley (of Nuns Cross Brook) and ascends the hill. Between gully and wall is the (dry) leat channel that once conveyed water from Whealam Stream to Whiteworks Mine – its site seen beyond the great mire, right – the channel also rounding the hill spur above Track 12. The way now converges on the brook, reaching it at the transverse wall; its further continuation on the hill slope is now seen to be exactly in line. *Eastward from ford: stay near brook's right bank until track diverges to round Whealam Hill. Keep always below leat channel.*

Cross the broken wall; ford Nuns Cross Brook; follow the path diagonally ascending the hillside ahead. The gradient is easy and the route excellent. Pass two granite boulders (right) near the (flowing) Devonport leat; continue to the clapper bridge over the leat, its site, like that described on p. 146, probably indicating the passing here of an ancient track remaining in use long after monastic times. Join the stony road ascending (left) from the wide and deeply worn Nuns Cross Ford. The way becomes sunken and crosses the newtake of the former Nuns Cross Farm; house and trees appear left and the head of † 12 ahead. Pass through a purpose-made gap in a transverse wall, then through an older wall; the way again becomes sunken on approaching † 12, where a gap in the outer newtake wall has been in-filled. *Eastward from † 12: pass through outer wall; follow sunken track; bear right to Nuns Cross Ford after passing through transverse walls. Visible from here left to right: Ter Hill, Fox Tor, Caters Beam, Stream Hill, Hand Hill, Eylesburrow, Forest boundary reave.*

The splendid old † 12 was recorded in 1240 at the Perambulation of the Forest of Dartmoor as *Crucem Siwardi*. Seven feet high, the monument bears a look of immeasurable age; engraven on its west face are the letters $_{LOND}^{BOC}$ and an incised cross, and on its east face, SYWARD, inscriptions relating to land boundaries, the former to that of the land granted to Buckland Abbey in 1278 (see p. 163). Track 12 is now joined for a short way by Track 4; 35 yards beyond the newtake corner it branches left as a clear, sunken way through heather. Now passing from the Forest to the south-western Commons near the head-waters of Newleycombe Lake (Mewy), the track makes a gradual descent into Mewy country, through which it passes for the remainder of its moorland course to the western escarpment. It runs towards a series of tinners' mounds (left), passing by the three nearest and most prominent. From here the crossing of the escarpment by the monastic way over the Yannadon-Peak Hill saddle is seen directly behind the tip of Down Tor. Lether Tor is truly impressive from here, too. South Hessary Tor and a wide, green track appear ahead, whilst Track 4 and PCWW stones are to the right. Ignore the green track, which connects with another passing through a transverse hollow ahead. Track 12, still traceable because remaining in use over the centuries, bears left in descending from the mounds to run along the right bank of the Devonport leat, and so join the track known as 'Uncle's Road' in the transverse hollow, a few yards above Older Bridge over the leat. *Eastward from Older Bottom: cross Older Bridge; follow leatside track, join Uncle's Road in hollow; turn right beside large boulder into shallow, heathery Track 12; follow uphill to largest mounds. Way becomes clearer on approach to Track 4.*

The scenic contrast here to the lonely stretches of the Forest is striking: Down and Sharp Tors, rising above Burrator reservoir, are etched upon a huge spread of western in-country reaching far beyond Bodmin Moor in Cornwall. All around are the pits and shafts of the former Nuns Cross Mine, and on the left in Drivage Bottom the Devonport leat, after flowing beneath Nuns Cross Hill, emerges from its granite tunnel to follow the south-west flank of Cramber. Uncle's Road, descending from Peat Cot, is a packhorse way used formerly for conveying peat to the south-west border villages; the two tracks, united for some way, cross the leat at Older Bridge and the headwaters of Newleycombe Lake at twin, shallow fords. Below, left, is the hidden dell of Newleycombe Bottom where the deep Newleycombe Gert opens; near the head of the gert, left, is † 13, which Crossing found broken some eighty years ago; it was subsequently re-erected a little way to the south of the existing hard track, though the loop path passing beside the cross could well be the original way. The walker descending west from here will clearly see † 14 on the smooth horizon of Clazywell Hill.

Down Tor is seen to dominate Newleycombe's south valley-side, and two other deep gerts cleave the land ahead on the north side: Cramber, the first, opens well above the track; but the cutting of the second, Clazywell Gert, has obliterated the track near † 14. At a sharp bend beyond a streamlet forded by Uncle's Road (less than half a mile west of † 13), the latter continues to descend towards Burrator reservoir, whilst Track 12 branches to run directly ahead as a clear, grass path towards † 14. This handsome cross is on the brink of the large, steep-sided Clazywell Pool, an old mine working, below which the gert dips to the valley floor; the course of the monastic way towards Mewy country enclosures at Raddick Gate must now be picked up as a grass path on the hill slope beyond the pool; here it makes towards a wall ascending Clazywell Hill from Cockle's Gate (where Uncle's Road becomes Norsworthy Lane) near the left extremity of the plantation ahead, and enters Raddick Gate and lane.

The picturesque old lane (Pl. 26) makes a direct descent to the Mewy riverside where, at Riddipit Gate (site of) it is joined by another medieval way (Riddipit Lane) to reach Riddipit Steps. The fine clapper bridge here was built as recently as 1833 and might have replaced an earlier one. One or two of the original stepping-stones lie on the downstream side of the bridge, four of them still *in situ*. From the river, the way climbs the west bank, passes Lether Tor Farm (ruins) and its trackside potato-storage cavern, crosses the Devonport leat and reaches † 15 on a valley-side shelf. (Parking is possible here at 562695.) In pre-reservoir days, when no conifers cloaked the valley-sides, † 14 and † 15 would have been intervisible; † 15 is unlike the rustic crosses common to Dartmoor's monastic tracks in having a slender, chamfered shaft; this replacement of the lost original – taken probably for use as a gatepost – supports the old, damaged head. The way is now absorbed by the tarmac road running westward; the scenically striking valley-side here is overlooked by the tors of Lowery and Lether opposed by Sheeps Tor across the valley. Crossing the leat and descending to a dell, the way throws off a branch (left) to the former Lowery Farm and Sheepstor, where † 16 once stood at the junction: the marking by OS, 'Cross-site', is correct according both to tradition and to R.H. Worth in his *Dartmoor*. From the site of † 16 the way climbs to the western escarpment at Yannadon; this junction of Track 12 with the old road coming up from Sheepstor Bridge (now submerged) is known as Lowery Cross; the name could be significant as denoting the original and expected site of a stone cross († 17) which within recent years was rescued from duty as a gatepost at a nearby farm and erected at Yannadon crossroads.

The way now descends from escarpment to in-country, passes † 17 in its modern position, crosses the B3212 Yelverton-Princetown road, here on the link of Track 9, and enters Long Lane, which points with arrow-like directness to the tower of Walkhampton church. At the foot of Long Lane, which bends to the right, it crosses Blacka Brook (Walkham) and becomes a grassy lane approaching the church. When a swollen stream and a steep, muddy lane offered arduous walking, travellers could follow Long Lane to Welltown Farm, the curving road making an easy ascent to the church; there exists a tradition indeed that 'the monks went that way' – a far better wet-weather route then, as now, than the often mud-clogged lane.

There are signs that the old path, ascending from Welltown, entered a field and emerged beside the cross-base (site of † 18) at

Walkhampton Church House. This is not a right of way, and walkers must follow the road running left above Welltown to its junction with the steep lane from the brook, and there turn right to the Church House. The rear of this fine old building is accessible from the churchyard in common with other Dartmoor church houses, a feature of convenience for the priest-monk, or any traveller, who wished to enter the church before taking bodily refreshment in the house. Walkhampton (locally 'Waketon') church,* like the church house, is a sixteenth-century rebuild of an older structure; the sight of its fine tower must have encouraged the westbound monk reaching the crest of Yannadon, and successive church houses on the site have preserved a tradition of hospitality reaching back to monastic times. The church tower is seen as a landmark from many places in the border-country, including points on both Tracks 12 and 13. Walkhampton was the first point on the long trans-moorland route, since leaving Holne, where an altar and rest and refreshment were available; here the monastic way branched to reach, with notable directness, the abbeys of Buckland and Tavistock. The base of † 18 is opposite the house. Parking (with discretion) is possible near the church gate for one or two cars.

Follow the hard track to the entrance (left) to Ward House, then continue on its line through a field gate and along a hedgeside path down to a stile with slotted posts. Cross the stile and walk to another, where an iron rail guards the approach to a single wall-step; seven steps on the further side descend into a narrow packhorse lane, directly aligned with Track 12, which is visible on the further side of the Walkham valley. There is an impressive view from here up the valley, topped by the tors of Pu, Cocks, Great Steeple, Great Mis and King. The packhorse lane, having associations with a former Walkhampton villager, is known as 'Jimmie Pickles's Lane'; 350 yards from the wall-steps, the lane meets the Walkhampton-Eggworthy road, beyond which the way formerly continued through a walled-up gap in the lower roadside hedge into Huckworthy Mill Meadow.† The farmer renting these – as the mill no longer works –

---

* Early in 1985 thieves broke into the church and took away the reserved Sacrament, it is thought for satanic rites. On Lady Day, 25 March, the Bishop of Plymouth rededicated the church in a reverent and moving ceremony, at which the author and his wife were present.

† Huckworthy Mill and the two meadows were leased by Sir Ralph Lopes on 23 June 1842 to 'John French and John Bartlett Gents of St Budeaux' for seven years at £51 p.a. (Maristow Papers 203).

expressed his opinion that a field path once connected Jimmie Pickles's Lane with Huckworthy Bridge, so providing yet another link in the chain. Do not enter the field, but turn left, then right into the road descending to the bridge.

This fine Tudor packhorse structure spans the often wild water of the River Walkham immediately below the old mill in the picturesque hamlet; recorded in 1665 as being in need of repair, it replaced a clapper and is of importance as the point of convergence of two monastic routes, Tracks 12 and 14. Cross Huckworthy Bridge; 240 yards up the hill bear right into a lane leading through a gateway onto Huckworthy Common, which the track crosses to reach Huckworthy† (19). This weather-beaten monument, with one short and one broken arm, stands over 6 feet high. The major road at the junction runs from Horrabridge to Sampford Spiney; Track 12 crosses the junction in line with the path over the common; behind is seen Long Lane climbing to Yannadon. This delightful and very ancient lane crosses a streamlet at Watery Ford – which is backed by Sampford Spiney church and village – and fringes Plaster Down to reach Warren's Cross.

I have long thought it strange that no sign of a stone cross remains at Warren's Cross, an important junction of ancient ways where the united Tracks 12, 14 and 16 crossed the old Plymouth-Okehampton road via Horrabridge and Harford Bridge (Tavy). Dom Leo Smith OSB, Abbot of Buckfast, recently brought to my notice the two old crosses, now in the abbey grounds, mentioned on p. 144. One of these – its dimensions are: height, 2 feet 6 inches; width of arms, 12 inches – was discovered in the old smithy at Moor by Miss Calmady Hamlyn JP and is likely to have come originally from a nearby site. The 1882 survey of OS shows a guide-post near the Moorshop smithy, and it seems unlikely that a granite cross would also have stood there – especially as the modern B3357 road was then a moorland track of far less importance than the ancient Horrabridge – Harford Bridge highway. The most logical site for the cross would have been alongside Track 12 at Warren's Cross, from where the next cross westward († 21) would have been visible. I am therefore including the cross here as † 20, despite the evidence being only circumstantial, as one of the monastic way series. Here would have stood at the track's entry upon Whitchurch Down, where the united ways begin their final lap to Tavistock. The down once provided a large area of pastureland for commoners and was swaled (burned) annually to control the growth of gorse and bracken, but the larger part of it now comprises a golf course (see p. 101). In slightly less than a mile west of † 20 (site of) stands Pixies'† (21), marking the junction of two ancient routes, Tracks 4, 8 and, united, 10 and 12. The route between crosses 20 and 21 still bears the semblance of a path, even in some places slightly sunken. It passes onto the common in line with the road from † 19 and Watery Ford and runs through a parting in the gorse bushes directly towards the side of a knoll mentioned on p. 101. Here it is joined by the well-marked strands of Tracks 8 and 10 from Moortown and Quarry Lane. Continuing from the knoll to † 21, observe the parallel motor road (Sampford Spiney–Tavistock) approximately 100 yards to the left. *Eastward from † 21: cross slope of knoll; observe definable grass road running through parting in gorse bushes towards Warrens † junction; passes low mound, joins Harford Bridge road just below junction.* Crossing writes in *Crosses* of † 21: 'It has a very rugged appearance, and the depth of the arms, which are roughly shapen, will at once strike the observe as being greater than is generally the case … its full height is seven feet nine inches. This venerable cross leans slightly on one side, and its rude fashioning presents a great contrast to the care displayed in the shaping of the Windypost … Though standing on the line of the "Abbots' Way", the appearance of this cross would seem to warrant the supposition that it is of earlier date than either of the religious houses of the moorland borders.'

Crossing's supposition is open to question, as both Tavistock and Buckfast were pre-Conquest Benedictine foundations; an inter-monastic track, therefore, is highly likely to have been formed and marked out by stone crosses of 'rude fashioning', and perhaps no other reason need be sought for the erection of † 21. Although granite preaching-crosses are not uncommon in Devon and Cornwall, they are not known to have been sited on waste land, such as was † 21, but in the centres of communities.

The reader is now referred to the sign * on p. 101, from which follow the continuing way via † 22 into the monastic and stannary town of Tavistock.

Tavistock Abbey

In 973/4 the Saxon Ordgar and Ordulf, Earl of Devon and Christian convert, founded a house beside the River Tavy for a community of the Benedictine Order. The monastery, dedicated to St Rumon, was completed by Ordgar's son Ordulf in 981 and in that year granted a

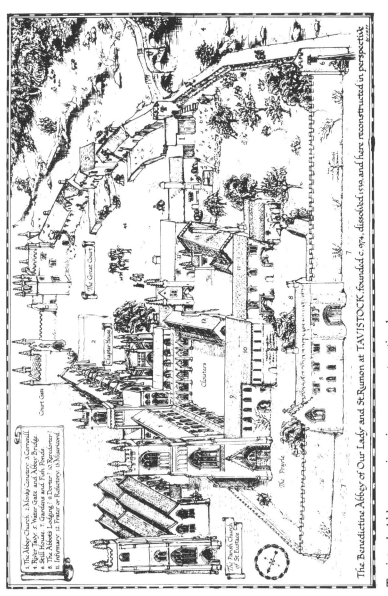

1. The Abbey Church 2. Monks' Cemetary 3. Cornmill
4. River Tavy 5. Water Gate and Abbey Bridge
6. Still House 7. Gardens and Fish Ponds
8. The Abbot's Lodging 9. Dorter ? Reredorter ?
11. Infirmary 12. Frater or Refectory 13. Misericord

The Benedictine Abbey of Our Lady and St Rumon at TAVISTOCK, founded c. 974, dissolved 1539, and here reconstructed in perspective

Tavistock Abbey – an imaginary reconstruction by Mrs J.P.R. Finberg.

charter by King Ethelred II. Almer, the first abbot, was destined to witness and survive the terrible events of 997, when marauding Danes sailed up the river in 997, sacked the monastery and put the monks to the sword. It says much for the vigour of monastic life then that the great task of rebuilding began almost at once. Livingus, a friend of King Canute, was successor to Almer; holding the sees of Crediton and Worcester concurrently, he died on 23 March 1046, and his body was brought back to St Rumon's Abbey for burial.

The establishment stood on the river's north-west bank and was approached by Track 12 over an arch-bridge leading through the Watergate into the Great Court. In *c*.1260, this bridge was demolished and replaced by Tavistock Great Bridge to serve the growing township, after which traffic to the abbey entered the precincts at Court Gate, the fine gateway standing today in Bedford Square. The Great Bridge was in turn demolished and superseded by the new (present) Abbey Bridge in 1764 – its name honouring the remarkable establishment that had passed into history over 200 years previously. The abbey of St Rumon became a 'mitred abbey', a privilege conferred only by the Pope, which entitled the abbot to wear a mitre and carry a pastoral staff in episcopal style. Some idea of the flourishing state of the abbey at the time of its dissolution (1539) may be judged from its possession of 22,000 acres of land, including scores of farms in many manors, with consequent large-scale moorland sheep-grazing and a necessary programme of travelling over Dartmoor and through the border-country. The rapacity of Henry VIII brought the great monastery to its knees on 3 March 1539, when, writes H.P.R. Finberg, '... twenty monks assembled with the abbot in their octagonal chapter house, and took their places for the last time in the accustomed stalls, "arched overhead with curious hewn and carved stone". Here they signed and sealed a deed surrendering the monastery and all its possessions to the crown. The church was speedily dismantled ...' Today the remains of the abbey are tragically scant and are dispersed among parish churchyard, twentieth-century town development, masonry fabric of a hotel, the vicarage garden and a Free Church meeting house. Mrs Josceline Finberg's imaginative reconstruction surely recaptures something of what must have been the former glory of Tavistock Abbey: Figure 4.

TRACK 13

MONASTIC WAY: BUCKFAST ABBEY – BUCKLAND ABBEY   18 miles

Oral tradition again plays some part in the delineation of this route, whose history and topography seem to provide a reasonable answer to the question 'Which way did they go?'

Following the Track (westward)
The Buckland-bound monk from Buckfast would have followed Track 12 as far as Walkhampton Church House, and there branched left for

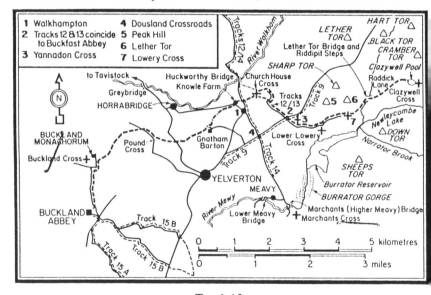

Track 13

his destination. The manor and church of Walkhampton were given to the abbot of Buckland by the Lady Amicia, Countess of Devon, in 1278. This resulted in much monastic travel between abbey and church, as well as over Dartmoor as far as Siward's † (see p. 152), across what is now Walkhampton Common, for the purpose of shepherding the abbey flocks and herds. (For parking, see p. 155.)

Take the churchyard path round the south side of the church, where a kissing-gate in the finely built boundary wall leads through a copse to a field enclosed by walls of densely packed stones. Follow the field path – pointing towards the Walkhampton-Horrabridge road above Knowle Farm – to another gateway. Descend over the next field to an iron gate, beside which seven slabs have been vertically set to narrow the passage; two other stones, now displaced, show that the original opening was even narrower than at present. The monastic way passes from the gateway into the Sampford Spiney road, where for a short way it joins Track 14. *Eastward: on passing through field above iron gate, observe path practically aligned with road above Knowle Farm and Track 12/13 ascending to Yannadon on moorland escarpment.*

Turn right into the road for 160 yards to a gateway (now blocked by a shed) in the left roadside hedge, where granite gateposts remain. (From here the original way descended to Knowle Ford and a clapper bridge on Blacka Brook before ascending the opposite valley-side to Knowle Down.) Do not enter the field, but return along the road to Walkhampton village; turn right at the cross and immediately right again into the Horrabridge road, when Knowle Farm will soon be reached. Go to the farm (Mr G. and Miss D. Eggins) and ask permission to follow the ancient way (i.e. Track 13) down to Knowle Ford, a pretty, secluded dell. The blocked gateway beside the Sampford Spiney road is visible from the brook's left bank. Return through lane and farmyard; turn right to the nearby rocks on the summit of Knowle Down, where a fine view is seen of the lower-reach valley of the moorland Walkham; below is the old leat from Blacka Brook to Furzehill Wood copper mine.

Mr George Eggins was of great assistance to me during my researches in this area (see also footnote to p. 114), and his is the third generation of the family to work the farm.

Return to the road and descend westward for 300 yards to the point where the wall (left) diverges from the roadside and is followed by a grass track. This again is Track 13, which enters a gateway at a wall corner. It then crosses fields in line with Buckland Down and reaches a flight of wall-steps near the by-road from Walkhampton to Gnatham. It must be emphasized that the fields, belonging severally to Knowle and Gnatham Farms, must not be entered without obtaining prior permission at both farmhouses. It is in this case simpler to return over Knowle Down to Walkhampton village; do not turn left to the cross, but right into the Yelverton road; less than half a mile up the hill is the junction of the farm road to Gnatham (pronounced 'Nattam') Barton. Pass by the farm (a large establishment, left) into a narrow way aptly named Watery Lane; the outflow from a vigorous spring near the farm has adopted the lane-bed as its course to join a stream below, where a gate leads to a ford. Near here and reached by another gateway (right) are the remains of Furzehill Copper Mine.

Follow the narrow lane ascending from the ford for 500 yards, to a junction of lanes and a bridge over the former GWR Plymouth-Tavistock railway line. The A386 highway, where a roadside stone is marked 'North Road', is 75 yards beyond the bridge. Turn right into the main road and notice an overgrown, green way (right) bounded by a wall; this, directly aligned with Gnatham and Walkhampton church, was a footpath following Track 13 before the railway cutting and bridge were made and North Road for access. On the opposite road-verge a gateway opens onto the northern extremity of Roborough Down. Enter; follow the broad path ahead between trees and workings of the old North Roborough Down Mine; it is sunken for a short way before emerging onto an open hillside, where it runs ahead as a wide, green way to reach the road junction at Pound Cross. Here its alignment is preserved in entering the gate and fields of Pound Farm – *where there is no permitted access*. Turn right at Pound Cross, therefore, and enter the third gate in Pound Square – the large grass clearing, left. Follow the footpath along the edge of a copse; it is shortly joined by the original route through the farm fields. At a gateway ahead is a stone post, rising perhaps to 5 feet above an earlier ground level; it is of regular shape throughout and has one short arm and a slight bulge on the opposite side where an arm could have been broken off; it is not impossible that it was once a cross removed from the Pound Cross junction and drilled to hold a gate-hanger. From here follow Fieldpath 1 to a wooden stile; mount and enter a narrow lane leading (left) to Stanley's Barn. Continue to a fine granite stile known as Uppaton Stile; from here the Buckland-bound monk obtained his first view of the tower of St Andrew's Church, Buckland Monchorum ('Buckland-of-the-monks').

Pass through a rusty kissing-gate and descend Fieldpath 2 to a similar gate. Follow Fieldpath 3 to a granite stile leading into an ancient lane bordering the north side of the churchyard: the old people of Buckland know the lane as 'Church Walk' and say that 'The monks came that way.' The upper horizontal stone of the stile could be a cross shaft, but there is admittedly no known tradition to support the suggestion. The sound of the swift little Buckland Brook is audible from the lane; Church Walk enters the village centre beside the fine old 'Lady Modyford's School', near which once stood a cross on the (now built-over) village green. The base of the cross now stands in the churchyard and supports the long, tapering war-memorial cross. The column nearby was made for the sundial now surmounting it and, Masson Phillips assures me, could have no history as a cross-shaft. On the further side of the church gate and, as usual, accessible from the churchyard, is the original Buckland Church House, now the 'Drake Manor Inn'.

From the village, the monastic way is likely to have been the basis of the modern road to Buckland Abbey; tradition would otherwise have presented an alternative. But perhaps it does! Alice J. Bere, in her privately printed *Buckland Monachorum* (*c*.1930), wrote: 'Several subterranean passages from the Abbey existed. One down to the Tavy and a tunnel under the river were marked in a survey as late as 1708. Another running from the present stables, which was blocked in late years, was believed to run to the village.'

As the road descends more steeply to the valley of Buckland Brook, which flows through the abbey grounds, a sharp (left-hand) bend occurs. At this point (below a lodge and drive entrance, right) a kissing-gate opens upon an overgrown footpath which drops to the rear entrance drive (reaching it at another kissing-gate) to the abbey. Its directness and avoidance of the bend make it likely to have been the original way.

Buckland Abbey

The monastery was founded in 1278 by Amicia, Countess of Devon, and colonized by Cistercian monks from Quarr Abbey, IOW. The Cistercians, traditionally successful sheep-farmers, were quick to utilize the spacious Dartmoor commons for their flocks, and the eastern limit of the land granted to the abbey by statute (the *boc-lond* – book-land) was Siward's†, the word BOCLOND being engraved upon its west face; 'Yannadon crosse' (see p. 154) is recorded as the northern limit. Despite such extensive grazing rights, it appears that the abbey shepherds did not unfailingly observe the boundaries, and in 1478 the abbot, Thomas Olyver, was answerable at Lydford Castle Court for allowing abbey flocks to stray onto the Forest of Dartmoor.

A considerable increase in traffic on the monastic ways must have followed the establishment by Abbot William in 1317 of a Tuesday market on Buckland Green (being within the abbey's manor of Buckland) as well as a cattle fair on the three days following Trinity Sunday. These markets and fairs would have been attended by scores of farmers from the Walkham and Mewy valleys, where the manors of Walkhampton and Sheepstor were part of the abbey lands. (Abbot White is recorded as having leased a cottage in Sheepstor village in 1513: Maristow Estate Papers 185.) The abbey also had a grange at Gnatham (Walkhampton parish, p. 162) beside Track 13. Track 15 was furthermore in use by monks and lay-brethren journeying to a fishery on the River Plym at Bickleigh, another of the abbey's manors, to bring back fish for the community.

The abbey church is a handsome building with a fine late fifteenth-century tower. It fortress-like appearance arose from steps taken by the community in 1336 to defend themselves against French pirates, who could so easily have reached the monastery by sailing up the Tavy river – but never did.

On 15 October 1538, in the eleventh hour of the monastery's existence, Abbot John Toker issued a lease 'To John Servyngton of Tavystoke of the grange at Gnatham excepting a tin-mill and $\frac{1}{2}$ acre held there by Thomas Ford, Philip Talbot and John Rykes at Way' (Maristow Estate Paper 261). Following the dissolution of the abbey (1538), Abbot Toker became Vicar of Buckland Monachorum, and in 1576 the abbey church was purchased and converted into a residence by the renowned Sir Richard Grenville of Bideford. In 1581 it passed into the hands of the even more renowned Sir Francis Drake,* in whose family it remained until the twentieth century. In 1947 the property was vested in the National Trust, and today it provides the ideal terminus for a trans-Dartmoor walk from Buckfast – though advisedly in easy stages!

---

* *Donn* shows the abbey as 'Place of Sir Francis Drake'.

TRACK 14

MONASTIC WAY: PLYMPTON PRIORY – TAVISTOCK ABBEY (WITH BRANCH TRACK TO MEAVY CHURCH)   14½ miles

Plympton Priory

A Saxon chapel existed on the site of Plympton Priory until 1121, in the reign of Henry I; a quay was situated nearby, at the head of a former tidal creek. The canons of the college were in that year replaced, on the orders of Bishop Warelwast of Exeter, by those of the Augustinian Order, and the priory of the Blessed Virgin and St Peter and St Paul was founded. The Reverend H. Wackett, writer of the Priory guidebook (1969 edition), speaks of Plympton Priory's growth '... in wealth and power. It was a favourite house of the Bishop and he was lavish in his gifts and endowments. When he was old and blind he retired to Plympton Priory and took the habit of an ordinary canon. Here the Bishop died in 1137 and was buried in the Chapter House.'

The monastery became a daughter house of Holy Trinity Priory, Aldgate, on 29 October 1311, and the many manors it acquired included Boringdon, Sutton Prior (now a part of the great city of Plymouth 4 miles to the west), Shaugh Prior, Dean Prior, Meavy and Sampford Spiney, which Bishop Grandisson granted to the prior of Plympton in 1334 as the 'Chapel of Saunforde'. In 1355 the hospitality of the prior was somewhat strained by the Black Prince, who quartered himself and a thousand men at the priory for several weeks while waiting for a fair wind to sail from Sutton Harbour to the French coast. There is likely to have been much travel between Plympton and both Tavistock and Buckfast, as the community enjoyed a high reputation for hospitality, and guests – royal, commoner and clerical – moved between the monasteries. with some frequency.

There must have been Augustinian dissatisfaction at the priory over the holding by the Tavistock Benedictines of nearby Bickleigh weir and fishery and many acres of fertile land at Plymstock – but this historical precedence remained unbreached according to Mrs Bray (*Tamar and Tavy*) for the very good reason that, 'By an agreement between the Abbot of Tavistock and the Prior of Plympton, the latter obliged himself and his successors to do certain acts of suit and service to the former: namely, to attend the abbot, at his own charges, whenever he made his visitation within the diocese of Exeter … and on the feast of St Michael to provide him with a chaplain … for the church of Plymstock.' Southern Dartmoor commons grazed by the priory flocks and herds included Shaugh Moor and the more distant Dean Moor, but their wool production was small compared with that of the great Cistercian and Benedictine houses, and inter-monastic travel was likely to have been more administrative and social than agrarian. Recognizable routes, however, connected Plympton with Tavistock, Buckfast and Buckland and are described here as Tracks 14, 15 and 16.

The splendid granite priory church of St Mary the Blessed Virgin, over a century in building, was dedicated on 19 October 1311. Among its many interesting features are tombs and memorials of the Strode family of which Richard, Member of Parliament from Plympton during the reign of Henry VIII, was the central figure in the drama of the Sandy Hole tinners' conduit (see p. 53). At the time of the monastery's dissolution on 1 March 1539 the prior was John Howe; the conventual buildings, which stood to the east and south of the church, were razed to the ground; the stone, lead, glass and timbers were sold locally, and only a few years afterwards Leland wrote that, 'The lower and first buildings of the Priory be almost choken with sand that the Torey (Torry) Brook bringeth down from the tin-works.' So came an inglorious end to an institution known to have been of outstanding benefit to people of all classes over a wide area.

It should be explained here that the lie of the land between Wigford Down and Meavy church includes the deep little valley of Lovaton Brook. For this reason the main Tavistock track beyond Wigford Down maintained a high level to pass round the head of the brook near Brisworthy, and made its first descent to the Mewy (OS River 'Meavy') valley before reaching Dousland and Walkhampton. This route, however, constituted an indirect approach to Meavy church, which the monks were regularly obliged to visit, and a branch track

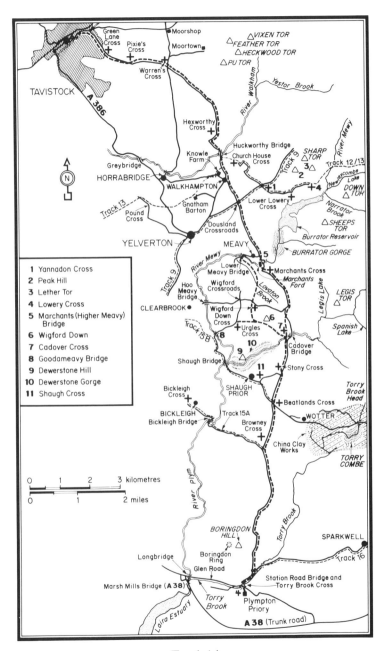

Green
Lane
Cross
Pixie's
Cross
● Moorshop
Moortown ■

△ VIXEN TOR
△ FEATHER TOR
△ HECKWOOD TOR
△ PU TOR

Warren's
Cross

TAVISTOCK
A 386

River Walkham
Yestor Brook

Hexworthy
Cross
Huckworthy Bridge
Knowle
Farm
Church House
Cross
SHARP
△ TOR
3 △
2
River Meavy
Track 12/13

Greybridge
HORRABRIDGE
WALKHAMPTON
Lower Lowery
Cross
1
4
Newleycombe
Lake
DOWN
TOR △

Track 13
Pound
Cross
Gnatham
Barton
Dousland
Crossroads
Narrator Brook
△ SHEEPS
TOR

YELVERTON
MEAVY
River Meavy
5
Burrator Reservoir
BURRATOR GORGE

Lower
Meavy Bridge
Marchants Cross
Marchants
Ford
LEGIS
TOR △
Legis Lake

Wigford
Crossroads
Hoo
Meavy
Bridge
CLEARBROOK ●
Wigford
Down
Cross
Lovaton Brook
△ 6
7

Track 15B
Urgles
Cross
8
10
Cadover
Bridge
Spanish
Lake

Shaugh Bridge ●
9
11
Stony Cross

Bickleigh
Cross
SHAUGH
PRIOR
Beatlands Cross
Torry
Brook
Head

BICKLEIGH
Bickleigh Bridge
Track 15A
Browney
Cross
WOTTER

China Clay
Works
TORRY
COMBE

River Plym

0   1   2   3 kilometres
0   1   2 miles

BORINGDON
HILL △
SPARKWELL
Track 16

Longbridge
Boringdon
Ring
Glen Road
Station Road Bridge and
Torry Brook Cross

Marsh Mills Bridge (A 38)
Torry
Brook
Plympton
Priory

Laira Estuary
A 38 (Trunk road)

Key

1 Yannadon Cross
2 Peak Hill
3 Lether Tor
4 Lowery Cross
5 Marchants (Higher Meavy) Bridge
6 Wigford Down
7 Cadover Cross
8 Goodameavy Bridge
9 Dewerstone Hill
10 Dewerstone Gorge
11 Shaugh Cross

Track 14

was used that descended over the west slope of Wigford Down into the Lovaton valley, from which the church could quickly be reached.

Following the Track (northward)
Park at 541566, the car-park mentioned below. The busy main road on the north side of the priory churchyard is Ridgeway; the site of the conventual buildings lies to the south of this, at the east end of the church. In the wall bordering the north side of Ridgeway is the pointed arch of a medieval doorway, its lower portion now buried beneath a raised ground level inside the walled area; still visible, however, are the heads of two arch-buttresses. That the original floor of the arch is at least 6 feet below present ground level may be judged from that of the road outside. The wall encloses the (public) grounds of Harewood House; walk through a nearby doorway in the wall and follow the footpath rounding the upper side of the tennis courts (left) where the monastic way formerly ran. Pass to the right of the house (now Plympton Borough Library); from the higher corner cross a public car-park, on the left side of which is Harewood†. This is a large stone slab on which the outline of a cross has been incised, and is considered by E. Masson Phillips originally to have been a tomb cover in the priory. A cottage that once stood here was demolished many years ago, and the slab-cross was found within, where it had been put to use as a fire-back. It also is of interest that a doorway from the conventual buildings of the priory – and perhaps the sole relic of the monks' quarters – was discovered not long ago in a Plympton garden and was given by the owner to be erected where passing townspeople could see it. It stands near Harewood House on the opposite side of Station Road.

There is little doubt that Track 14 swung left where Harewood House now stands and descended to Torry Brook through the grounds of a new housing estate on the west side of Station Hill, so making a direct approach to the site of a clapper at Station Road Bridge over the brook. From the car-park, descend Station Hill and turn left opposite Earl's Mill Road into Station Road to reach the bridge. The modern structure is of iron, but old masonry seen below the right bank remains from the earlier bridge.

A few yards downstream in the left bank of the brook is the octagonal shaft of Torry Brook†. Now lacking both head and arms, the shaft is set in a socket stone with a chamfered upper edge partly embedded in the bank, which is frequently obscured by mud and the high-water level. To view the cross easily, stand on the verge of the highway (Glen Road). The former ford may have lain between the (clapper) bridge and the cross. From here cross Glen Road at a pedestrian crossing; follow the footpath, opposite, below the railway bridge known as 'Black Arch'. The path, reaching Boringdon Road, is here aligned with the village street in Colebrook; at Golden Square a short way ahead, the Sparkwell road bears right, but Track 14 runs directly to the foot of Boringdon Hill to commence a long ascent past Elfordleigh hamlet to Dartmoor. NOTE: if the way is followed throughout on foot, it may prove tedious from Colebrook to Shaugh Moor, on which 4-mile stretch it coincides with the modern motor road.

At the top of Boringdon Hill, on the north edge of the Forestry Commission's 'Plym Stand' plantation is the Iron Age earthwork of Boringdon Camp – locally 'Boringdon Ring'. It may be visited by telephoning Mr D.C. Turner of Higher Collard Farm (Shaugh Prior 231) for permission to cross the field where the earthwork is situated; enter the field beside the bungalow named 'Fernhill'. The camp, which fortunately has remained unplanted, occupies a pleasant, level site from where interesting views are seen: the tors of Bodmin Moor appear beyond the Derriford Hospital chimney (west of the Plym valley); the Royal Marines 42 Commando establishment at Bickleigh is nearer, backed by the line of Roborough Down; in the foreground are Dewerstone Hill, Shaugh Beacon, Hawks Tor, Collard Tor, Wotter village, the Lee Moor clay-tips and the high ridge of Shiel Top and Pen Beacon. The single rampart of the camp, which describes an almost perfect circle, is on average 8 to 9 feet high and has a diameter of 200 yards. The main entrance faces towards 'Fernhill' and, beyond, to Collard Tor.

Just beyond Fernhill is the former level crossing of the Lee Moor Tramway (closed 1947) where one gate still stands. A mile further is the road junction where Browney† once stood (545608); the left fork leads down to Bickleigh Bridge on the River Plym and formed the best route (Track 15) for monks travelling via Bickleigh church to Buckland Abbey (to which the manor of Bickleigh belonged). Stones lying on the green triangle at the junction include the socket stone of Browney†. A small plaque reads: 'These stones are the relics of a medieval cross, which was one of ten which marked the route of an ancient track from Plympton Priory to Sampford Spiney.' Sampford Spiney, a manor of Plympton was reached by following the Tavistock way to Huckworthy†, and there turning right for the village (see p. 156). Half a mile east of Browney† are the very ancient farms, in north-south succession, of Lower Collard, Coldstone and Truelove, the two last architectural gems. The local tradition linking all these with Plympton Priory is very strong: it identifies Lower Collard as a monastic grange – an outpost farm of the monastery – Coldstone as a chapel, and Truelove as a hospice.

At Browney† fork right; Hawks Tor is in view as the road passes over the cattle-grid at Neil Gate and mounts to Beatlands Corner, where the socket stone of Beatlands† lies on the right roadside at the junction. Here the monks could turn left for Shaugh Prior, the first of their moorland manors on this route, passing the tenth-century Shaugh† before reaching the church of St Edward, King and Martyr. The lands of Shaugh were presented to Plympton Priory in 1134 by Roger de Nonant, and the church (then a small chapel on the site) by Bishop Grandisson in March 1334, after which the village became known as Shaugh Prior. The church is a typical, sturdy structure of moorland granite with crocketed tower and contains a fourteenth-century octagonal-basin font. The remarkable oak font cover, 9 feet high, has an elaborate carving of particular relevance to the monastic way, in that eight monks are portrayed looking down upon the scene of Christian baptism below. Nearby is an ancient door leading to the porch chamber, which provided accommodation for a visiting monk due to celebrate Mass next morning. A memorial on the wall of the south aisle is of interest to all Dartmoor-lovers: 'Sacred to the memory of N.T. Carrington, Author of *Dartmoor, Banks of Tamar, My Native Village* and other poems. He was born at Plymouth 19 July 1777 and died at Bath 2 September 1830 Aged 53 years. He lies buried in the churchyard at Combehay, near that city. Distinguished by his literary works, he won the regard of his countrymen. Mild and meek by nature, his heart overflowed "with the milk of human kindness". A humble and earnest champion.' In his *Dartmoor*, Carrington captures the sombre mood of the great upland with remarkable success.

The road branching east at Shaugh† is Brag Lane, joining the Plympton-Cadover Bridge road at Brag Lane End below the crest of Shaugh Moor. On the crest stands the 7-foot Stony†, visible from Beatlands Corner. Views from here north of the moorscape, west to the border-country and south to Plymouth Sound and the English Channel, are striking. Beyond the † occurs another division of ways: whilst the main track (practically identical with the line of the modern road) descended to the valley floor and Cadover Bridge, the Meavy church way branched left and, river level allowing, crossed Plym at Dunstone Ford. Upstream from here the river has for many centuries been bridged beside the still visible ford, the Cad-a-ford, or Cadover. The main track swings left on the north bank and approaches Cadover† as a sunken way; it is a fine monument nearly 9 feet high. Beyond the cross the Meavy branch ascends Wigford Down beside the Cadworthy enclosure wall, but the main (Tavistock) track, here obliterated by a large pool of the workings of the old Wigford Down China Clay Works, aligns with a further length of the modern road to Brisworthy Corner, from where it rounds the bend of Lovaton Brook and continues (still with the road) across the south foot of Ringmoor Down to Lynch Hill and descends to the River Mewy.

The prospect from Lynch Down is very fine and includes the beautiful woods of Burrator Gorge, the large tors above Mewy's middle reach and the granite wall of Burrator dam. At the foot of Lynch Hill (near a cattle-grid) stands the splendid old Marchants†;* 8 feet 2 inches high, the monument bears on each face an incised cross central to the shaft. 'Marchant' is the local pronunciation of 'merchant' and here could reasonably be assumed to signify a meeting place between merchants and customers. It also marks the river crossing just below, where the scenic delights of Marchants Ford attract countless picnicking visitors. The massive steps are still in place beside the sandy ford, and the arch of the ancient bridge stands a little way upstream; this was found by surveyors in 1665 to be crumbling and in need of immediate repair. The road passes to the north end of Meavy (once 'Mewe') village beside school and council house, reaches Dousland crossroads at the intersection of Track 9 (now the B3212 road) and descends to Walkhampton village. Within a short distance the independence of the old way ends; firstly, Track 13 comes down from Walkhampton Church House and is united with it for 260 yards; secondly, it is joined at Huckworthy Bridge by Track 12 and so continues to Tavistock Abbey.

Branch of Track 14 to Mewe (Meavy) Church
NOTE: that portion of the route between Dunstone Farm gate and the ford must not be entered upon without the express permission of Mr

---

* The cross was knocked over by a vehicle, out of control on Lynch Hill, in late 1984, the second such occurrence this century. It has since seen expertly repaired and re-erected by the DNPA.

Kenneth Kingwell, obtained by calling at the farm.

This branch path to Meavy church was marked by two granite crosses and offers a pleasing moorland walk over Wigford Down. It is particularly with this branch track and with Track 15 that I associate Dunstone Ford, which would have provided the most direct route to both Meavy and Buckland.

Following the Track (northward – on Wigford Down, a route rather than a defined way)

North of Stony† the roadside wall, left, diverges from the road and marks an ancient way now enclosed and obliterated in the Dunstone farm fields. Its line is virtually represented by the farm lane at whose foot it enters (through an iron gate) a field beside the farmhouse and runs between a very ancient hedge, right, and a tinners' gert, left, to reach the hidden, picturesque Dunstone Ford on Plym. This wide, shallow crossing, little more than a foot deep at normal river level, shows signs of having received constant use, probably by packhorses, long after the monks had ceased to walk or ride the Moor; a clear track leads from the right bank to a gateway (of packhorse rather than wagon width) beside a small enclosure into a narrow lane. In an oak-tree glade the track branches, left to Cadworthy Farm and right to Wigford Down; it crosses the modern Cadworthy Farm drive from Cadover Bridge and mounts to a moorgate, where it becomes a sunken way. There are steep gradients at the riverside approaches; Dewerstone Gorge opens immediately below the farm, and the next practicable crossing would have been at Shaugh Bridge (formerly a clapper) at the foot of the gorge. Pass from the moorgate through the funnel opening between enclosure walls and ascend towards a dip in the crest of Wigford Down, ahead. This portion of the route is clearly shown (as presumably then still in use) on *OS 1809*. In a short way, join the main track (here ill-defined) coming up from Cadover† (right); follow it to the crest where it runs beside a reave. Wigford Down was once crowned by four very large cairns – one with a circumference of 105 yards; reave and and track crest the down well to the west of the cairns. Continue beside the reave until the track bears away right to descend towards a field-system reave containing two prominent stones, one entirely of quartz. Pass between them near a large hut circle (1), right, and walk towards hut circle 2, with a thorn tree growing on the wall. Not far distant is hut circle 3, of massive construction, with a thorn tree in the centre. Stay below on the green path in order to see (left) the clear outline of an unrecorded medieval longhouse; this certainly would have been occupied when monks were passing between Plympton and the village then called 'Mewe'.

The track, clearly marked along the edge of Blacklands Mire, now heads towards the tree-backed Meavy rectory (beside a triangular plantation surrounding a white house); the gushing spring at the head of the mire would certainly have accounted for the siting of the longhouse. Pass below another large hut circle, 4, and enter the right-angle corner of a field system. From here the erect Greenwell must have been visible. An ancient leat channel is seen, left – it took water from Blacklands Mire to Greenwell Gert – with which the track converges. They meet at hut circle 5 (with thorn tree) where the leat actually bisects the hut. The track now loses definition but descends towards the Cadover Bridge-Yelverton road at Greenwell† (base: 544656) within view of a roadside gateway. *Southward from Greenwell†: make for hut circle 5 (with leat and thorn tree visible from Greenwell†). Cross field system to far, upper corner, leaving leat channel right. Remain near verge of Blacklands Mire; pass hut circle 4; observe longhouse; pass below hut circle 3 (with tree), then 110 yards further to hut circle 2 (also with tree). Enter another field system and pass beside the two reave stones; notice hut circle 1 nearby, left. Make for clear dip in hill crest above; notice ascending reave, right, converging with path. Join it; indistinct path to Dunstone Ford passes through bracken field at south end of reave as ground declines towards Plym valley; descends to funnel opening between Cadworthy walls in direct line with Dunstone farm road beyond valley.*

Greenwell† (with massive remaining socket stone) is near the great tinners' gert of that name, excavated in post-monastic times, at the source of Greenwell Brook. The cross long ago disappeared; it may once have stood on the north side of the road, for Mr Arnold Cole of Greenwell Farm tells me his father found the huge base an inconvenience to carts entering his fields and moved it to its present position. The monastic path crossed the road,* entered the gateway opposite (see above) and followed an ancient field hedge, right. Passing a large mining pit and gerts on Catstor Down (in a copse below the field centre), it descended to Lovaton Ford below Durance

---

* To be exact, there was at that time only a rough moorland track to the head of Shadycombe; the track to Gratton and Elfordtown branched from it and ran beside the enclosure wall to the site of a moorgate (at the present cattle-grid).

Farm. There is no right of way on this portion of the route between Greenwell† and Lovaton Ford, all the land (including Catstor Down) now being enclosed. Follow the Yelverton road to the first right turning; continue to Lovaton; park, with discretion, near the brook. Walk to Lovaton Ford.

At Lovaton Ford is a (modern) clapper bridge; cross; ascend the lane ahead to Lovaton hamlet. Follow the valley road to the next bridge over Lovaton Brook, then mount a stile (right) and battle with a muddy path leading through an oak wood where scurrying squirrels, and bluebells and anemones in spring, compensate for the mud. Pass an upright stone resembling a Hepworth sculpture (I write this with respect). The hill slope is Callisham Down and marks the border of the granite in this locality. Follow the path to a stile near Callisham Ford and clapper bridge – originally of two openings, but one is now blocked. Cross; continue through a green glade; the buildings of the ancient Callisham Farm are left. Mount the next stile at the head of Callisham Lane (a former packhorse way); hedges are high, mud abounds, but so do wild flowers, and the view of Meavy church and village is quite beautiful. Pass through a gateway at the foot of the lane into the tarmac road (from Callisham Cross to Meavy). Cross the unbeautiful bridge over Mewy – properly Lower Meavy Bridge but locally 'Iron Bridge'; pause and look down at the river banks above the bridge, where signs remain of a medieval clapper bridge; also at the approach from Callisham Lane (left bank) and traces of a track crossing the field (right bank) and aligned with the site of the ancient bridge; the track ran towards the old mill and is, of course, now superseded by the modern road from Iron Bridge.

A stone's throw from the old mill are the lych gate, steps and path to St Peter's Church. Rosemary Thomas writes in her guide-book of the church: '[The fifteenth century] ... was the last time that Meavy Church had a major rebuild: today's church is much as the 15th century workmen left it. Details have altered, but the overall shape is the same. Perhaps an expending population, combined with increased prosperity from the wool trade and the tin mining encouraged the villagers to expand their church.' The tower can be entered from the exterior through a beautifully carved doorway; near it is an outbuilding of Meavy Barton, with a window containing a chamfered granite lintel $53\frac{1}{2}$ inches long, and a vertical iron bar still in place. The church house, as usual, could be entered from the churchyard. The house, now the Royal Oak Inn, faces the village green where stands the great and ancient oak of Meavy; under its branches, year by year, the children of Meavy Church of England Primary School perform a pageant with song and dance on the day of the annual Meavy Oak Fair. According to the Register of Bishop Grandisson (thirteenth century) the cellarer of Plympton Priory at one time was John of Mewe; the bishop removed him from office 'for divers reasons upon which for the benefit of religion I [Grandisson] will not enter'. On 8 January 1434 (12 Henry IV) a grant of land and tenements at 'Mewy' was made by 'Nicholas Prior of the Apostles Peter and Paul to Richard Myleton' (the name later became 'Middleton'). Tithe charges on the parish in 26 Henry VIII, when Thomas Harding was rector, were 'In the Spiritualities of Plympton Priory in the Deanery of Plympton' sheaves, wool and lambs; dues owed to the Prior by the rector were –

Prior	13s.	4p.
Archdeacon	6s.	0p.
Synodal	2s.	6p.
Bishop's Visitation	2s.	2p.
Rental for Mewy Park, parcel of Barton of Mewy	3s.	4p.

This amounted to the then substantial sum of £1.7.4. (From *Valor Ecclesiasticus*.)

Travellers wishing to reach Tavistock from 'Mewy' would take the road between the green and the church house; a typical, high-banked Devon packhorse lane, this passes both old and new rectories – and so is named Rectory Lane – and joins the main Track 14 here climbing from Marchants Ford to Dousland.

TRACK 15

MONASTIC WAY: PLYMPTON PRIORY – BUCKLAND ABBEY $10\frac{1}{4}$ miles

Two satisfactory routes linked these monasteries, Route A via Buckland Abbey's manor of Bickleigh, and Route B via that of Plympton Priory at Shaugh Prior. Route B included alternative crossings of the River Plym, according to river level, detailed here as B1 and B2.

Following the Track (northwestward): Route A
From Plympton Priory to Browney† as detailed in Chapter 14. At Browney† (see p. 170) fork left and descend to Bickleigh bridge, a late medieval structure typical, except in the absence of pedestrian refuge bays, of those built in the Dartmoor border-country to carry traffic in the early years of expanding medieval commerce. Bishop Stapledon of Exeter had in the early fifteenth century bequeathed 25 shillings for the upkeep of Bickleigh bridge, which was recorded in 1665 as needing repair, and in 1809 it was ivyclad when seen by traveller James Green. The village centre and church of St Mary the Virgin are some way beyond the bridge; later restoration of the church has obliterated much of the fourteenth-century work, but a twelfth-century south doorway remains, thus pre-dating the gift of the church to Plympton Priory in 1271. The foundation date is not known, but evidence of a much earlier building is provided by a Norman font, not now in use but exhibited near the tower, and by the recorded dates of 1278 and 1288 during its period of use. The font that now serves the parish stands near the south door and dates from 1589, the year following that of the Armada. The tower with its fine pinnacles was built in the fifteenth century and probably postdates the church, which has granite monolith pillars and four arches on either side of the nave.

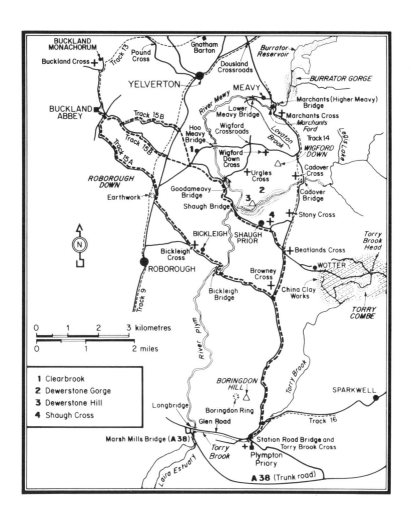

Track 15

Windows now are of clear glass, and the church interior gives an impression of light and height. Numerous wall monuments in the building commemorate members of the Lopes family, of which the head is styled Lord Roborough (of Maristow), and the striking modern altar and altar rails are of local granite. Since 1950 the church has had close links with the Royal Marines, whose 42 Commando barracks are situated at the south-east end of the village.

On the village green near the churchyard wall is Bickleigh†. This beautiful old granite monument stands 9 feet above its base, which rests upon two massive plinths. From Bickleigh, the track is represented by the road running north-west, and the second lane branching (right) from it beyond the village centre, known as Little Down Lane; this crosses the track of the old Plymouth & Dartmoor Railway near Combe Park. At the bridge over the (disused) Plymouth leat, the tarmac road bears away left towards Roborough Down and Maristow; follow the rough path (Track 15) along the leat's right bank for a short way until it diverges to reach the crest of Roborough Down. Cross the A386 Plymouth-Tavistock road 150 yards south of the Bere Alston road junction, where the track is traceable on each side; it is sunken in passing the summit earthwork on the summit of the down and is aligned with a bend in the Bere Alston road. A late sixteenth-century map, copied from Spry's *Plot* at Hatfield and published in TDA 66 of 1934 with Dr E. Symes Saunders's article on Roborough earthwork, shows this medieval track branching from the packhorse way from Plymouth to the area of modern Yelverton. It shows a 'Broken Cross' east of the forking tracks; this was in later times replaced by a bond-stone bearing the letter 'B' (for Bickleigh) which, in its turn, has disappeared. The track is then shown running beyond Roborough Down to another fork – right for Buckland Monachorum village, left for the abbey, which is marked (as the domicile of) 'Sr Fr: Drake'.

The private estate wall, park entrance and woodlands seen on the left from the Bere Alston road are those of Maristow House, the property of Lord Roborough. From here the way follows an unbroken, direct line to the south-east entrance to Buckland Abbey grounds, situated at Buckland Abbey crossroads at the junction of the roads from Milton Combe to Crapstone and Buckland Monachorum village. Thus the route is motorable between Browney† and the abbey with the exception of the short portion lying between Combe Park and the Bere Alston road on Roborough Down.

Route B
This provided alternative ways 1 and 2, according to which crossing of Plym was used.

B1: descend from Stony† (p. 170) to Cadover Bridge. Cross; branch left from the road; pass Cadover† and follow the contour of Wigford Down's south flank to join with the track ascending from Dunstone Ford.

B2: descend from Stony† to Dunstone Ford; here a reminder that it is essential first to obtain permission at Dunstone Farm. Cross; ascend through the Cadworthy funnel walls to Wigford's south flank;* join B1 and curve left to climb diagonally to a dip on the south crest. Its westward continuation from the dip, past some prehistoric enclosures, to the corner of Blacklands Newtake is well marked. It then becomes a wide grass track used by moormen over the centuries. Follow the wall, left; ford Blacklands Brook; continue through the sunken way to Urgles† (Pl. 19). Crossing (*Crosses*) mentions this path over Wigford Down as part of the track to Buckland Abbey – though only the base of Urgles† was *in situ* in his day; the restored cross is a rather striking monument, despite its proportionately short arms. Noted in the margin of the relevant *Spencer* is: 'Base only 1902: Broken Head and Shaft repaired OK 1912. Broken under arms and cemented in socket stone.' Below Urgles† follow the road descending to Goodameavy Moorgate (cattle-grid) and the farming hamlet of Goodameavy. Cross Mewy at Goodameavy Bridge. Note interesting features nearby: the county bridge stone; the ancient ford beside the bridge where steps lead down to the river's right bank; the still intact railway bridge of the former GWR Marsh Mills-Tavistock line: downstream, the huge stone embankment and sole remaining bridge pier constructed to carry a branch railway from the Tavistock line to the granite works at Dewerstone Quarry: as things transpired, this was never built.

The road at the junction beyond the bridges is based on an ancient way between Shaugh Prior and Buckland Abbey; this descended from Shaugh church to the former clapper where Shaugh Bridge now stands and joined Track 15 to reach Buckland. Turn right, climb the steep Market Hill to a cattle-grid and the open common of Roborough Down; about 75 yards beyond the grid (site of Market Hill Gate, 524649) the road bends to the right, but its former alignment is

---

* This portion of the route is shown on *OS 1809*.

continued onto the common by a sunken way. Follow this; cross an old (small-capacity) leat channel and bear right to follow the leat. A pile of stones comes in sight on the further side of the motor road as this climbs out of a hollow. Running left from the pile is a ditch, which gradually converges with – but does not actually touch – Track 15; this drains the Plymouth leat, just above, which today carries drainage from the war-time Harrowbeer airfield at Yelverton and discharges it at this point. Cross two or three converging green tracks; keep an eye on the approaching ditch and, when very near it, pass a heap of rubble, left, and notice the clapper bridge directly ahead – evidence in most cases for the passage of an old way. The leat was completed in 1589 by Sir Francis Drake to carry water from the Mewy to Plymouth. *Southward from leat bridge: Dewerstone Hill on horizon, Goodameavy Farm and enclosures left; Blacklands Newtake below dip on Wigford south crest.* Cross the bridge; summertime bracken and heather make it impossible to distinguish one path as unarguably the right one among the many on the down. Three appear to lead away from the bridge; take the path directly ahead (maintaining the general direction of Track 15) and the roof of an old building will come in sight beyond the path. Pass a pointed set stone beyond which the path is joined by a wider grassy way (right) and converges on the leat to cross the Clearbrook road beside a vehicular bridge and a signpost. The old building near the bridge was the Plymouth & Dartmoor Railway depot, now used by Yelverton Golf Club. The tramroad was built in 1823 by Sir Thomas Tyrwhitt for transporting granite from his quarries near Princetown to the Laira (Plym) estuary for shipment. Iron rails were bolted to granite sets (blocks) instead of sleepers, to provide a walkway for the towing horses. Some sets may be seen near the crossing of Track 15, and a short way upline (northward) is milestone 12, showing the distance to Sutton Pool, Plymouth's ancient harbour.

Beyond the depot, both Plymouth leat and tramroad bear away to the right, while Track 15 begins a gentle ascent of the higher part of Roborough Down and crosses a clapper cart bridge over the Devonport leat (dry portion), which was cut in 1793-4 to carry drinking-water to 'Dock' (Devonport Dockyard). Reaching the 650-foot contour, the track affords magnificent views of south-west Dartmoor and Plymouth Sound opening into the English Channel. On the crest of the down beyond the leat, the way bears right and passes some old quarry pits (right) and two tall, standing gateposts (hidden by bushes until near approach) which once formed the quarry entrance. From here the way makes a diagonal crossing of a clear, green patch of ground and, near trees, reaches a further patch scored in parallel grooves. It remains clearly marked beyond this in approaching the roadside fence, which it reaches opposite Yeoland Lane junction (513663) on the further, west side. The fence may be climbed (but the road is dangerous), and a slightly sunken way leads from the west verge through bushes to Yeoland Lane, before reaching which it intersects Track 9 (see p. 106) here branching from the Plymouth-Buckland Monachorum road. *Southward from A386: keep right of quarry gateposts; join wide grass track from right; cross leat bridge; pass P&DR depot; cross Clearbrook road; bear slightly right; pass pointed set stone; approach clapper bridge beside leat spillway channel; notice Urgles Farm and track from Blacklands to dip on Wigford south crest. Beyond bridge, path curves slightly away from spillway; cross broad, green track; Goodameavy road just ahead; track joins it near spillway.*

That portion of the monastic way now described on Roborough Down would have received regular use in the pre-motor age as a path between Yeoland and Clearbrook; it was naturally abandoned when the highway was fenced in and traffic became increasingly fast. At Yeoland Lane, the signpost points to Milton Combe. The ancient, high-banked lane was the obvious route to Buckland Abbey from Goodameavy Bridge over Roborough Down. Pass Yeoland House and Higher and Lower Hellingtown; at Green Lane turn left; at a crossroads where the signpost shaft bears the parish name, Buckland Monachorum, turn right; descend to the valley of Miltoncombe Brook, a clear stream rising near Crapstone and flowing through Milton Combe village. At the bridge, pause to look down at the ancient ford and a few remaining slabs (imposts) of the former clapper bridge. The way now ascends to Buckland Abbey and enters the abbey grounds on the north side of Buckland Abbey crossroads.

TRACK 16

MONASTIC WAY: PLYMPTON PRIORY – BUCKFAST ABBEY   Route A: 18 miles   Route B: 17½ miles

Here are alternative routes (detailed as A and B) eastward from Spurrell's†, perhaps one for fair weather and one for foul. The moorland route from Harford Gate to the cross is shown on *OS 1809*, and the entire moorland route B on *Donn*.

Following the Track (eastward)
Proceed as in Track 14 (p. 168) from the priory to Golden Square, Colebrook, from where the route is motorable as far as Harford Moorgate. At the square bear right for Sparkwell; continue to Lutton and Cornwood; at the Cornwood Inn crossroads go straight ahead; cross the River Yealm at Vicarage Bridge ('Parsonage Bridge' on *OS 1809*); ignore left turnings and follow the road bending south-east at Tor Farm. Cross the River Erme at Harford Bridge, which in 1668 surveyors found to be in need of repair; turn left at the picturesque old church where Harford† stands at the road junction (just within the churchyard wall); continue up the lane to the moorgate (644595); drive through the gateway and park in a disused gravelpit facing the gate.

The gravel pit appears to have swallowed the last link of the track between Harford Gate and the open moor. Ascend to the moor on the south side of the pit – when the line of the track may easily be picked up – and walk a little to the left of Hangershiel Rock (below the crest of the high ridge ahead). A Bronze Age retaining circle (unrecorded) is visible about 100 yards to the left; eight or nine stones of the circle remain, all but one fallen; the position of the kistvaen is clear and there are traces of the barrow that once covered the interment. In a short

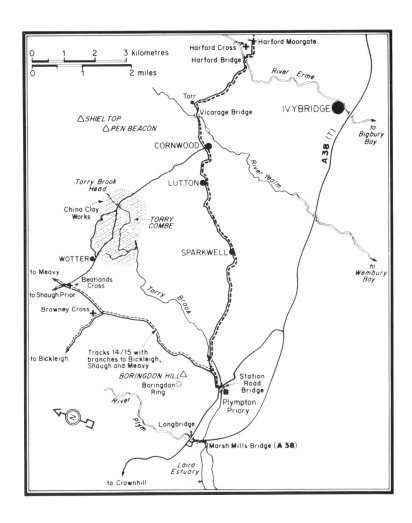

Track 16 – West

way a low, pointed stone will come in sight and the track becomes a shallow, sunken way. An alignment of four (low) stone heaps will then appear, marking the way clearly towards the next waymark on the horizon ridge, a grassy mound north of Hangershiel Rock. Pass the four aligned stone heaps and notice others ahead leading towards the Butter Brook valley. The heaps, now very overgrown by moss and turf, were stated by Crossing to have been placed beside the track as waymarks; others appear near Butter Brook Head.

Again slightly sunken, the track approaches the little valley between a rockfield, left, and the source-mire of Butter Brook, right. The grassy mound on the further high valley-side acts as a useful waymark and is approached by a grassy strip (the northern of two) on the hillside. The high-level Red Lake Railway (RLR) is seen approaching from the west flank of Wetherdon Hill (right); it was built in 1911 for light-engine steam haulage of workers and materials to the remote Red Lake clayworks. Work came to an end in 1934, when the line was closed and the track lifted. The old trackbed passes behind (east of) the mound and converges on the $1\frac{1}{4}$-mile-long Butterdon Bronze Age stone row, into which bond-stones marked 'U' and 'H' (indicating Ugborough and Harford parishes) were later interpolated. Views from the row over southern Dartmoor and the English Channel beyond Ugborough Beacon Rocks are good; small wonder that Ugborough was one of the Armada beacons of 1588; Hangershiel Rock, too, can be seen from here as a fine example of a granite hillside outcrop. Notice also the prevalence of Bronze Age burial cairns on the surrounding heights. *Westward from near mound: track sunken on either side of RLR; follow green strip down to rockfield near Butter Brook Head; stone heaps soon appear, swinging direction of track momentarily towards prominent border-country round plantation, Hanger Down Clump. Butter Brook reservoir nearby, left. Track regains westerly direction and again becomes faint; the four clearly aligned heaps appear, followed by pointed stone and shallow sunken way. When track again becomes faint, stones of Bronze Age cairn are seen on right and cornditch wall of enclosures just ahead. Descend to moorgate.* Follow the well defined way here; crossing stone row and railroad, Track 6 descends through a sunken portion from the ridge-crest to Spurrell's†, which I have described in *High Dartmoor* as 'a patchwork relic ... unique among Dartmoor crosses in having traces of ornamentation'.

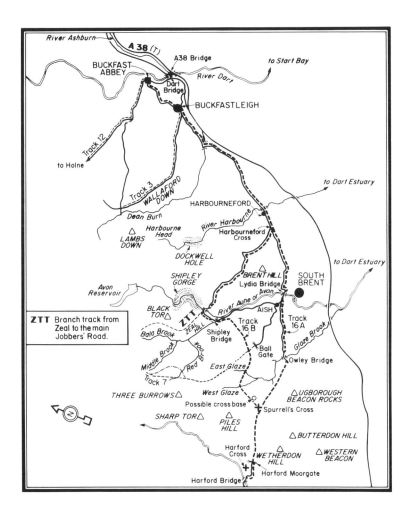

Track 16 – East

Route A (southern): Spurrell's† – Buckfast Abbey via Lydia Bridge
The track is clear in descending the east flank of Beacon Plain from the cross and offers a view over the Scad Brook valley (left) and the beautiful wooded basin of Glaze Brook backed by Coryndon Ball, Wacka Tor and the great, domed Three Burrows. At the foot of Beacon Plain ignore a grass track branching right (to Wrangaton Moorgate). Cross the (flowing) Owley leat; reach Owley Moorgate at the head of Owley Lane. Follow the lane to Owley Farm; from here, excepting two short lengths of footpath, the tarmac road coincides with Track 16, and the remainder is motorable to Buckfast. Turn left at the farm; cross Glaze Brook at Owley Bridge; pass Bulhornstone Farm (left), and at Aish turn downhill to Lydia Bridge (Avon), where formerly was a clapper; the present structure was originally a very narrow packhorse bridge with refuge bays, widened early in this century; when Polwhere saw it in 1797, it was ivyclad. Beyond the cascading river turn left, then right at Splatton and continue past Underhill (literally the farm under Brent Hill) to join the old South Brent-Buckfastleigh coach road at Leigh Cross. (A short length of footpath here represents Track 16 approaching the road junction.) Another junction follows at Harbourneford Cross before the road descends to the old-world hamlet where, until recent times, it crossed the Harbourne river at a ford, now concealed under a concrete way. The delightful clapper footbridge, of four openings, however, remains alongside.

From the high ground east of Harbourneford is seen a view (left) across the wooded gorge of Dean Burn to the south-east escarpment of the Moor. On the high plain here, a lane branches west to Zempson; within the fork stands a well-stone marked on maps as a guide-stone, but it bears no directional letters. The road next passes Whitehead Cross and Higher and Lower Dean; crossing Dean Burn near the junction of the road (the old A38) to Buckfastleigh Lower Town, it runs ahead to Higher Town to cross Mardle at Mardle Bridge in Market Street, and follows a footpath descending from Church Cross to Buckfast Abbey as detailed on p. 188.

Route B (northern): Spurrell's† – Buckfast Abbey via Shipley Bridge
Stranded paths lead north-east from the cross to Glascombe (pronounced 'Glazcum') Corner and point to the north slope of Coryndon Ball; the best-defined strand passes an interesting circular formation of stones such as could have formed a base-surround for

either a stone cross or a guide-stone. It is not until one actually reaches this point that Glascombe Corner is visible, so that a 6-foot-high guide-stone here would have been intervisible from Spurrell's† and the Corner; also it would have been conspicuous from Owley Gate, when the westbound traveller on route A would have treated it as a convenient marker to the locality of Spurrell's†. The hill, Glascombe Ball, has a smooth, almost stoneless east slope; hillside drainage has in two places eroded underlying granite and exposed areas of small boulders, the source of the stones used to make the circular setting. *Westward from Glascombe Corner: start with 'blind' diagonal ascent of Glascombe Ball (there being no guiding feature when hard track from ford ends); make towards distant cairn to reach stone setting and see Spurrell's† ahead. Path westward from sunken† crosses RLR between two curves in trackbed.*

Descend the hill diagonally to the visible hard track approaching Glascombe Corner, where pine trees grow. Glascombe Ford shows every sign of long usage. East of the stream (West Glaze Brook) the track crosses a deep tin-working and runs parallel to, but some distance from, the cornditch wall, right. The set stones of a Bronze Age row soon come in sight, part of an interesting group of sepulchral monuments; there are two triple rows, one double and one single row; several ruined cairns, a retaining circle and, oldest and most striking of all, a ruined neolithic dolmen, or chambered tomb, the huge coverstone of which lies alongside. Amidst the antiquities the monastic way fords both East Glaze Brook and the (flowing) Coryndon leat and runs past the dolmen to a meeting of tracks at (Coryndon) Ball Gate. Notice here the ancient court for sorting animals. The grass track running from the gate towards Brent Fore Hill (left) is Track 7, whilst Track 16 follows the cornditch wall (right) past Merrifield Plantation. Between Merrifield Farm and Brent Fore Hill it enters a pleasant green lane between enclosures, fords the (flowing) Badworthy leat (now used only for field irrigation) and, passing through a gateway, makes a direct descent of the steep, rugged and often very wet Diamond Lane. (This part of the route must surely have called into question the physical fitness of pedestrian monks as well as the surefootedness of palfreys and packhorses!) The lane opens upon the Zeal-Brent road south of Zeal Bridge over Bala Brook; from here the way crosses Avon at Shipley Bridge and runs east to Yalland Cross and Yalland Farm.

William Crossing (*Guide*) states that the monastic way probably ran through the Dockwell enclosures, and both route-direction and enclosure walls between these adjacent farms support his surmise. In addition, such a route is actually marked by *Besley*, but there is now no right of way. The original Track 16 ran through Dockwell Bottom, where it intersected Track 26 and passed beside Dockwell Farm to reach the River Harbourne at an ancient ford and clapper bridge where Gidley Bridge stands; one or two slabs lying in the river here could well be remnants of the clapper. A short ascent leads from the bridge (which both walker and motorist – the latter parking at 704649 – must now approach from Yalland Cross and Gingaford Cross) via Reddacleave Kiln Cross to Moor Cross; at this remote spot in the southern border-country an ancient track descends from the Moor at a gate, left; the old road to Totnes runs (right) via Mill Cross and Tigley, while the 550-foot descent to the valley of Dean Burn, which must be crossed before Ashburton or Buckfast is reached, lies ahead. The four ways are indicated by a weather-beaten guide stone (Pl. 46): 704640

T

P □ A

T

The letters represent, in clockwise order from the top, Tavistock, Ashburton, Totnes and Plympton. It is interesting to note that the Tavistock track from Sandy Gate crossed Skerraton Down to Water Oke Corner, and there joined the Jobbers' Road (Track 3). Track 16, the basis of the present road to Buckfastleigh, reached the Burn near Deancombe hamlet and ran through its beautiful valley before rising to Coxhill Cross. At the next road junction, at Fullaford, it joined Track 3 and crossed the River Mardle in Buckfastleigh Higher Town at Mardle Bridge in Market Street. The monastic way traveller should park his car near the bridge and enjoy the satisfaction of completing the ancient route on foot.

From the bridge ignore left turnings and fork right to walk up Church Hill. At Church Cross, the hilltop road junction, the way swings left and enters a roadside kissing-gate and field path on the opposite side of the junction. Follow the path alongside the hedge, left, directly aligned on the tower of Buckfast Abbey. Pass through a second kissing-gate into a narrow, enclosed lane from where the land drops away sharply (right) to Bullycleaves Quarry, where building stone was obtained for both abbey churches – medieval and modern.

The next gate opens onto a path hedged only on the left side, allowing pleasant views, right, over the Dart valley and open countryside beyond. The fourth and last gate heads a tarmac road serving new houses on the hillside; this reaches the Buckfast-Dart Bridge road opposite the entrance to the abbey car-park and would have provided for the monk as convenient an approach to the conventual buildings of 1485 as it does to those of 1985.

Part II

Inter-Moorland Tracks

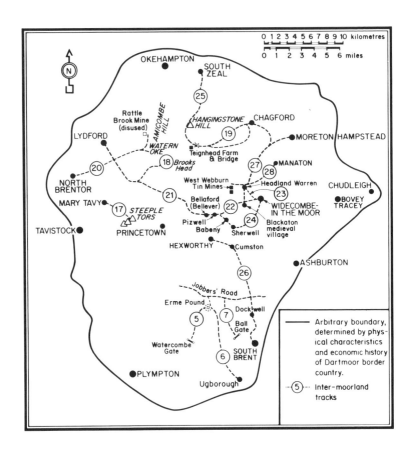

Map C – Disposition of Inter-moorland Tracks

TRACK 17

QUARRYMEN'S PATH: MARY TAVY, PETER TAVY – MERIVALE QUARRY   4 miles

Route according to William Crossing and to a tradition received by the author from George Penrose of Peter Tavy.

In the heyday of the Victorian granite industry in the middle reach of the moorland river Walkham, quarrymen's paths crossed the Moor in several directions. Well-defined paths can be traced from Sampford Spiney to Merivale, from Princetown to Foggin Tor (See p. 115), from Walkhampton to Swell Tor and King Tor and from Mary Tavy and Peter Tavy to Merivale, the subject of the present chapter, to give only four examples. The path from the Tavyside villages, one of the longest, is chosen for description here by virtue of its ascent of the Steeple* Tors ridge and the marking of the way by the quarrymen themselves, who laid down a combination of paving and kerb. In the early days of the Walkham quarries, granite was transported by horse and wagon to the quay at Morwellham for shipment down the Tamar estuary. The construction by Sir Thomas Tyrwhitt in 1823 of the Plymouth & Dartmoor Railway, and the opening of the Tavistock Canal in 1817 facilitated quicker and easier handling of the stone from Foggin Tor, Swell Tor and King Tor quarries by the railway to the Laira (Plym) Estuary, and from Merivale, Heckwood Tor and Pu Tor quarries by a shorter wagon journey to the canal basin at Tavistock. Many hundreds of men were employed in the quarries, some, with their families, occupying cottages at the works, others walking to their work from Princetown and Rundlestone on the high moor and from the border villages of Walkhampton, Sampford Spiney, Mary Tavy and Peter Tavy. The Walkhampton men followed a well-beaten track

---

* Steeple, or stone tower, the characteristic feature of Great Steeple Tor. The broad vowel, 'ea' for 'ee', has been mistranscribed by OS as 'Staple'.

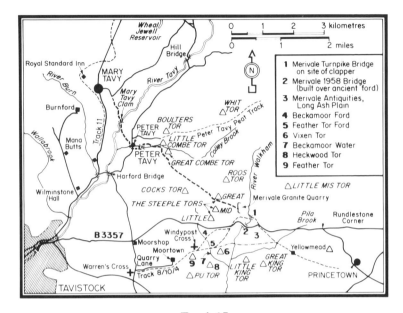

Track 17

up the Walkham valley, those from Sampford had also a clear route to their destination via Pu Tor, Heckwood Tor and Vixen Tor Ford, while quarrymen from Mary Tavy crossed Tavy on Mary Tavy Clam and followed Track 17. Mrs Bray writes of 'one of those light wooden bridges called clams. This, near Mary Tavy, is a great height above the stream, which, as usual, tumbles over vast portions of broken rock, and nowhere in greater beauty than near this clam.'

Mr George Penrose of Peter Tavy has recalled for me the daily walks of the quarrymen. His father, Frederick Penrose (born 1870 and an employee at the quarry), lived as a young man at Higher Godsworthy Farm above the head of Peter Tavy Combe. Each morning he awaited his workmates coming through the combe from the village, and together they would follow the Quarrymen's Path – its local name was the 'Sheep Path' – to their day's work. Reaching home in the evening, a meal and rest would be followed by an hour's hard work in the cottage garden.

Signs of granite-cutting abound on the commons of Peter Tavy, Whitchurch, Walkhampton and Sampford Spiney, and in the early days of the use of Track 17 men were walking not to the great quarry (now the Dartmoor Granite Company) on the valley floor but to the south and east slopes of the Steeple Tors ridge where, at little stone benches known as 'bankers', they knelt to shape slabs for roads and paving stones. The track and cart clapper bridge over the (disused) Grimstone and Sortridge diversion leat below Mid Steeple Tor, by which the finished slabs were brought away, are still visible today, and many of the paving slabs that started their journey here are now trodden daily by the citizens of Plymouth. Speedier transport of the quarried granite resulted in 1859 from the opening of the South Devon & Tavistock Railway, and in 1883 that of the Great Western branch line from Yelverton to Princetown. Throughout this period of industrial and transportation development – horse wagon, canal, railroad, traction engine and the Foden and Sentinel steam wagons of the 1920s and 30s – the quarryman continued to walk to his work over Track 17 until, as in so many fields of activity, the motorcycle and later the car reduced his daily test of physical endurance to a more tolerable level.

Following the Track (eastward)
The ancient village of Mary Tavy beside Cholwell Brook – here rushing past cottage, farms and church to join Tavy at a highly scenic confluence – was the home of both miners and quarrymen. The latter, passing the fifteenth-/sixteenth-century church of St Mary – 'drastically restored in 1878-9, but nevertheless pleasing in feeling' (Hoskins) – followed the old lane descending to the river, which they crossed on Mary Tavy clam; this spot, with a gate at the foot of the lane leading to a wide and potentially dangerous ford, is now as it was when Mrs Eliza Bray visited it in September 1833 (see p. 193), except for the proximity of mining works of a century later, and the replacement of the original 'clam' by one of iron. The old bridge abutments were used again, so that the new bridge is still 'a great height above the stream'. From the village, therefore, drive down the lane, where there is ample parking and turning space for one or two cars at 509785; continue on foot; cross the bridge and bear right (a DNPA fingerpost stands here) for Peter Tavy.

The walker with time to spare ought, before following the Peter Tavy path, to turn aside to look at mining remains upstream, which include leats, wheelpits, adits, shafts, machine-beds and ruined buildings, all a part of the huge Wheal Friendship enterprise which worked well into the present century, though arsenic mining became more profitable than copper during the mine's last decades.

The Peter Tavy path now climbs the east valley-side and brings into view a remarkable rockpile on the river's left bank, in character and situation resembling Looka Tor in the Double Dart gorge. Cross the field* below the path (by using a gateway at the top of the lane) and inspect the pile at close quarters – Longtimber Tor. This is a place of particular attractions: two rushing streams meet here, one the River Tavy, the other, Cholwell Brook, its surprising volume due to the release from the hydro-electric power-station above of water leated from high Dartmoor and here greatly augmenting the brook. The combined waters rush through a rocky declivity, a scene enhanced by trees and bushes sprouting from rock-crevices in Longtimber Tor – some of surprising age and size.

Return to the path, now a narrow, hedged lane; passing a small barn (right), the lane widens and has a tarmac surface: the tower of St Peter's Church rises ahead, flanked by Boulters Tor (left) and Great Combe Tor (right). Reaching Harewood House, it enters the village between the church (left) and the Peter Tavy Inn (right), which at the end of last century was kept by the author's wife's great-grandparents, named Salter. Inn, vicarage, post office and village shop, smithy (now closed), Methodist church, church hall, cornmill (there were two working) and the cottages built for agricultural labourers, miners and quarrymen – all these collectively set a traditional borderland village scene. A daily part of this scene once was the quarryman, in bowler hat and hobnail boots and with cord trousers tied below the knee, joined by his workmates from Mary Tavy and setting off to work. Walking beside Colley Brook – the villagers' name for Peter Tavy Brook – through the beautiful glen of Peter Tavy Combe, he passed under Great Combe Tor and Sharp Tor (locally 'Sharpator') to reach the open moor at the foot of the huge Cockstor Hill. The walker is recommended to visit the church, a building mainly of fourteenth-century work, with several additions of the following century such as the crocketed tower, north aisle and south porch. *Notes on the Church of St Peter Tavy* ('B.D.W.' 1972, revised 1977) tell us that: 'The tower is particularly handsome and the pinnacles are larger than usual, to allow for an interior staircase in the N.W. pinnacle, which gave access to the tower roof. It is now blocked up and an iron ladder from the bellchamber leads one through a trapdoor

---

* It is emphasized that access here, although unimpeded, is not a right, and discretion should be exercised by using it only to visit the tor.

to the leaded space above.' Also that, 'There is no visual evidence of Norman or Early English work anywhere in the building.' The font, having the Keys of Peter carved on one of its facets, is ancient, perhaps made for an earlier church on the site.

Follow the path passing the post office; notice a stone step (consisting of two chamfered stones) near the Methodist church; reaching the (no through-) road at Peter Tavy Mill, turn left, cross the bridge over Colley Brook, notice the unspoilt character of the former mill (Peter Tavy Higher Mill) where Mr Frank Collins lives in 1985, and a mounting-block, millpond, wheelpit and grindstone remain. Mount the hill. Pass Combe Cottages; enter a gateway, turn right at a DNPA fingerpost and descend to Peter Tavy Clam. (This is a DNPA blue-spot route only as far as the Godsworthy road – see below). Cross Colley Brook. Ascend the steep path to Great Combe Tor, a craggy mass of metamorphosed slate, giving views over the Tavy valley and of Little Combe Tor on the opposite valley-side, its east face weathered into huge, leaning slabs like a stack of prefabricated gable-ends. Near the lower side of Great Combe Tor, a gate and sunken track lead to the ruin of Huntingdon Farm where Peter Holmes last farmed and which appears in the Peter Tavy Tithes Apportionment of 1839. The path rounds the higher side of the tor and reaches another gateway into a lane between enclosures; at the first gateway beyond this, DNPA have marked the path (left) across an area of rough grazing; it is more interesting, however, to continue on the line of the medieval lane – from which one hedge has been removed – and turn left near a gateway (right) to walk alongside the base of another demolished wall. The path now passes at the foot of Sharp Tor and reaches a DNPA fingerpost at a junction of walls. The tor, also a mass of metamorphosed slate, affords a detailed view of Peter and Mary Tavy villages and Blackdown hamlet, backed by Brent Tor. Boulters Tor and Whit Tor are to the right and the distant northern heights beyond. Return from the tor to the wall-side path; do not wander across the newtake, where sheep are usually grazing, especially if you have a dog. The gate ahead, with another fingerpost, is beside the Pork Hill-Godsworthy road, and the high, open moorland portion of Track 17 lies ahead.

The moorland path – middle one of three – appears as a clear, green way heading over Godsworthy Plain towards Great Steeple Tor. Passing over the foot of Cocks* Tor (right), it bisects a large prehistoric village (many huts having double walls) built from metamorphic rock. The track climbs well above Wedlake Combe (left), and 130 yards beyond the easternmost hut of the village the quarrymen's causeway begins (Pl. 24 and 25). Heading now towards the south slope of Great Steeple Tor, it consists of a succession of flat stones. Notice in climbing the magnificent sweep of tor-crowned moorland and the remarkable series of rock-streams (from the Great Steeple Tor clitter) through which the track passes as it bears right towards the Great-Mid Steeple Tors col. Rounding the head of Beckamoor Dip (right – the hollow between Cocks and Mid Steeple Tors where Beckamoor Water rises), the causeway is succeeded by a kerb like series of set stones verging the track

On approaching the Steeple Tors col, notice the grotesque 'steeples' of the great tor, left; in contrast, the piles of Mid and Little Steeple Tors, right, trace a more regular outline – though the ruin of Mid Steeple Tor makes clear its original immense size. From the col, the sound of the Merivale quarry machinery is audible, and a splendid vista unfolds of that notable feature of middle Walkham country – the torscape: indeed, the immediate surroundings here, on this breezy col, are by any standard altogether impressive. The path passes a large pit and two set stones and descends the hill towards the north end of the large Merivale granite tip, bringing into view the enclosures on Long Ash Hill and the B3357 Tavistock-Ashburton road. The walker who observes a red flag flying on Roos Tor (left) and beyond the Walkham valley on Great Mis Tor may be reassured that it does not affect him, as Track 17 does not enter a military range area.

From the set stones the quarryman could pass to his work at the large quarry below, or direct to the slopes of Mid Steeple Tor (right), where he was employed in making paving sets.

It is worth reflecting on the lot of the nineteenth-century quarryman from the Tavy villages, walking to his daily work across this exposed col, often in cruel conditions. Lucky was the man who could sit astride a moorland pony, or even a willing donkey, as a few are known to have done to reach the scene of their labours – which were fatiguing enough without having to endure a lengthy return walk at the day's end.

---

* Authentic spelling given by *Donn* and *Greenwood* and used by Crossing in all his writings.

TRACK 18

BLACK LANE (NORTH): PETER TAVY – BROOK'S HEAD (OUTER RED LAKE) FROM BAGGATOR GATE   2 miles

Peter Tavy village was, in times not so long past, a distribution centre for peat. The commodity was cut at Blacka Brook Head (served by a branch of the Peter Tavy Peat Track), on Stooky Moor (served by part of Track 21 and the Peter Tavy Peat Track) and at the head of Red Lake (Tavy), from where it was carried, over the track now to be described, by packhorses to the village, much of it being taken on to local mines as well as to Tavistock market. Just as the rich, deep peat on the east edge of the northern fen was accessible by reliable routes from Chagford and South Zeal (Tracks 19 and 25), so here on the west edge it could be reached by Black Lane (North) from Peter Tavy. 'Over this old road', writes Crossing (*Guide*), 'very large quantities of peat were formerly annually conveyed on the backs of packhorses, as I have learnt from old men who at one time worked at the turf-ties to which it leads.'

Gradients on the track are moderate, the way is well marked as a road, views are magnificently wild. For the experienced Dartmoor walker, too, Black Lane offers the shortest and easiest approach to Vur Tor and Cut Hill in the centre of the northern fen – but such a walk should not be undertaken alone by an inexperienced walker. The difficult terrain of the fen must never be under-estimated – and the military firing programme for the week should be consulted before setting out to follow Black Lane.

Following the Track (northward)
From Peter Tavy take the road to Cudlipptown and Wapsworthy ('Waps' rhymes with 'taps'). It is a long lane, but old-world and

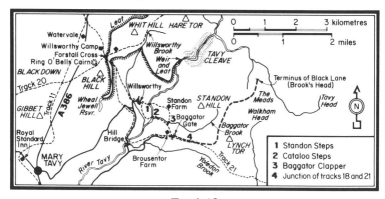

Track 18

attractive, with pleasant views over the Tavy valley through lengthy breaks in the hedge. Hill Bridge, with salmon ladder and leat headweir (see p. 233), is only a quarter of a mile from the lane junction south of Wapsworthy. At Wapsworthy hamlet the lane crosses Yoledon Brook to begin its long ascent to Baggator Gate (park here at 546805), beyond which the track becomes a rough road and coincides for a short way with Track 21. Bagga Tor is beside the track and easily climbed, giving good views towards the big tors overlooking Tavy Cleave.

Pass through a second gate, installed as an outer moorgate when the large newtakes in this area were enclosed; it is named Roundwood Gate from the round plantation on the valley-side below. Beyond the gate is Wapsworthy Common where the track forks – left, Black Lane, right, Lych Way (Track 21). Fork left; follow the wall (left) of Baggator Newtake; notice that the diverging Lych Way also is accompanied by a wall, known as Longbetor Newtake. At the end of the Baggator wall, Track 19 curves northward and becomes a sunken way on the long, 600-foot climb to Brook's Head; it is from here onward Black Lane. As it climbs west of Lynch Tor, it throws off two (right-hand) branches, one south of the tor, the other, north, leading to Walkham Head; a peat works was established here early in the nineteenth century by the owners of Wheal Betsy copper-mine on Black Down, in order to ensure a constant supply of peat for the mine. In this case no tramroad was built, and the peat cut was, as the quotation above from Crossing's *Guide* makes clear, transported by packhorses to Black Down. The stones that once supported the roof of the peat store – the workmen called it the 'Turf House' – are still there, but only one remains standing (1985).

To visit the old peatworks take the first right branch south of Lynch Tor; notice a fine rock basin on top of a large boulder, left of the track. Return from the peatworks via the summit of Lynch Tor: as a rockpile it is unremarkable, but views seen from it are widespread and impressive, reaching far into Cornwall. Black Lane, seen below, is easily rejoined.

The track becomes deeply sunken and very rough on approaching the hill-crest, the easiest walking being along its west verge. At an acute bend ahead it tops the 1,600-foot contour and opens up a panorama of the extraordinary terrain of north Dartmoor. Less than three-quarters of a mile east of the bend, on the plateau known as The Meads (Pl. 27), a branch of the track turns downhill to Homer (or Wester) Red Lake Head; remain on the upper track until it similarly turns downhill, this time to Outer Red Lake Head, or Brook's Head, as it is always known. Views from any point near this eastern terminus of Black Lane – especially from the upper track before its final descent – extend over the huge middle-reach basin of Tavy to High Willes, at over 2,000 feet the 'roof of Devon'. Vur Tor and Cut Hill rise ahead, and the walker will both see and sense the particular character of this wilderness that sets Dartmoor apart from other English highland zones.

At the terminus in this solitary place, beside the brook, a former moorman of Brousentor Farm named Reg Fuge drove an iron stake with attached tethering ring into the bank; it is sometimes necessary for the moorman to traverse the fen on foot to bring in wandering sheep, and to find that one's pony also had wandered would be an anti-climax to a task already difficulty enough. Thus 'Fuge's Post' marks the terminus of Black Lane (North).

TRACK 19

THE TEIGNHEAD ROAD: TEIGNCOMBE GATE – TEIGNHEAD FARM   5 miles
ALTERNATIVE ROUTE VIA FERNWORTHY (WITH EXTENSION TO WHITEHORSE HILL)   6 miles

Route according to tradition received by the author from the moorman Will Jordan of Moortown, Dick Perrott of Chagford (grandson of the celebrated Victorian Dartmoor guide Richard Perrott) and the late moormen Reg and Jack Rowe of Great Frenchbere and George Hutchings (last moorman of Teignhead Farm).

The large-scale cutting of peat on the north moor, for both mines and border-country vending, gave rise to numerous place-names now enshrined in Dartmoor tradition. Whitehorse Hill, remote whale-back ridge between the rivers East Dart and North Teign, almost certainly took its name, at least two centuries ago, from the baring by peat-cutters of the underlying granite on its east shoulder in the haphazard outline of a horse. Here, at over 1,900 feet, is the ruined shelter of Moute the peat-cutter, since known as 'Moute's Inn'. Beyond the foot of Great Varracombe and south of the Teign river is that of Stat, hence 'Stat's House' and 'Stats House Hill'. At the east foot of Watern Down are the walls and fireplace of the sturdy little building in which Chagford peat-merchant Will May lived while cutting peat on Manga Hill: thus, 'Will May's House'. Sammy Arnold brought down countless packhorse loads of 'turf' (peat) from Dinger Plain for Knack Mine in the upper Taw valley; his route, now providing a wild and scenic walk, has ever since been known as 'Sammy Arnold's Lane'.

Following the building of Teignhead Farm in the upper North Teign

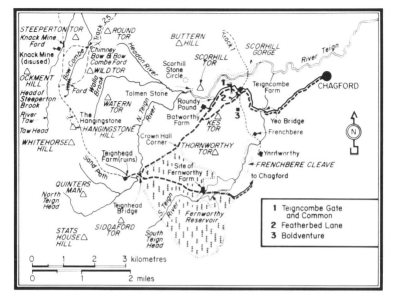

Track 19

valley in 1780, and the enclosing of Teignhead Great Newtake, an already existing peat track from Teigncombe Gate to Whitehorse Hill received increasing use between farm and moorgate. It is probable that the farm was actually sited near this track for convenience of access, so giving rise to the traditional label, 'the Teignhead Road' (Pl. 28). The name applies also to the ancient route from Chagford via Waye Cross, Metheral Farm and the former Fernworthy Farm, meeting with the Teigncombe track at Teignhead Bridge. (This is not detailed here as it coincides with the motor road from Chagford to Tawton Gate and Fernworthy, with the exception of a short portion now submerged by Fernworthy reservoir. From Fernworthy (site of farm) it continues as a forest road over Froggymead Hill and descends to the plantation boundary at Langridge Gate, from where its remaining brief course to Teignhead Bridge can be seen below the looming ridge of Whitehorse Hill.) The main Teignhead Road, however, crosses open moorland, the enclosures encountered offering unrestricted access from either Teigncombe Gate or Teigncombe hamlet, from where the ancient approach to the moor was the packhorse way known as Featherbed Lane. Left to decay and unrestricted erosion by storm drainage after earlier centuries of use, possibly it had become too rough and sunken for regular use as long ago as the mid-eighteenth century. The lane may be followed from Teigncombe hamlet to a gate opening on the common and a wide stroll. It then becomes a sunken way verged by set stones and runs along the east fringe of a large Iron Age village on Teigncombe Common. Running parallel to a wall, left, it climbs toward the north slope of Kes Tor. Its junction beyond the tor with Track 19, which superseded it, occurs near the Shoveldon fourfold stone circle.

The use in comparatively modern times of Track 19 is shown in plate 28, in addition to which it received regular use by successive moormen of Teignhead Farm on horseback and in pony-trap until the last occupant, George Hutchings, who was born at the farm, was (much against his will) evacuated to Chagford in 1942 when the War Office requisitioned the area for troop-training. The track was ridden over almost daily by the late moorman Jack Rowe of Great Frenchbere, who rented and supervised the huge newtake until his death in 1984, and today it is still used by riders and walkers.

Following the Track (southward)
Drive from Chagford via Waye Cross, Thorn, Yeo and Teigncombe; here notice the branch lane, left, leading into Featherbed Lane. Reaching Teigncombe Common at the moorgate (cattle-grid), observe the field system and hut circles of the Iron Age village on either side of the Batworthy road. This leads to a particularly massive hut circle within its own enclosing pound; known as Roundy Pound, it was excavated in 1952 by Lady Aileen Fox of the University of Exeter, who found evidence of iron-smelting. (Her Report was published in *TDA* 86 of 1954). Park on the open space, right, just beyond the pound (663868). The walker will now hear the North Teign river rushing through Scorhill Gorge, beyond which are seen the fine range of tors and hills bounding the middle-reach basin of the river, and the bold rock of Kes Tor, above left.

To visit the tor, follow the ascending path opposite Batworthy Bridge. The rock is an interesting example of cohesive granite, with several rock basins, including the largest on Dartmoor; there are wonderful views across the Teign basin and southward over the eastern highlands to Hey Tor, also over the in-country to Chagford town, Castle Drogo (the last castle to be built in England, 1910-30, masterpiece of Sir Edwin Lutyens) and the hilltops above Fingle Gorge. The overgrown, shallow ditch crossed on the ascent to the tor is the ancient Southill leat, its cutting recorded in 1505 and its course seen twisting through the prehistoric fields and hut circles on Teigncombe Common.

Westward from Roundy Pound the way – a rough track beyond Batworthy Bridge – runs parallel with the Batworthy Newtake wall, right. Keep the wall and Batworthy Stream to the right; from Batworthy Corner follow the green, sunken way (left) towards a cluster of standing stones. The track passes above the cluster, comprising a ruined fourfold retaining circle of the remarkable Shoveldon Bronze Age sanctuary. The alignments of several stone rows are visible pointing towards majestic Cosdon. The track intersects a double row and mounts to the crest of Shoveldon; some prominent set stones 50 yards to the right belong to a Bronze Age field system, and involved in the south boundary reave of the system is a large hut circle, its size suggesting an origin in the Middle or Late Bronze Age. The hut has a double wall with an inner diameter of 26 feet and is worth turning aside to see. It is also a fine vantage point from which to view Quinters Man, Whitehorse and Hangingstone Hills, Watern, Wild and Steeperton Tors, and Big Whit Hill rising towards Cosdon; of particular relevance to Track 19 is the small, circular plantation of trees now seen ahead, pinpointing Teignhead Farm.

Descend from the crest of Shoveldon to reach Stonetor Gate, where the track converges with the wall (left) bounding the plantations; this comes up from Crown Hall Corner and is paralleled by the track as it passes through Little Langridge Newtake. On the east side of the gate are Two Stones, a pair of set stones marking the junction of the east and north Quarters of the Forest. The bank tracing a horseshoe curve round the site of the stones is the dry channel of the Southill leat: from here notice the wind-resistant, 'lacework' pattern of the Stonetor Newtake wall.

Pass through the newtake; on the right are Stonetor Marsh and the green patch of Langridge Field where, say the moormen, corn was once grown. As the track reaches Little Langridge Gate (the next south-westward), it becomes sunken. This area lies at the foot of the river's upper reach where it passes smoothly to the edge of its peneplain before dropping into the gorge of Manga Hole. Ahead and across the valley are bold, lofty hills – all between 1,700 and 1,900 feet in elevation. Siddaford Tor rises beyond the ruined Teignhead Farm, now not far ahead, from which Track 19 takes its title: windbreak plantation, enclosures, approach stroll and access clapper bridge mark the valley-side around the settlement. On the further hillside, right, is the lane leading to the intriguing ruin of Manga House, deserted, tradition relates, before the building of Teignhead Farm in 1780, and last occupied by the Endacott family.

A hundred yards below Little Langridge Gate, and on the east side of the wall among tinners' works, is the ruin of a blowing-house or mill first recorded by the author in *High Dartmoor*. The tumbled walling unfortunately conceals what internal features might remain, but the leat from the river and the wheelpit are traceable. After viewing this little ruin, follow the leat beyond the wall to regain the track; this descends to the bridge as a sunken way and is joined by the Fernworthy branch track from Langridge Gate (see p. 203).

Extension from Teignhead Farm to Whitehorse Hill via the Sand Path and Whitehorse Cut   1¾ miles
Cross the fine clapper bridge of three openings, built for the track in 1780, then the smaller but equally sturdy clapper over Great Mire Stream, and follow the stroll (left, Pl. 29) to the farm court. The dereliction of Teignhead Farm is unfortunately complete, the chief interest now remaining in external features, such as bridges, sheep-dip and some impressive slotted gateposts. *Eastward – taking in the Longstone (Shoveldon): from hollow east of Stonetor Gate, track stranded. Walk towards south end of Shoveldon crest along strand that becomes clear, green track (Teignhead Road bears away left towards centre of crest). Fernworthy reservoir below, right, overlooked by Thornworthy Tor and detached logan stone, backed by eastern highlands. Kes, Middle, Frenchbere Tors ahead; tip of Longstone appears between them. Menhir is south terminal of much-robbed double row: 10½ft high; bears letters 'C' (Chagford), 'G' (Gidleigh), 'DC' (Duchy of Cornwall) indicating meeting point of parishes with Forest. Turn left; follow ruined row. Path beside it leads to grave heading highest placed of Shoveldon rows. Descend; cross Track 19; go to fourfold retaining circle; follow row from it to Batworthy Corner.*

Extension to Whitehorse Hill via the Sand Path and Whitehorse Cut
NOTE: this walk enters the Okehampton military range area; be sure to check the firing programme before setting out.

Pass through the gate at the rear of the farm and ascend the newtake, keeping the valley of Great Mire Stream right. Make for the gateway in the transverse wall below the steep of Whitehorse Hill, known as 'Big Gate', near which is a military range-board. Views from here are panoramic, southward as far as Ryder and extending over the eastern highlands to Blackingstone Rock, the tower of Moreton-hampstead church and the north-east escarpment of the Moor.

From the gate, continue to climb north-west over good ground for about 300 yards, when some set stones are seen (left), possibly the relics of a row and circle. Ahead is the beginning of the Sand Path (Pl. 30), a stone causeway penetrating the blanket of fen on the hillside. Although broken in places, the causeway is clear and easy to follow. Near its commencement is a ruined peat-cutters' house (right), one of several in this locality of deep peat (see p. 202). Quinters Man, left, rises steeply above the great cleft of Varracombe, and Stats House Hill and its little building are visible beyond. From the north end of the Sand Path, a continuing track approaches the head of the large basin of Watern Combe; below it, right, is a small, sheltered hollow where a moorman of Teignhead is known to have cultivated raspberry canes; it is consequently known as 'Raspberry Garden'. The track shortly reaches a large peat hag where a Phillpotts post indicates the opening to Whitehorse Cut, the peat pass leading to the summit of the hill. Ahead, beyond the post, the continuing hillside track is wide and stony in following the scarp to Hangingstone Hill, so providing for the walker an excellent link with Track 25 and a challenging long-distance walk over high, remote moorland.

To enter Whitehorse Cut, turn left at the post and follow the rough granite way between high peat banks. The pass, like the track to Hangingstone Hill, was illegally widened by military agency in 1963 to facilitate the passage of overland vehicles. At the higher, west end are a cairn and another post. The whaleback summit of Whitehorse Hill (1974ft) is largely denuded of peat; its northward, fen-covered ridge culminates some 10 feet above at Hangingstone Hill, third highest of Dartmoor's hills.

NOTE: the walker wishing to explore further should cross the Whitehorse summit plateau south-westward towards another Phillpotts post; this, also set on a peat hag, marks the opening of Dart Head Cut, a pass leading into the upper East Dart valley a short way below the source of the river. But this is wild, isolated country, and it is inadvisable for the lone walker to extend the walk in this way without having left notice of his intention before setting out.

TRACK 20

THE SOUTH ZEAL TRACK: SOUTH ZEAL – HANG-INGSTONE HILL   5½ miles

Route according to tradition received by the author from Will Jordan of Moortown, and the late John Spencer of Plymouth and Sam Madders of South Zeal.

The inns of South Zeal are mentioned on p. 39 as ports of call for mariners with the price of an ale in their pouches. There must have been a greater certainty of patronage from the South Zeal and South Tawton peat merchants at the end of their long haul from the skirts of the northern fen at Hangingstone Hill. We might also include in that stratum of society the miners of Bow Combe and Knack, for D. St Leger Gordon gives evidence in his *Under Dartmoor Hills* to show that South Zeal – the south hall of South Tawton manor – came into existence principally as a miners' settlement. The 'long haul' may readily be appreciated by the walker who, perhaps transported by car to the head of the military ring-road from Okehampton Battle Camp, walks southward to Hangingstone Hill – third among Dartmoor's principal heights – then turns about and resolutely follows Track 20 to South Zeal village. He, too, will be glad to have with him the price of a pint.

From OP (observation post) 'Hut 15' at the head of the ring-road loop, follow the rough track running south-east and descending from an elbow-bend to Taw Ford; a quarter of a mile beyond and east of the ford the track joins that ascending from Knack Mine (Taw); turn right at the T-junction and follow the track to the looming hill ahead: the ascent is excessively rough.

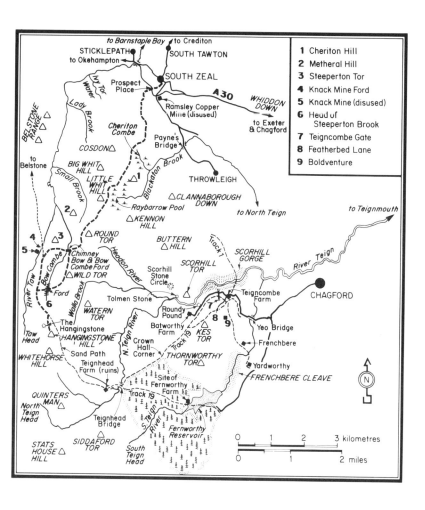

Track 20

Following the Track (northward)
Hangingstone Hill (1,983 ft)
Nearest parking – OP 15 on Ockment Hill (603878). At the north end of a lofty ridge, extending from the upper Teign river at Great Varracombe, a ruined cairn is surmounted by a military flagpole and observation hut; they scarcely enhance the summit of this majestic hill of the 'hanging stone'. Running from the cairn along the east flank of the hill is a wide, stony track; this – its artificially bald character also the result of military operations – points initially to the south boundary of the Fernworthy plantations, then veers southward to reach the Phillpotts post at the entrance to Whitehorse Cut. Moormen from the Zeal and Tawton areas intending to cut rushes at East Dart Head could therefore use the route as a convenient extension of Track 20 to reach that location; it also provides an exceptionally scenic link with Track 19 and forms an exhilarating through-route from Fernworthy to South Zeal.

Views from the summit of Hangingstone are sensational: a wide area of the northern fen surrounding the remote Cut Hill and Vur Tor; huge, tor-crowned ridges above the valleys draining the fen; the hollow of Cranmere Pool westward – if one knows where to look; the fissured ground (southward) penetrated by the peat pass on Whitehorse Hill; the whole moorland area traversed north-eastward by Track 20 to the point where it disappears beyond Cosdon's shoulder; an amazing spread of country far beyond Dartmoor in the east to Somerset and west Dorset.

On the west slope of the hill is a large granite slab. Descend to this (as a pleasant alternative to the rough track of ascent); the slab, protruding from the hillside and visible from many points on the north moor, was a moveable logan stone within the author's memory but has twice been capsized during military exercises. The goodwill of the South Western Command, however, has each time been manifest in restoring the logan. It no longer logs, or rocks, but at least it surmounts its pivot in virtually the original position – a protruding slab or 'hanging stone', giving its name to the great hill above.

Rejoin the track, below right. It crosses two gullies carrying water from the peat bog into the headmire of Steeperton Brook, visible in the steep-banked, bow-shaped valley, right, known as Bow Combe. Above the gullies, left, a pleasing summertime sight, unusual on Dartmoor today, is provided by a working turf-tie and stacks of drying peat. Relevant and fortuitous in the context of the present chapter, the peat is harvested by Mr Keith Brook of South Zeal (see p. 214).

Follow the ascending road to Ockside Hill, marked by several set stones on each side. The great hollow of Taw Head appears, left, as the walker approaches the junction with the track ascending from Taw Ford. Beside the junction are the remains of an OP, recently demolished, and 100 yards beyond it is an area of granite bedding across the width of the track. A nearby red range-board provides the only distinguishing feature of Ockside Hill's summit. Branch right from the stony track (which leads to Knack Mine Ford and Belstone) into a clear, grassy path descending the east flank of the hill to Bow Combe. The path soon breaks into sunken strands, but three valley-floor features provide a sure guide: 1, the floor is traversed by a conspicuous black peat bank, left; 2, also by a nearer, curving line of rushes approaching a ford on Steeperton Brook between two areas of mire – the curving line being the rush-filled Track 20 approaching the crossing on the neck of the Bow Combe hour-glass; 3, on the further side of the neck, is a small rockfield bisected by a lane-like passage; here the track swings northward between parallel tinners' burrows and the hill under the rocks of Wild Tor, opposite. Descend any one of the sunken strands to the curving line of rushes; follow this across the valley floor to the ford; cross, pass over the hour-glass neck – though not mire proper, it will be wet – towards the passage through the rockfield. Enter this; pass a pointed stone; the track is sunken and well defined in passing between the burrows (left) and the Wild Tor hillside (right) – the tip of the tor rocks being visible above. After mounting the bank slightly, the track becomes a grassy way descending towards a wide crossing place on the brook; this is the picturesque Bow Combe Ford, much used during last century in the working days of Knack Mine, and approached by men from Zeal and Tawton along Track 20 to this point, where they would ford the brook, cross Steeperton Hill and turn down into the Knack Mine track. This crossing of Bow Combe and passage over Ockside Hill, still in use in John Spencer's day, was drawn by him on his 6-inch map and appears here in Plate 31.

Track 20, remaining on the east bank of Steeperton Brook, is joined by the branch from the ford and continues ahead as a sunken, grassy hillside track. On the further bank 50 yards below the ford is a tinners' house with a small wall cupboard; there has been interference with the ruin, as there all too often is, by walkers, and inner partition wall has been erected by removing stones from the exterior walls; the still remaining height of those, however, suggests that peat-cutters using the South Zeal Track rebuilt and reroofed the little house as a shelter.

Continue towards the rounded tor ahead; named on OS maps as 'Hound Tor', this is known on Dartmoor only as 'Round Tor'. The Steeperton Brook valley now deepens as the brook falls picturesquely from its upper reach at the falls known as Chimney Bow into the trough below. The southernmost pile of the lofty Steeperton Tor (left) is Eagle Rock; Reaching a point opposite this, the track becomes stranded; follow the highest strand, which curves below a dip in the Wild Tor-Round Tor ridge to become a clearly defined track passing below and west of Round Tor. Views from here over the brink of Metheral Hole (the deep little gorge of Steeperton Brook) and across the great amphitheatre of Taw Plain to the Belstone range are fine indeed. Metheral Hill is the gentle dome rising above the Hole on the left of Round Tor.

Round Tor's mound of partly grass-covered bedrock has weathered mainly into horizontal jointings; the High Willes-Yes Tor ridge appears in the west, and the stones of the prehistoric Whit Moor Circle are nearby, practically alongside the track as it crosses the Taw-Teign watershed. The tract on which the circle stands – also the menhir 210 yards to the south-east known as the 'Whit Moor Stone' – is Whit Moor Mead, extending north-east to the verge of the great mire of Raybarrow. The menhir is marked 'DC' (Duchy of Cornwall Forest boundary) and 'TP' (Throwleigh Parish).

As the track approaches a wide hollow on the Mead, it becomes deeply sunken and is clogged by peat-silt washed down the hillside in which bog vegetation has taken root; make a diversion over the higher ground, left. (The prominent spur seen ahead is Big Whit Hill, south-west shoulder of Cosdon.) The track remains sunken for some way and allows one to appreciate the extent of the lethal Raybarrow Pool below. Beyond it are Cheriton Hill and Kennon Hill (the higher), between which the waters of the swamp escape over a lip to initiate Blackaton Brook (North Teign). The upper edge of the mire has in places encroached upon the track; avoid this by another diversion. However severe the drought, the pools of Raybarrow never fail to glisten in the sun.

When the track is again walkable, notice four large, cut granite slabs laid alongside, obviously awaiting collection by a horse-and-cart that never came. Again sunken, the way rises to cross the east shoulder of Cosdon; Raybarrow is passed; Shilstone Hill and Clannaborough Down are seen beyond the Blackaton Brook valley; the eastern border-country and the tops of Fingle Gorge carry the view towards the distant Creedy and Exe valleys. Rounding the head of Cheriton Combe (below, right), also with an extensive mire, the track descends from Cosdon's shoulder to a pleasant, grassy plain stretching eastward to the hill known as Balls (which on its south side drops to Blackaton Brook in the scenic Blackaton Hole). On the plain, it intersects a remarkable stone row of the early Bronze Age, known locally as the 'Graveyard' but formerly as the 'Cemetery' (Pl. 36). The triple row, 447 feet in length, with a damaged kistvaen and retaining circle at the higher end, was restored from a ruinous state in 1897. It is a striking monument in a striking place, the shoulder of huge Cosdon looming above and countless miles of in-country spread in the east and north-east. Beyond it, the old peat road, again sunken, reaches the brink of civilization and its final, long descent to the border-country terminus (Pl. 32).

A wide stroll opens between two newtake corners ahead; the southern corner was presumably a lookout post during the Napoleonic Wars, as it is marked 'Sentry Corner' by *Spencer*. Enter the stroll, observing the villages of South Zeal and South Tawton (with prominent church tower) in the Taw valley below. The way is grassy, the walls close in to form a wide lane pointing directly towards Zeal, and the left-hand wall shortly ceases on the edge of a hollow channelling a stream. Cross a low, wide clapper bridge where approaches are mire-covered, when the left-hand wall reappears in more ancient guise. Pass the ruin of a granite linhay, left, and follow the high-walled lane, now a very rough watercourse. Beyond a branch lane, left, conditions underfoot improve and a tarmac road arrives from the first dwelling-house nearby, left. Notice from here the spoil dumps of the former Ramsley copper mine, which was worked profitably well into the present century.

Descend to Prospect Place at the intersection of Dartmoor lane by the A30 highway,* below which it is known as Prospect Lane. Continue to the bridge over the streamlet at 'Washing Place'. At Coopers Cottage turn left into Ramsley Lane, then left again at the Beacon Inn into the village centre. Cottages, many of cob and thatch, shops and inns form a cluster on each side of the village street, which

---

* This bypass for the village resulted from a Highways Act of 1829.

was the old coaching road from Exeter to Okehampton and Launceston. The steep eastward approach to the junction with the A30 occurs a short way beyond milestone 5 and the Rising Sun Inn.

South Zeal was a medieval borough found in 1299 (*The Archaeology of Dartmoor from the Air*). The building of chief architectural interest fronts the village street, the Oxenham Arms, named from the South Tawton land-owning family of Oxenham; on the opposite side of the street is the King's Arms. The church, quaintly sited in mid-street, was built as chapel-of-ease to South Tawton church (the manor of South Tawton appearing in the Devon Domesday of 1066) and from 1773 throughout more than a century served not only as the village school but also as the schoolmaster's residence. Although medieval, its scholastic adaptation and in 1877 its Victorian 'restoration' have unfortunately left it as a place of very little interest.

The peat markets for the Track 20 men of Zeal and Tawton were towns and villages to the north, such as North Tawton, Chudleigh, Hatherleigh and possibly Crediton. It is good to know that peat-cutting is continued by some of the moor people. Mr Percy Brook of South Zeal, having venville rights permitting him to bring turf from the Forest, has been cutting Hangingstone peat for sixty-four years, and his son Keith has inherited his father's expertise. Percy's horse-and-cart trips as a boy with his father, using the military ring-road, are succeeded now by speedier ones in Keith's motor van. Percy's most interesting memory, so relevant to this chapter, is of John Holman, the last peat-cutter and vendor to use the ancient Track 20 exactly as it is detailed here – and that with a horse and cart! He also recalls that another South Zeal peat merchant, 'Laddie' Lentern, carried spare wheels of different sizes in his cart when setting out for the turf ties, as did Frank Williams of North Brentor (p. 216).

TRACK 21

THE DARTMOOR PATH: NORTH BRENTOR – RATTLE BROOK VALLEY 6 miles

NOTE: the greater length of the track crosses the Willsworthy military range, therefore check the firing programme before setting out.

The Church of St Michael de Rupe (of the Rock), Brentor, is perhaps the most striking English example of a church on a height. Tristan Risdon described it in 1625 as 'a church, full bleak, and weather beaten, all alone, as it were forsaken'. But this has never been quite true and today it is far from true. Although only in regular use for worship for five months of the year, it is visited at all times and during a year receives well over 20,000 visitors.

The church stands 1095 feet above sea level on what is believed to have been once part of a volcanic cone. The hill is now surrounded by the remains of earthworks, the outer wall being nearly complete with an entrance on the southeast. Lady Aileen Fox has tentatively dated this hill-fort as late Iron Age (between 150 BC-AD50).

> (from *Saint Michael of the Rock* by permission of the
> Reverend Peter Apps, Vicar of Lydford and Brentor)

It is satisfying to start at this lofty point to follow the Dartmoor Path, for it overlooks the greater length of the track to the head of the west Dartmoor escarpment – on the Sharp Tor-Hare Tor col – 4 miles away and 600 feet above Brent Tor. The first church was built on the rock in *c*.1130 by Robert Giffard for the villagers of North Brentor; later in the century it was presented to an abbot of Tavistock to ensure

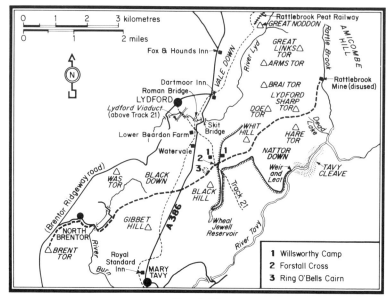

Track 21

that his monks served the church. Originally little more than a small chapel, it was rebuilt in the early 1300s and re-dedicated by Bishop Stapledon of Exeter on 4 December 1319. The hearths of the Norman village of North Brentor were warmed by Dartmoor peat nearly seven hundred years before its menfolk began walking out in groups to work at Curbeam and Rattle Brook mines, and it is highly probable that the discovery in early post-Conquest times of the Amicombe Hill peat deposits resulted in the formation of tracks for peat-carrying packhorses to North Brentor, Lydford, Bridestowe and Sourton villages. Similarly, the rich deposits of tin-ore in the Rattle Brook valley drew men from the border villages before even the blowing-house evolved in the fourteenth century.

A former resident of North Brentor, Charles Bennison, recalled for me the horse-and-cart journeyings of a peat merchant named Frank Williams along the Dartmoor Path 'semty or eighty year agone'. Frank customarily carried spare wheels of different sizes in his cart; arriving at the turf ties, he would change one wheel of the cart to a smaller in order to stabilize it on the steep hillside.

John Tindall, curate of 'Brent Torr' from 1736 to 1764, writing to the Precentor of Exeter Cathedral in *c.*1750, stated that; 'The air was sharp and very often foggy, but wholesome. Wheat, barley and oats were grown, all sorts of cattle reared. About 40 hogsheads of cyder were brewed, mostly rough, and some very good. The wood was mostly oak and ash and the land valued at 10s. an acre' (*Saint Michael of the Rock*).

Richard Polwhele in *History of Devonshire* (1806) wrote: 'It has been shrewdly said of the inhabitants of this parish, that they make weekly atonement for their sins. For they can never go to church without the previous penance of climbing up this steep, which they are so often obliged to attempt with the weariest industry, and in the lowliest attitude. In windy or rainy weather, the worthy pastor himself is frequently obliged to humble himself upon all fours, preparatory to his being exalted in the pulpit.'

It is perhaps not surprising that the development of mechanized mining in the Rattle Brook valley in the late eighteenth century, attracting workmen from the border villages who had to walk out to that remote valley, coincided with a movement in North Brentor village to promote the building of a chapel-of-ease; miners who had walked, lived and worked out their hard lives on Dartmoor during the week would not, however God-fearing, have relished a Sunday afternoon climb to St Michael's. A small chapel was consequently built in the village centre in 1825 which sufficed for over thirty years, until, in 1856, the foundation stone of Christ Church was laid, and the Bishop of Exeter consecrated the new church in 1857.

Following the Track (north-eastward)
A few decades ago a long, dusty, white lane led from North Brentor village to the London & South Western (later Southern) Railway station, heading towards the long line of Blackdown as it dropped over the hill. Now a tarmac road leading past the former station (today a residence), it is the link between village and Dartmoor Path. Cross the three parallel lines traced by the former railways (SR and GWR) and the River Burn; branch left at the old school (also a residence) and, at the site of the former Station Moorgate at the top of a small rise (490813), park on the roadside; follow the green track, right, which continues in line with the road just ascended. The borderland Was Tor (Was rhymes with 'gaz') overlooks the old rail tracks in the Burn valley at the former Lydford Junction (left); but further ahead is seen

the fine range of western tors from Sourton to Hare, a challenging reminder of the 1,000-foot climb lying before the walker, who must breast the Sharp Tor-Hare Tor col. The initial ascent of Black Down is in direct line with St Michael's, and on reaching a level plain the track heads towards Hare Tor. Many tracks cross Black Down, most of them in regular use in William Crossing's day and detailed in his *Guide*. The shoulder of Gibbet Hill rises on the right, and the track soon becomes a stony road. Near Lydford Junction is the Manor Hotel, the whole scene enhanced by the lowly but craggy Was Tor. Beyond is the deep cleft of Lydford Gorge.

The track, well up on Black Down, bears towards Great Links Tor; this great pile, highest of the range, rises north of Hare Tor to over 1,900 feet. Eventually the enclosures of Henscott come in sight, left, and the line of the track swings back towards Hare Tor. Traffic soon becomes visible on the A386 Tavistock-Okehampton highway, and the walker crosses Track 11 before reaching it. First, however, Track 20 forks; the right branch, wide and stony, leads to settlements under the east side of Black Down: therefore follow the grassy left branch heading towards Hare Tor. Track 11, meanwhile, cuts through an old reave-bank (left) running from Henscott Corner to the highway; also approaching the latter and converging on Track 20 is a line of telegraph poles, the track passing between them, while the intersection of 11 and 20 occurs 100 yards before reaching the road. Track 21 crosses the road obliquely 300 yards north of Barretts Bridge and becomes a forked, sunken way: fork right towards Hare Tor. *South-west from A386 highway: follow grass track until road and cottages visible in Burn valley; track forks; branch right in line with road ascending to North Brentor village.*

The track is well defined on the plain of Black Hill and bears left towards Lydford Sharp Tor and Rattlebrook Hill; southward, it is still in line with St Michael's Church. Distant rockpiles visible north-eastward behind the frontier range are Higher and Lower Dunnagoat Tors. On the east side of the plain are a flagpole, a Willsworthy range bond-stone and a military warning board. Here, too, is the low, circular bank of the cairn known as Ring o' Bells; this offers a fine view extending from Sourton Tors (left) to Great Mis Tor, the 'steeples' of Great Steeple Tor and the mound of Cocks Tor (right). Track 21 now descends from Black Hill past Forstall Cross and the north (left) side of the Willsworthy range shooting butts: passing out of sight for a mile or so, it reappears ascending to the high col between Lydford Sharp and Hare Tors. In descending from Black Hill the track passes two tin huts and a concrete base, and brings into view the Wheal Friendship leat passing through the old Redford fields (right); this formerly continued southward to supply the waterwheels of Wheal Friendship but now flows into the Wheal Jewell reservoir. As the gradient levels, a small (flowing) leat is crossed (on a buried conduit) also carrying water (from Walla Brook, Lyd) to the reservoir. The buildings seen on the right are connected with a target railway.

From the crossing of the Walla Brook leat, observe a track ascending (right) from the old enclosures of Yellowmead in the Willsworthy Brook valley. It crosses the Wheal Jewell leat (near an elbow-bend) beside a footbridge, intersects Track 12 at the conduit (Forstall Cross) and continues (left) towards the unsightly buildings of the range camp. This is the historic Lych Way (Track 22).

The Willsworthy military camp and firing range were established shortly after 1900; farming at Redford was phased out, and by 1910 the old farmhouse was in ruins. Its outline, set within overgrown enclosures, is seen below (right) beside the Wheal Jewell leat. The outermost cornditch reave-wall runs for some way beyond the butts beside Track 21, which now passes over the south flank of Whit Hill and crosses a plain; 80 yards from the north side of the track are set stones forming a semi-circle, which, as I have suggested in *High Dartmoor*, may be the remnants of a stone circle with a possible diameter of 165 feet.

Track and reave-wall now diverge, the latter curving above the source-mire of Willsworthy Brook to mount the high ground under Hare Tor and enclose Palmer's Newtake; the track, meanwhile, bears left to round the head of Walla Brook. Visible ahead are the tors of Great Links, Brai (topped by Widgery†) and Doe, the remote Dunnagoat Hill, the Doetor Brook valley, Lydford Sharp and Hare Tors and (right) Ger Tor. The track forks beside a large, flattish stone; branch right to another fork; again branch right (the left-fork paths lead to the old Foxhole Mine in the Doetor Brook valley) and cross a feeder of Walla Brook draining a mire high on the hillside. The track is clear as it climbs beside the streamlet (north side), pointing first to Sharp Tor, then to Hare. The ascent is a stiff, direct one of 400 feet, and the track becomes sunken on the high slope, with a serpentine course to ease gradient. The walker nearing the crest will see in detail the castle-like rocks of Sharp Tor (left) and the lofty piles of Hare and Little Hare Tors (right). *Southward from col: track clearly seen under south slope of Whit Hill and passing flagpole and noticeboard at Ring o' Bells cairn; reappears beyond on plain of Black Down north of Gibbet Hill and heads towards St Michael's. Lydford village and associated features appear above unsuspected depths of gorge, backed by vale of Tamar and Cornish moors.*

Track 20 crosses the plain known as Dead Lake Head; this declines eastward from the col between the two major tors and introduces the walker to the wilderness of northern Dartmoor. During field work for the present book in the spring of 1984, my wife and I were confronted by the sombre sight of countless undulations of blackened ridges after the raging fires of April.

The descending track points to the centre of Amicombe's long ridge, passes near bond-stone wd and crosses a streamlet flowing from a subsidiary mire (left) into Dead Lake Mire (below, right). Beyond are stone mounds and pits, and below them is a deep gert; all are workings of the former Rattle Brook Mine – and the gert offers shelter to the walker in an otherwise very exposed landscape. Beyond the gert, stranded paths lead (left) to turf-ties on the slopes of Rattlebrook Hill above the valley-side steep. The main track, retaining good definition, curves round the head of the gert and descends for 200 yards in the direction of a group of Bronze Age hut circles on the west slope of Watern Oke, opposite; it then abruptly regains its former north-easterly courses and descends obliquely – here the shell of Bleak House can be seen upstream – to a ford on Rattle Brook opposite the foot of Green Tor Water. This tributary of Rattle Brook receives a sub-tributary, known as the Scad, a short way above its confluence with the principal stream. A track leads from the ford to turf-ties on the lower plain of Amicombe Hill, crossing both Green Tor Water and the Scad. Medieval tinworks, including a tinners' house, occupy the valley floor below the ford; these, together with access to turf-ties on the high valley-sides, suggest the formation and regular use of the Dartmoor Path by peat- and tin-workers during the Middle Ages. Relics of latter-day mining in the valley include a short leat and a wheelpit on the left bank; further downstream is another ford at the crossing of the track from Lane End Gate.

Upstream from the ford on Track 20 are the surface workings and scant remains of the Curbeam and Rattle Brook Mine buildings, which were reached easily from the track. Curbeam was at work in 1790, and Rattle Brook Mine (Pl. 32) half a century later, each doubtless including Brentor men in its workforce; the tradition concerning the latter was current when Crossing was writing: 'On its [Rattle Brook's] bank is the deserted Rattle Brook Mine, and it was by the workmen who were there employed that this track [Dartmoor Path] was chiefly used.'

What shelter existed for the men at either of the mines it is difficult to determine; the medieval tinners had their 'houses' and, similarly, the Industrial Age miners their 'barracks'; at Rattle Brook Mine one must assume that the ruined building was a barracks, whilst the men of Curbeam could have used the earlier house on the right bank below the Track 21 ford, where the positions of fireplace and doorway are still clearly seen and the miners have adapted and strengthened the structure of the building rather as earlier tinners are known to have adapted and reinforced prehistoric hut circles to their needs. Atkinson, Burt and Waite write in *Dartmoor Mines*: 'The only records found relating to the site refer to the North Dartmoor Mining Company being launched in 1872 with John Symons as manager. The company was formed to work a sett covering 4 square miles on the Rattle Brook with a nominal capital of £20,000. The mine failed to appear in any returns after 1873 so it was probably a failure. In view of this, it is probable that the scanty remains at the site consisting of a few ruined buildings, openworks and tips belongs to an earlier working. A company known as North Dartmoor Streams produced tin in 1864-5 and it is possible that it was located in the Rattle Brook area.'

TRACK 22

THE LYCH WAY – THE WAY OF THE DEAD: BELLAFORD (BELLEVER, DARTMOOR CENTRAL BASIN) – LYDFORD
Using Tavy crossing A $11\frac{3}{4}$ miles   crossing B and C $11\frac{1}{4}$ miles

Travellers from the more easterly settlements of Cator would cover an additional 2 miles.

The sombre duty of carrying the dead over wild, open country on foot for Christian burial at the parish church once lay upon dwellers in remote areas through highland Britain. Nowhere more than on Dartmoor was this onerous duty of a punishing nature, a circumstance created by its unique topographical shape. Whereas the deceased cottager in a Highland glen, a Cumbrian valley, a Yorkshire dale or a Welsh mountain pass could be carried without the undue exertion of his bearers *down* to the parish church, on Dartmoor the Lydford-bound cortège must needs climb out of the central basin in order to cross its rim and negotiate transverse river valleys separated by long, steep ridges between basin rim and outer escarpment of the Moor.

The settling of Devon by the Saxons in the late seventh century – they were soon to become Christianized – and the establishing in Norman times of the central basin Ancient Tenements results throughout more than five centuries in a steady increase in church-bound traffic to Lydford, ancient capital of the Moor. The rise of commerce in the early thirteenth century was accompanied by a questioning attitude to many established customs – both religious and secular – and to practices that formerly had been tacitly accepted; one of these was the gruelling journey to Lydford, not only to bury the dead but to receive all the Sacraments of the medieval Church. The distance by the most direct route from the tenements of Babeny and Pizwell in the east central basin was about 12 miles; when adverse weather compelled travellers to use a route less arduous and consequently less direct, the distance increased to 17 miles. In 1260, therefore, the easterly Ancient Tenements successfully petitioned the Bishop of Exeter (Walter Bronescombe) for permission to attend the much nearer Widecombe church instead of Lydford for all sacramental purposes, whereupon the Church Way (Track 22) began to receive regular use for that purpose, and the vicar of Widecombe to receive tithes which properly were due to the rector of Lydford.

Lydford church has nevertheless remained to this day the parish church of the 76.6 square miles of the Forest of Dartmoor. From Norman times until the early nineteenth century the Forest courts were held at Lydford Castle, which was also the official prison of the Stannary (Tin-trade) authority. New farms that sprang up in the central basin in the fifteenth and sixteenth centuries – Smithill, Cherrybrook, Stannon, Crockern are examples – did not enjoy Ancient Tenement status and privileges, but the religious and administrative circumstances that shaped the lives and livelihood of the farmers and their families were identical to those of the tenements, and Lydford was the hub of their universe. We should therefore regard 1260 not as the year in which traffic on the Lych Way ceased but as marking a period of *increasing* use until the construction of the turnpike roads, the commuting of tithes and the transfer of the Duchy of Cornwall's Forest administration to Princetown, all within a few years of the turn of the nineteenth century. Even the tenement dwellers of the eastern central basin, excused after 1260 from attending Lydford church, and, for several centuries to follow, their descendants, had to attend the Forest and Stannary courts at Lydford, journeys in all probability made over the Lych Way as their most direct route, the old track thereby carrying more secular traffic than, when the basin had been so sparsely inhabited, it had churchbound travellers. In his dispensation to the eastern Forest dwellers, Bishop Bronescombe had ruled that the vicar of Widecombe should receive tithe lambs from those using his church. This directive appears to have been honoured more in the breach than the observance, for the lambs due to Widecombe were reaching neither there nor Lydford. In 1610 the rector of Lydford, William Hunt, brought a lawsuit for the recovery of tithes which he considered properly to be his. The suit was never satisfactorily concluded, and in 1702 rector Thomas Bernaford

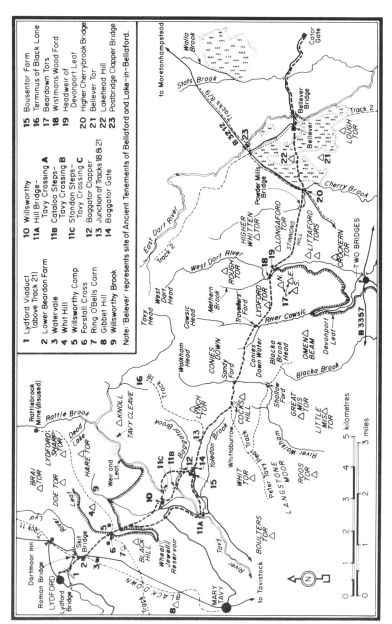

Track 22

Legend:

1 Lydford Viaduct (above Track 21)
2 Lower Beardon Farm
3 Watervale
4 Whit Hill
5 Willsworthy Camp
6 Forstall Cross
7 Ring O'Bells Cairn
8 Gibbet Hill
9 Willsworthy Brook
10 Willsworthy
11A Hill Bridge - Tavy Crossing **A**
11B Cataloo Steps - Tavy Crossing **B**
11C Standon Steps - Tavy Crossing **C**
12 Baggator Clapper
13 Junction of Tracks 18 & 21
14 Baggator Gate
15 Bousentor Farm
16 Terminus of Black Lane
17 Beardown Tors
18 Wistmans Wood Ford
19 Headweir of Devonport Leat
20 Higher Cherrybrook Bridge
21 Bellever Tor
22 Lakehead Hill
23 Postbridge Clapper Bridge

Note: 'Bellever' represents site of Ancient Tenements of Bellaford and Lake-in-Bellaford.

resurrected the case; in spite of vigorous opposition on all sides, he won the day. The hornets' nest he stirred up would not have endeared him to the Dartmoor people, and his benefit in kind from this hollow legal victory is likely to have been meagre.

The original, extreme easterly termini of the Lych Way were Babeny and Pizwell. The route from Babeny was via Loughtor Hole and a junction with Track 2 south of Bellaford tenement. Pizwell dwellers would have travelled down the Dury Brook valley by an old track linking the tenements, and joined the main Track 21 east of Bellaford. In the late fifteenth century the Riddon tenement was established, access to the Lych Way also being by the inter-tenement track. 'Bellaford' is the ancient form of Bellever, current until the twentieth century and strictly applicable to the Ancient Tenement on East Dart's right bank; both Bellaford and Lake-in-Bellaford date from the mid-fourteenth century. The hamlet, to which so many ancient ways led, is the historical main east terminus of the Lych Way, and description will begin at Bellever Bridge, where links converge from Pizwell, the later tenements of Runnage and Dury, the very ancient venville tenements of Cator and end at the church and castle of Lydford. Moormen and their families bound for Lydford from the more westerly tenements of Sherberton, Dunnabridge, Broom Park and Prince Hall (the westernmost) are likely to have used the track across Muddy Lakes to join the ancient route of Track 8 (see p. 97); branching right from this on the Beardown ridge, they could then pass up the Cowsic valley to Travellers' Ford on the main Lych Way.

Three alternative crossings of the River Tavy are described as A, B and C. Finally the reader should note that the track crosses both the Merivale and Willsworthy live-firing ranges, and it is important to check the firing programmes before setting out. The walk is perhaps one of the most satisfying of historical ways in Britain's highlands, beginning as it does in the insularity of Dartmoor's central basin and crossing wild moorland, often turbulent rivers and lofty, tor-crowned ridges that offer a vista far into Cornwall, to terminate in the beautiful and still sparsely populated western border-country declining to the Tamar valley.

Following the Track (westward)
A car should be parked just within the forest at 655772. At the crossing of the East Dart river by the ancient road from Cator Gate

stands the medieval clapper bridge of Bellaford. Links with Dury and Pizwell reach the bridge on the east bank and from Babeny on the opposite, west bank. An early nineteenth-century arch-bridge now carries traffic, leaving the clapper a picturesque ruin on the downstream side, and the ford virtually disused. The curve of the right bank wall is aligned with ford and clapper and reaches a gate in the conifer plantations; here Track 2 arrives, carrying with it the Babeny link via Win Ford; it intersects the Lych Way and crosses the east verge of Bellever Green to run northward.

Continue past the entrance (right) to Bellever Youth Hostel and Bellever Farm. Here, once, stood the two great longhouses of Bellaford* (1355) and, on the south side of the way, that of Lake-in-Bellaford† (1347-8). Of the original buildings of the three farms, all that now remains is at Lake, where the road becomes a steep, rough track. Pass through the gate above Lake and look back over the gentle East Dart valley; enter the trees and turn right (the track ahead leads to Dunnabridge), where Track 22 is marked by re-tipped posts as far as the second (very wide) transverse forest road. Interesting antiquities exist of the plain of Lakehead Hill; to see them, continue ahead to the wide, unplanted crest of the hill, where Bellever Tor is seen to advantage (left); to visit the sites, including the Lakehead great kistvaen, turn right.

Return to the track and follow the small guide-stones across the crest. Beyond dense tree-growth is the west boundary of the plantations and a sighting of the B3212 road; the Cherry Brook valley appears left, backed by the southern hill-chain and, on the right are the houses, ruined works buildings, chimneystacks and wheelhouses of Powder Mills. Beyond the old mills is Stinnons Hill, culminating in the tor-crowned ridge running northward from Crockern Tor, which is crossed by Track 21 *en route* for Wistmans Wood Ford.

Descend from the plantation gate, pass through another gateway, cross the highway – here on the line of Track 8 – and enter a gate on the further side. Mr Jeff Coombes, the present occupant of Powder Mills Farm, is kindly willing for walkers in ones or twos to cross his grounds; dogs must be kept on a lead, and intending party organizers must telephone Tavistock 88202 to obtain permission. It is wise not to

---

* John Coaker was moorman at a Bellaford tenement in 1840 and James Hamlyn at Lake (Lydford Tithes Apportionment).
† (Lydford Tithes Apportionment 1839)

cross the valley tract ahead during a spell of wet weather – it is difficult enough when dry – but to walk along the farm drive. The original way continued its descent towards Cherry Brook's left bank and is now represented by an old, broken wall, left, which runs north-west to a corner where a gate stands, the trackbed now being a watercourse. The line of the wall was almost certainly dictated in Tudor times by that of the Lych Way when in regular use by moormen travelling to the Lydford Forest courts; in other words, the wall pre-dates the powdermills' establishment by several centuries. Cross the wet tract where convenient towards the corner; pass through a broken transverse wall into a small stand of rowan trees, from which a sunken way leads direct to the clapper bridge on Cherry Brook (Pl. 34). Here observe the alignment of sunken way, old trackside wall and ascent of Lakehead Hill beyond the highway.

Ruined works buildings near the brook were served by a hard track leading (left) to the terraced buildings visible from the highway. These include the former works manager's house (now the farmhouse) and a barracks, with a fireplace at each end, for the accommodation of workmen living at a distance. Objects of interests at the old gunpowder factory – the old wheelhouses especially – include a powder-testing bombard and a craft workshop in the old smithy run by Mr Jeff Coombes. Large quantities of gunpowder were manufactured here from the 1840s-80s for blasting in mines and quarries. The massive clapper bridge is likely to have replaced an earlier structure; built, however, as a part of the Powder Mills development of less than 150 years ago and wide enough for the passage of horse-drawn carts, it is inappropriately marked by OS in Gothic lettering (*cf.* p. 71).

West of the bridge the way ascends the valley-side obliquely from a wire fence (an access gateway is seen, left, between two old works buildings); its ascent is marked by kerbstones towards another ruined building, and the ancient path was evidently adopted during the factory years as the best way of ascending from the bridge. The way makes a compensating elbow-bend (now scarcely definable, right) to a gateway, where it crosses a disused leat channel on a small, overgrown bridge. On Stinnons Hill ahead is Withy Tree Clitters, where the Lych Way ascends the ridge beside the extreme north verge of the clitter. The route appears from the gateway as a wide, light-coloured stripe on the hillside reaching the ridge-crest at a shallow dip slightly nearer Littaford (left) than Longaford Tor.

From the Powder Mills gateway follow a clear path towards the north verge of Withy Tree Clitters (the withy trees grow only in the densest clitter and do not reach the north verge). When the path becomes stranded, make for a triangular boulder among tinners' pits; continue to the clitter verge and mount the hill to a break in the (Stinnons) newtake wall above. No gateway exists near this point as the land was not enclosed until direct journeys from the central basin to Lydford had almost ceased, the turnpike roads had become available and the old path would already have been fading fast. (Hunting-gates north and south of the broken wall are not relevant.) *Eastward from Stinnons newtake wall: stranded path beyond clitter verge leads to triangular boulder, then clear path to Powder Mills gate; alignment of visible overall route excellent; Bellever Tor appears slightly right of gate.*

Beyond the wall, despite the direct course suggested by modern maps, the path doubtless described a south-north curve to ease gradient: no sign of either now remains. The walker should navigate his curve to reach the ridge-crest a little to the north of Littaford Tors. Stranded paths intersect the well-defined ridge-crest leading (left) to Two Bridges, and the OS marking may be taken as correct from here on for a considerable way. The track is, however, less clear than the marking suggests, and careful attention to detail is needed in order to retrace it. In crossing the west flank of the ridge, pass a small, flat rock outcrop, right, and a set stone ahead. The Beardown Tors now rise impressively beyond the West Dart valley. Beyond the set stone is a blunt, westward spur of the ridge (topped by rocks); pass to the right of this and make an oblique descent towards the highest, furthest trees of Wistmans Wood, near which the way joins another track coming out from Two Bridges. The remarkable primeval oak wood of Wistmans, comprising three groves of gnarled, deformed trees clinging to life amidst the sheltering, lower clitter of Longaford Tor, is a haven for wildlife and has been a reserve of the Nature Conservancy since 1961. Rabbit buries above the wood and foundations of a small building here are those of a former sporting warren established in 1895.

The way makes a gradual approach to the West Dart river; pass between the highest-placed bury and the outermost oak tree; when opposite the headweir of the Devonport leat, cross a rough, shallow gully at a well-marked fording place (the only satisfactory one) and cross the flank of a small hill with a scattering of rocks; the path, now clear, passes below the largest group of rocks. Ahead is the wall of Longaford Newtake, where a hunting-gate gives access to Wistmans Wood Ford on the river. No signs remain of steps – though the velocity of West Dart makes it more than probable that they once existed – and the continuing path on the right bank, slightly sunken and partly obscured by mire, points to the foot of the south gully of two on the flank of Beardown, the northern being a tinners' gert. The south gully is without doubt the route of the track; it has become badly eroded over the centuries by stormwater but still provides the most convenient ascent of Beardown. Clearly the gradient of the way both here and on Stinnons Hill must have posed a challenge to litter-bearing, pedestrian travellers, but the topography of each ridge ruled out convenient alternatives.

The wild surroundings of Wistmans Wood Ford must often have daunted Lydford-bound travellers entering upon the fringe of north Dartmoor's great waste, the frowning tors of Longaford and Beardown (north), Lydford Tor and the grotesque Crow Tor serving only to emphasize the solitude. (Each of these fine tors is, of course, worth a visit.)

Track 22 emerges from the gully at a slight dip in the hill-crest quite near the outlying rocks of Beardown Tor (north). Lydford Tor now appears ahead, a landmark of importance to travellers in either direction on the Lych Way. Near the military range-pole, right, is a ruined kistvaen discovered by the author over thirty years ago and marked on the OS 2½-inch map. Traces of a hollow way, although faint, are now discernible. Pass 90 yards to the south of the range-pole (it is near the wall of Beardown Newtake), where the way becomes poorly defined; it passes along the north verge of a small mire, some 50 yards below a pointed stone, right. The stone stands near the lower edge of the Lydford Tor clitter, and several remarkable rock canopies appear at the base of the tor. *Eastward: walk towards the dip in the hill, aligned with Higher Whiten-Longaford Tors ridge beyond West Dart; ignore track bearing right towards Beardown Tor (north).*

Verging the small mire, Track 22 points towards the domed hill of Blacka Brook Head beyond Cowsic, before veering right on the contour below Lydford Tor to point towards the valley of Conies Down Water (Cowsic). The way becomes better defined in passing a leaning slab, a large bedrock boulder and a small rockfield on the edge of wet ground, where a series of ten flat stones has been laid to assist in crossing. Pass through a hunting-gate in the newtake wall (which crosses Beardown on the north side of Lydford Tor). The Cowsic valley branch is seen southward skirting the wet flats on the valley floor and fording Beardown Brook to join the main track at the gate. Beyond the gate the track follows the edge of the steep east bank above the river, from where it is seen beyond Cowsic threading the natural pass of the Conies Down valley. Becoming a stony way on the hillside within sound of the river, it reaches the hidden, rocky hollow, overlooked by Conies Down Tor, where Conies Down Water joins the river at Cowsic Fork and the Lych Way crosses the picturesque Travellers' Ford (Pl. 35) at the head of Broad Hole. To make a diversion to Conies Down Tor would offer the walker little by way of recompense, for views are restricted by the superior heights around – though the series of river meanders below Broad Hole forms a sight unusual on high Dartmoor. At Travellers' Ford, sitting one day long ago in the company of a remarkable man possessed of extra-sensory perception, I was astonished to hear him say that many, many people had passed this place in former times, burdened by a great sorrow. A German prince, he was a complete stranger to Dartmoor and its, history. This instant revelation of the true purpose of the Lych Way was, I realized from his demeanour, the result not of telepathy between us but of genuine ESP.

The ford is some way below the foot of the tor; follow the path past a brilliantly coloured mire cushioning a sparkling spring; continue parallel with Conies Down Water, and for some way well above it. The track becomes clearly defined when passing miry ground, left, and a large, flat bedrock (with horizontal jointing) right. It then describes an S-bend to avoid the source-mire of Conies Down Water (above, right) and reaches a wide, stony ford on the stream's upper reach below the mire. The OS marking 'Spring' with commencing stream symbol on the *south* (left) side is misleading as, except during very dry weather, a considerable flow of water crosses the ford. The double stone row on the north side of the track, just short of the ford, is a poor specimen and remarkable only in its superiority in elevation, at 1,660 feet, over all other accredited Dartmoor monuments of the type.

The track remains clear beyond the ford, sunken between stony banks and follows the south verge of a rockfield. It crosses the Cowsic-Walkham watershed on a wide plain, from where its continuation to Whittaburrow west of Walkham is visible as a sunken, grassy way. Lynch Tor rises in the near distance, right, and the huge mass of Great Mis Tor dominates the Walkham valley, left, with

Great Steeple Tor to its right. *Eastward from crest of Conies Down: Beardown range appears formidable; Longaford ridge (beyond) not visible; homeward travel after rigours and emotions of funeral journey must have been very wearisome; 5-mile stretch Whittaburrow-Cherry Brook most gruelling for family travel.*

Descend westward past a pointed, leaning slab; remain on the track round a double bend, cross the Dartmoor Prison leat on a wide cart bridge and observe a smaller footbridge downstream. At the foot of the hill is Sandy Ford on the river, named from the gravelly approaches; a stone heap above the right bank downstream is the spoil from an excavated mine adit – its higher opening in a shaft seen on the hillside above. Upstream, also right bank, is the old building which was the centre of tin-mining operations here. Dr T.A.P. Greeves has researched the mine's history* and finds that the site was first worked in 1806 under the name Wheal Prosper and operated in spasms until the 1850s. A final, abortive plan to work the sett in 1872 by two Peter Tavy men named Crocker and Burgoyne represents Wheal Prosper's last claims on the pages of history. (I have, for reasons given there, including the working in *High Dartmoor* as 'Rowse's Mine'.) The wide ford with its curving, stony approaches, the dominating tors of Lynch and Great Mis, the soft grey of the old mine building and the heather and whortleberry dressings laid by Nature upon old mining scars make this lonely place one of great attraction.

Follow the track ascending Stooky Moor and pause on the hilltop to inspect Whittaburrow – or, of greater interest, the view from it. This large, despoiled cairn with a few stones piled on one side and the central hollow once occupied by the grave, is a recorded boundary point of the Forest of Dartmoor. On Track 22 alongside, the walker leaves the Forest and obtains his first sighting of the western border-country and his destination 1,000 feet below; appearing from this lofty point as of insignificant elevation are Brent Tor, Gibbet Hill, Whit Hill and the Lyd valley against the backdrop of Cornish moors. Without doubt the Lych Way provides the walker with a deeply satisfying challenge over wild and remote country. *Eastward from Whittaburrow: pointed slab visible near Conies Down crest; track clear ascending from Sandy Ford and Prison leat bridge.*

Less than 100 yards west of Whittaburrow the broad, stony road from Sandy Ford bears away south-westward; this is the Peter Tavy

---

* Published in *Plymouth Mineral and Mining Club Journal*, Volume VI, No. 1, 1975.

peat track. Its worn, road-like character is due to the great quantities of peat formerly carried over it by packhorses from the upper Walkham valley. Follow the well-defined grass path forking right; this is Track 22; it leads to a ford on the upper verge of a large patch of rushes at Yoledon Head, where the first water of Yoledon Brook flows from the peat to feed the headmire. Ahead appears the outer wall of Longbetor (pronounced 'Long-bettor') Newtake, the Peter Tavy track passing its higher corner, left, and Track 22 running towards the lower corner – the intermediate portion of the wall is as yet not visible. From the ford, the track follows the north verge of Yoledon Head and, when the valley steepens, achieves a more gradual descent by curving from right to left. The entire length of the outer newtake wall soon appears, diving into and out of the valley bottom. The track approaches the lower corner, follows the wall and with it curves inward to drop to the plain of Bagga Tor. The route of the track, in avoiding the deep Yoledon Brook valley, clearly dictated the line of the north Longbetor wall. Both pursue the same line for half a mile, the track deeply rutted in places; the fine skyline to the right comprises the boulder-strewn mass of Standon Hill and tors of Hare, Great Links, Ger and Lynch. The humble cone of Bagga Tor marks the plain, and Track 18 is seen, right, descending under Lynch Tor to unite with the Lych Way at the opening of the wide stroll created by the Longbetor and Baggator Newtake walls. A leat enters the stroll beneath the wall, left, carrying water from a spring in the newtake to Brousentor Farm, a mile ahead. The stroll soon narrows to reach Roundwood Gate (see p. 200); the trees of the circular plantation nearby, are the first trees seen since leaving Wistmans Wood.

Beyond Roundwood Gate, Bagga Tor is easily accessible from the track and gives rewarding views towards Tavy Cleave. Baggator Gate, the ancient moorgate, stands at the head of the road ascending from Peter Tavy, Cudlipp Town and Wapsworthy. Passing by the gate, the track becomes a grassy way leading down to the tree-shadowed Brousentor Gate. So Track 22 reaches the parting of ways; the valley ahead is that of the tempestuous River Tavy, marked by John Spede (map of 1610) as 'Tavy Flud'. According to Tavy's state of flow – which could be pre-judged from the rivers so far crossed – the traveller could choose one of three ways. The walker needing an intermediate parking place should use Baggator Gate (see p. 200).

Tavy Crossing A: Hill Bridge

If travellers had reason to fear that Tavy was in spate, they would choose route A and pass through Baggator Gate to follow the Peter Tavy road for a little over half a mile.

Pass the entrance to Brousentor Farm (right); at a bend in the road is a DNPA fingerpost (right) with yellow dot; inserted in each side of the modern roadside wall here are steps, a concession to local users of a path in continuous use for at least a thousand years. Mount the steps into Field 1; cross diagonally to a gateway in the higher, left-hand corner; enter Field 2; follow the wall (left) to an opening in a transverse wall ahead. Audible now is the sound of Yoledon Brook which, like the track, has dropped 800 feet since leaving the ford at Yoledon Head. The foundations of medieval walls are seen everywhere in this locality, where the history of settlement is a long one. Enter Field 3; the bulky hill, left, is Cudlipp Town Down; bear away from the Yoledon Brook valley to a pointed set stone; pass two conspicuous boulders and a wall corner (right), and descend a steep bank to Hill Bridge on the river below. The original approach to the bridge lay through a nearby gateway, but a bridge-side stile has been substituted. (The tarmac road crossing the bridge branches from the Peter Tavy-Baggator Gate road near the hamlet of Wapsworthy and runs to Willsworthy and Lane End.) A large clapper bridge is known to have preceded the present structure, and it is probable that successive bridges have occupied the site since at least early Norman times. Yoledon Brook enters the river on the left bank 70 yards below the bridge; a former mine leat draws its water supply (now chanelled to a hydro-electric power-station) at a weir and a salmon ladder has been built below the bridge: it is a beautiful glade (Pl. 37).

Cross the bridge; mount the hill, pass Hilltown Farm (right). At lane junction 1, turn left (signposted 'Mary Tavy'); at lane junction 2 continue ahead; 140 yards on, at an abrupt bend in the road, the stony Snap Lane takes up the line of Track 22; follow it, pass through Yard Gate – once known as Seven Stars Gate due to indecipherable markings on one gatepost – and follow the clear track alongside the cornditch wall past a range boundary stone (WD 20). On reaching the minor crest known as Snap, pause to look back: the track is clearly seen passing Bagga Tor and following the Longbetor wall to disappear at a skyline chink – the sunken way near Whittaburrow. Looking westward, the summit of Black Hill rises, left, and the well-defined Track 21 is seen flanking Whit Hill; beyond this is a fine range of heights: the tors of Great Links, Lydford Sharp, Hare, Tavy Cleave Sharp, Knowle and Standon Hills. The nearer of two flowing leats on the side of Black Hill, left, are useful guides when the track becomes stranded; branch left from the wallside track (leading to the former valley settlements of Yellowmead and Redford) and ascend Yellowmead Hill towards an elbow-bend in the leat (beyond a leatside waterworks hut). The way is joined on the hillside by the more direct, main Lych Way emerging from the Yellowmead enclosures below.

Tavy Crossing B: Cataloo Steps
Follow the grassy way from Baggator Gate to Brousentor Gate and descend the rough Brousentor Lane (normally a literal water-course) to its junction below Brousentor Farm, left, with the concrete road to Standon Farm. Descend the road for 250 yards; turn left into a green track curving to follow the left (south) valley-side of Baggator Brook. Mount a stile (DNPA yellow-spot route); the leat seen left of the track drives a turbo-generator to supply electricity to Brousentor Farm. Descend the clear grass track to one of the loveliest sylvan glades under Dartmoor's edge, with the sight and sound of the brook, right, overshadowed by oaks – sessile and pendunculate – rowans and sycamores, and with luxuriant ferns sprouting from crevices in the lichen-tinted rocks on either side. Pass through an old gateway; cross the steps over Baggator Brook near its confluence with the river – the stream bed is ruggedly picturesque here – and walk straight to Tavy's Cataloo Steps, of which five substantial stones remain in place, though gaps caused by raging spates are inconveniently wide for the walker unless the river is low. Significantly, the woodland above the river's left bank here is named Coffin Wood and the medieval lane, with crumbling walls on the west bank, Corpse Lane. The lane curves slightly left at the head; mount Stile 1; cross a transverse lane and mount Stile 2; follow a sunken way, another medieval lane from which the north wall has been removed to foundation level (Pl. 38); pass through an open gateway and mount Stile 3; notice a sheep-creep in the wall, right. From here the original way crossed a field diagonally to a corner gateway, opposite, where a sheepfold has been built; the consequent diversion crosses the field to Stile 4, in the hedge of the lane ascending from Standon Steps to Willsworthy, and the junction of crossings B and C occurs only a few yards east of the original.

Tavy Crossing C: Standon Steps

Start as for Crossing B; mount the DNPA stile; follow a branching sunken way (right) to the bank of Baggator Brook, which was crossed here by travellers making for Standon Steps on the further side of the extensive, very wet Baggator Marsh. At the brook, Time has stood still. Before the present Baggator Bridge and road to Standon were built early in the present century, this place was the crossing for riders and pedestrians between Peter Tavy and Standon. A ford, now destroyed by the spates of the brook, lay alongside the clapper bridge, which is an archaeological relic of Dartmoor travel in medieval times, one known to very few people today: see Figure 5. The brook has changed its course during the present century by cutting down some 3 to 4 feet beneath the right bank, leaving the remaining portion of its ancient bed high and dry. The impressive imposts A and B, therefore, now span a dry channel choked by leaves and driftwood. The stream has piled stones beneath the right bank, where evidence remains of built-up masonry to support the westernmost span (impost E in Fig. 5) and receive the track approach from the bank, now overgrown. Study Fig. 5, a sketch made from a photograph taken many years ago by

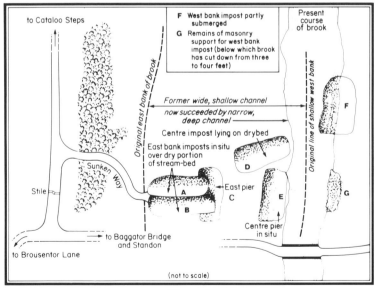

Figure 5

R. Hansford Worth and published in his *Dartmoor*, captioned 'The Clapper Bridge on the Lych Way, over Baggator Brook'. The picture was taken from the left bank, so that imposts marked A and B in Figure 5 are those in the foreground. One impost of the second span, C, now displaced, lies in the brook, as does that of third span (E) visible in Worth's photograph. In the interests of accuracy, it should be mentioned that the Lych Way does not run 'past the menhir on Langstone Moor', as Worth states, that being the route of the Peter Tavy peat track.

As the track leaving the right bank has for some way lost all definition, start for Standon Steps as follows: cross the brook at the modern Baggator Bridge; leave the road to reach a cornditch wall corner 40 yards below; ahead is a line of boulders, presumably intended as the foundation of a medieval wall; cross it midway and walk to a thorn tree – the largest of any in this area of Baggator Marsh – over-shadowing a small group of boulders. The original track (from the clapper) now becomes traceable passing the tree; follow it towards another cornditch corner. Pass through a break (made to admit the track) in an ancient reave and cross a patch of miry ground where stones have been laid to provide a firm path. Pause here to align lengths of the track: behind – Brousentor Lane and Bagga Tor rising to its left; ahead beyond Tavy – the walled lane ascending westward from Standon Steps to Willsworthy Farm; the huge, stony mound of Standon Hill is dominant, right, as one crosses the marsh. Reaching the corn-ditch corner, observe the stroll, right, through which the ancient way from Baggator clapper to Standon enters the farm enclosures. Bypass this and follow the wall running north-west from the corner, until an overgrown gateway, 1, appears in a hedge, left; the path leading to it, still traceable, is joined there by a well-defined one from the farm's home fields, right. This ends the passage of the track along the verge of Baggator Marsh, and good ground lies ahead. The way leads to Gate-way 2; notice sheep-creeps on either side; 75 yards ahead is Gateway 3; no gate remains and the way has been paved; the track is clear to Gate-way 4 (Pl. 39) – again, paving remains, but no gateposts; beyond the gateway is a line of flat boulders on the north side of the track; I would interpret these as the foundation of a medieval wall (perhaps demolished in later times), its line dictated by the Lych Way; 45 yards below it is Gateway 5, giving direct access to the ford and steps on Tavy.

The simplest way to explain the remarkable Standon Steps is to quote the relevant passage from *High Dartmoor*:

The alarming rapidity and volume of Tavy (prior to depletion by the large-capacity Mine Leat) was the motive in laying down immense stepping-stones unique in the Dartmoor country; they are of sufficient width to allow two corpse-bearers to cross abreast rather than fore and aft, a very necessary safety measure. Most unfortunately the bridge is built on the steps; it was erected by German prisoners-of-war (World War II) for Jack Evans of Standon, range-clearer at Willsworthy range, because the river level at the ford was often too dangerous for horse and rider. Inexpertly built, it was severely damaged by flood; incredible though it may seem, it was rebuilt *on the same site* by the Ministry of Defence, thus perpetuating the spoliation of the historic steps.

The width of the steps may be judged by looking over the bridge parapets.

Follow the rugged lane ascending from the steps over a large spread of granite bedding; at the top of the rise, notice the stile (left), where route B enters the lane; at the gateway ahead, the original route B and C unite. Pass through another gateway and pause at the entrance to Higher Willsworthy Farm to see the medieval chapel window incorporated in the wall of a barn, left (Pl. 40); the actual site of the Domesday manor and chapel of 'Wilfleurde' is probably nearer Lower Willsworthy Farm, and this ecclesiastical relic may have been inserted in the barn, perhaps during Tudor times, to provide ventilation for the hay-loft. The interesting statement in White's *Directory of Devonshire* for 1878-9 that 'An ancient chapel at Willsworthy has long been used as a cowhouse' does not invalidate this suggestion. I have always regarded as important the question of rest-stages on Dartmoor's long-distance tracks which were not specifically formed by, or for, mounted moormen; such stages have been specified for Tracks 1, 12 and 13 and doubtless existed in border villages or farms on Track 16 and 27. Here, on Track 22, is Willsworthy, the first large farm settlement on this arduous route since leaving Bellaford. Rest and refreshment for the living, a hallowed place for the dead, feed for any horses in the cortège – all this would have been available at Willsworthy.

Continue to the junction of the lane with the Mary Tavy-Lane End road; turn left; at the ancient manor pound beside Willsworthy Brook – to cross which the road bears left; turn right; follow the green Willsworthy Lane to a clapper bridge; cross; follow the grassy way, right, to a stile; mount it and take either high or low path along the stream bank to a fence gateway; pass through this into the well-defined way leading to the south-west corner of an old cornditch wall ahead, where WD boundary stone 37 stands. (The wall above left is that of a post-medieval enclosure.) Continue beside the ancient wall to reach a corner where it meets another; mount the stile ahead; the waterworks hut beside the leat on the flank of Black Hill (left) is now visible, as also are Whit Tor, right, and Great Mis Tor rising behind Langstone Moor.

Junction of Tavy crossings A, B and C
The main route C (with B) is joined by route A from Snap on the flanks of Black Hill. Continuation to Lydford is now straightforward. The track mounts Yellowmead Hill and approaches the elbow-bend of the leat; cross the footbridge nearby. Cross the plain ahead, intersecting Track 21 at the junction known as Forstall Cross and make slightly right of the Willsworthy Camp building, passing a low-level army telephone box. Traffic is now visible on the A386 road descending north from Black Down; Lydford church and castle stand above the deeply indented Lyd valley, and the way reaches the camp road to the right of the buildings; cross the road; the continuing track is sunken for some way, deepening were eroded by stormwater; at the head of a small mire (source of Sounscombe Brook) it is crossed by a military track from the camp buildings to a ruined observation post 100 yards away to the right. Descend a hillside track aligned on church and castle (another path joins it from the OP, right). Also visible from here is Lydford Mill Cottage, site of the old village grainmill, and the Lych Way ascending from the cottage and passing below Lydford Viaduct. *Eastward: at the mire-head ignore tracks right and left; follow only the sunken way towards the camp bar-gate.*

A cornditch, left, gradually converges with the track; beside it are seen WD stones 4, 5, 6 and 8; follow the rounded cornditch corner ahead and join a track from Barewalls Farm (right) which passes through Beardon Gate into Down Lane. Track 22 here leaves high Dartmoor and plunges into the Lyd border-country.

Follow Down Lane; cross the A386 road (warning: traffic is very fast here) and descend to a lane branching left below Lower Beardon Farm (opposite). From this point, where Track 22 joins the highway to a sharp bend in the branch-lane below, it is on the line of the King Way, Track 11. Pass Take-off stone and milestone (see p. 132) and follow the lane through the yard of Heatherdale Farm (right of way).

Descend a rough track to a woodland path through the workings of the old Kitts Tin Mine to a stile beside the River Lyd; here cross a tributary streamlet and another stile, and follow the woodland path along the river's left bank. Lydford Mill Cottage appears through the trees; cross the river footbridge and follow the track passing before the front of the cottage, under the looming viaduct and down to a cross-lanes beside another cottage. Mill Lane continues ahead as a motorable road entering Lydford opposite the war memorial; Track 22, however, turns left at the cross-lanes and follows a steep, stony lane over solid bedding of borderland slate.

Lydford

At the head of the steep lane, a terrace of council houses marks the beginning of a tarmac road into the village centre; this portion of the ancient way is still known as Silver Street after the Saxon mint; it reaches the village street opposite the Nicholls Hall at the site of the former South Gate. A huge earthen rampart above the road – containing a gap where the South Gate once stood – is the former Saxon defensive earthwork once surmounted by a stockade. The strategic advantages offered by this site on a spur of land between the deep Lyd gorge and another deeply cut valley to the west were first realized by prehistoric settlers. Lydford's defences were strengthened in Saxon times by the rampart and stockade mentioned, above the neck of the spur. In 920 Lydford was granted a market and became a borough – second in size in Devon only to Exeter. Seven years later, during the reign of Aethelred II, a mint was built, and pennies were minted from locally mined silver for more than a century to follow; a specimen of the ancient borough coinage is kept in the Castle Inn, nearby. The Saxons had already built a wooden church on the present site and a defensive wooden fort on a motte.

In 997 Vikings sailed up the Tamar and Tavy rivers and sacked the town (see also p. 159). In the process of time it was rebuilt, and the Normans replaced wooden church and fort by stone buildings. A stone castle was built on the present site within a few years of the Conquest and was superseded by the massive castle keep, seen today, of 1195; this was granted to William Brewer in 1216 by King John. The first known reference to a stone-built church, dedicated to St Petrock, is in 1237, when it consisted only of chancel and nave. Soon after that it was enlarged and in 1261 – dedicated by Bishop Bronescombe. 'Michael the Priest' is recorded as the first rector of

Lydford in 1237, and it is satisfying to have the name of at least one priest who administered the Sacraments to parishioners from the far corners, the Dartmoor Ancient Tenements, of his vast parish in the days of church travel over the Lych Way. It also is of interest that Bishop Bronescombe should himself have ridden to Lydford – he is known to have travelled his huge diocese widely – to dedicate the rebuilt church in the year following that of his dispensation to the eastern ancient tenement dwellers (see p. 223).

St Petrock's Church is well cared for and contains numerous features of interest. Above it towers the grim keep of the castle of 1195, which became the seat of the Forest of Dartmoor courts and the stannary prison. The traveller Leland visited Lydford in *c.*1540 and wrote that it 'is now only a poor village, but was formerly a considerable place, as it appears from the Conqueror's Survey book that it could be taxed only when London and Exeter was taxed and in the same manner; and the custody of this castle was given to men of the greatest quality. They formerly sent members to Parliament, and it is said that all Dertomore is in this parish.'

TRACK 23

THE CHURCH WAY: ANCIENT TENEMENTS IN EASTERN SECTOR OF CENTRAL BASIN (HARTLAND, LOWER MERIPIT, WALNA, RUNNAGE, PIZWELL) – WIDECOMBE-IN-THE-MOOR
Distance from Pizwell: $3\frac{1}{2}$ miles
Distance from Runnage: $3\frac{3}{4}$ miles

In the Accounts of 1491 (7 Henry VII) of the Baliff of the Forest of Dartmoor appears a charge on Richard Canna of a rent of 2d 'for a certayne parcell of lande (beside Walla Brook, East Dart and reaching to) the Churchway of the said Richard from his tenement towards the Church of Widdicombe'; Richard Canna's tenement was most probably Pizwell. This historic documentary reference to Track 23 occurs 231 years after it had begun to receive regular use by Ancient Tenement dwellers whose ancestors had had to undertake the formidable journey over the Lych Way (Track 22) to Lydford church.

Tenements north of Pizwell, such as Hartland and Lower Meripit, were linked to the Church Way by the inter-tenements track mentioned on p. 225. Description begins now at Runnage and Pizwell, the two branches uniting at Grendon Top Gate. Tenants at Dury could choose between travelling to Widecombe via Cator and the Rowden Church Path or, perhaps more conveniently, via the inter-tenement track to join the Church Way at Pizwell. The basis of the modern road to Widecombe branching from the B3212 at Postbridge also is shown by *Ogilby* with the direction 'A stone wall on both hands'.

Following the Track (eastward): A – from Runnage
Little remains of the ancient longhouse at Runnage. The path from Walna tenement entered the court and joined with the Runnage

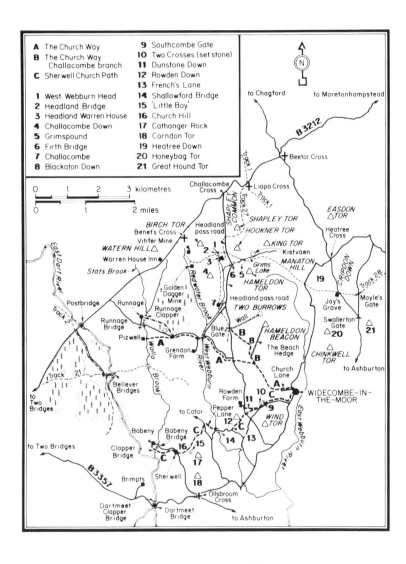

Tracks 23, 24 and 25

branch to cross Walla Brook. The crossing consists of an interesting clapper bridge with ford alongside (Pl. 41). A lane runs from the farm court to the bridge and is linked to it by a raised way verged by a wall. The bridge is of two openings, the west opening being a narrow flood channel; the (main) east opening spans the normal course of the brook and is a granite slab 8 feet 9 inches long and over 3 feet wide. Walla Brook is sylvan and placid as it crosses the grassy plain of Runnage Bottom to Pizwell. A sunken way passes from the ford through a hunting-gate on the left bank to a gateway in the (Soussons Down) plantation boundary wall. Beyond this it has been overplanted and cannot be identified with any existing forest ride. It may have joined the Postbridge road (which crosses Walla Brook at the modern Runnage Bridge) near the fine Bronze Age retaining circle near the hilltop east of the bridge; this has a diameter of 28 feet and encloses two remaining stones of the kistvaen, and there are traces of the barrow that once covered the grave.

To view the ancient Runnage Ford and Clapper, park near the road bridge (668789) and walk upstream beside the plantation boundary wall. The walker may inspect the clapper and unusual raised way but must not follow the private lane into the farm court. Return to the road and ascend to Runnage Circle; turn aside to see this. Continue along the road, beside which (left) is a large and conspicuous 'C' stone, indicating the limit of the County authority's responsibility two hundred years ago for the bridge and approach road. The hill is known as Ephraim's Pinch, after one Ephraim (locally pronounced 'Effram') who wagered he could carry a sack of corn over the 5 miles from Widecombe to Postbridge; reaching this point, however, Ephraim 'felt the pinch' and had to lay down his burden. At the foot of the hill, near the standing posts of the former Grendon Top Gate, the road bends and is joined by the branch track from Pizwell.

B – from Pizwell
Drive south from Runnage Bridge to Pizwell Green; park away from the road.

The beautiful cluster of old grey buildings at Pizwell, originally an ancient tenement of three farms, stands today as a classic example of Dartmoor's medieval past, its atmosphere in no way diluted by slate and pitch-covered roofing in place of thatch. On the lower side of the hamlet near Pizwell Green flows the peaceful Walla Brook at Pizwell Steps and across the ford on the Church Way; there is to be seen no bridge, no tarmac, no concrete to violate this striking scene of entirely natural conservation (Pl. 42). Follow the stony track from the steps, over the moor; traffic will be visible on the Postbridge road, left; the junction with the Runnage branch occurs near Grendon Top Gate (posts only), and the way continues past the foot of Grendon Strips (plantations) and descends to the West Webburn valley.

Ahead now is the huge ridge of Hameldon, its lower flank bearing impressions of ancient fields, highlighted always by the evening sun. Below, left, is the old warren of Soussons (pronounced to rhyme with 'ploughsons'), now a farm where practically every vestige of warrening activity has vanished through levelling, ploughing and tree-planting, but where the ancient warren house, in use as a barn, remains. The road passes the site of Grendon Bottom Gate (one post remains), and the south spur of Challacombe Down appears as a peninsula between Redwater Brook and the West Webburn river. Ahead in the near distance is the little pile of Blacka Tor. Pass Grendon Cot, a Victorian lodge at the entrance to Grendon Farm, and cross the river at Grendon Bridge. The road branching left and the unusually straight course of the river here are due to the 'improving' operations carried out in the 1870s by Mr Frederick Firth, who also built the house known as Blackaton Manor and the pass-road joining the B3212 road at Challacombe Cross (see p. 263).

The way now mounts Blackaton Hill and makes a steep, zigzag descent on the further side past Lower Blackaton Farm and the (cattle-grid) entrance to Blackaton Manor. It passes Gamble Cot and crosses Broadaford Brook (West Webburn) at Blackaton Bridge to reach Lower Blackaton Cross in 200 yards. Park at the roadside at the T-junction (698778) where Track 23 enters a gate (right-hand of two) on the further side of the road and becomes a steep, rough lane climbing Gore Hill, a foothill of Hameldon. Much pink granite is noticeable in the lane, which passes a granite post drilled to receive a horizontal timber which could be used to block the lane. Views westward, including the Church Way on Gore Hill, become increasingly interesting as one ascends to the lane-head and open moor beyond. Track 24 arrives here from Blackaton Down, and ahead the united way crosses the ridge of Hameldon some 400 feet lower than Hameldon Tor. Views (west) of the central basin and (east) of the eastern highlands are especially fine; eastern tors, left to right, are Honeybag, Chinkwell, Sharp (below Chinkwell), Bel, Holwell (distant), Bonehill Rocks, Hey and Saddle (distant), Top, Rippen (distant), Pil Whitaburrow, Halshanger (the last two being hill-summits rather than tors), Buckland Beacon, Auswell Rocks: fifteen points in all, thirteen of them tors.

Ahead now is the outer hedge of the Kingshead Farm enclosures on Langworthy Hill; a ridge-crest path runs the entire length of Hameldon and is here briefly joined by Track 23. At Kingshead Corner, however, the latter is sunken and bears left to commence a clearly defined descent towards the tower of Widecombe church in the vale below. Ignore a path forking from it, left, that runs close beside the descending Kingshead hedge. The view seen from here of the church and the further range of tors above the trees of Church Lane is delightful. The approach to Church Lane Head is sunken and stony; beyond it, notice the 'featherbed' granite in the lane, in a wet season a swift water-course. Beyond the entrance to Bowden's Barn (right) the lane has a tarmac surface and reaches the Natsworthy road opposite the car-park on the site of the former North Hall café, from where the village green and churchyard lychgate are only 400 yards distant.

The Church of St Pancras, with its magnificent early sixteenth-century, 120-foot-high tower built by the thriving local St Pancras Guild of tinners, has often been referred to as 'the Cathedral of the Moor'. Certainly it commands admiration from visitors and parishioners alike, and undoubtedly from the moorland people of the central basin, who were permitted to use it for worship and sacramental purposes from 1260 onward (see p. 223). Historical notes on the church may be obtained at the bookstall in the nave; to follow the Church Way merely as a physical exercise without entering the church would constitute an anti-climax to the walk. The village itself is charming, and the preservation and maintenance of the former Church House are assured by National Trust ownership; where formerly village 'ales' were held and hospitality was dispensed – including to mariners on Track 1 – books are now dispensed embracing every subject connected with Widecombe in particular and the Moor in general. A car-park lies on the north side of the green, its capacity inadequate only on the second Tuesday in every September, when Widecombe Fair brings a quite extraordinary influx of people from afar, most of them travelling to the fair in greater comfort than the legendary characters who rendered it famous.

TRACK 24

CHALLACOMBE BRANCH OF THE CHURCH WAY: HEADLAND WARREN – CHALLACOMBE – WIDECOMBE-IN-THE-MOOR $3\frac{1}{2}$ miles

Route according to tradition received by the author from moormen Wilfred Irish of Grendon, Peter Hannaford of Sherwell and Gordon Hambley, last warrener of Headland.

Both Gordon Hambley, formerly of Headland Warren, and the late Peter Hannaford, whose uncle worked the warren in the late nineteenth century, knew it to be a traditional custom at Headland to attend church at Widecombe rather than at Manaton, in which parish the warren lay, for reasons of distance and ease of route. Whereas the route of Track 23 necessitates only one climb before the descent to Church Lane Head, the undulations of a journey to Manaton may be judged from any contoured map, as Headlanders wishing to reach the village would have to follow Track 28 across three successive ridges, before reaching their journey's end. The main Church Way (Track 23) was used by the dwellers at Grendon in the West Webburn valley, whilst Mr Wilfred Irish of Grendon, who was born at Challacombe, tells me his mother in her childhood in the later nineteenth century walked, together with other children of the hamlet, daily over Track 24 to school at Widecombe, which then was held in the Church House. Traditions, events and customs of this nature show that the twentieth century has dealt harshly with many of Dartmoor's ancient tracks still in use less than a century ago and that it is historically important to record and preserve them while they are still traceable. The scenic virtues of Track 24, including views over the West Webburn valley and the central basin, are notable.

I have also recorded in *High Dartmoor* the last funeral cortège from

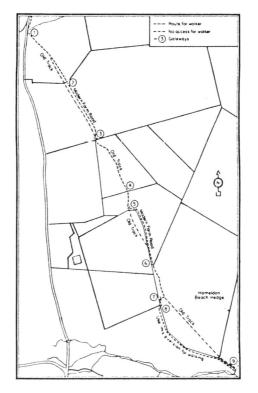

Map 32

Headland to Widecombe, that of James Hannaford (uncle of Peter) in 1899. The route was that of Track 27 as far as Blue Gate beyond Challacombe, from which point the description of Track 24 begins.

Following the Track (south-westward). See map on p. 242.
Park beside the road near Grimspound at 697810. Walk to Challacombe. The route from Headland Warren to Challacombe is described in reverse on p. 266. At the old village centre, turn left; cross Challacombe Bridge; turn right, pass the link road known as Straight Mile to Grendon Bridge, and continue to the site of Blue Gate. On the south side of this is a modern gate, left, at the foot of Blackaton

Down. Enclosure walls, fences and modern gateways seen on the down ahead are on the manor lands of Blackaton. The present owner, Mr Rupert Jones, is kindly willing to permit *bona fide* walkers *in ones or twos* to retrace the old way across his land on three conditions. Firstly, the intending walker should telephone Mr or Mrs R. Jones on 036 42 244 and request permission to walk the track exactly as detailed in this chapter; secondly, it is vital that every gate be securely fastened if the privilege is to remain in force; thirdly, since Mr Jones has allowed me to publish this map of his estate showing gates, fences, walls and tracks as in 1985, on which I have based the following guiding text.

Enter Gateway 1 beside Blue Gate. Follow the track across a gert; ford Broadaford Brook (here in its upper reach). Pass through Gateway 2; remain on the track (it is modern), though the old way lies below the fence, right, for a short distance before 'crossing' the fence to rejoin the track at Gateway 3. Beyond this the way diverges from the wall (right) and crosses an open field diagonally some 65 yards above the wall to reach Gateway 4. Walk to the gateway, beyond which is a well-defined stretch of track, part of the original way. Follow it to Gateway 5. Do not enter, but follow the fence upward (left) and onward (right) from its corner. This leads to Gateway 6 and another original stretch of the way. An abrupt bend further along the track marks the point where the old way continued straight ahead but has been obliterated by cultivation since World War II. Do not enter the field, but follow the track round the abrupt bend to Gateway 7, which is seen to be approached by a modern farm road ascending from the valley floor. Views from here over Lower Blackaton and Blackaton Manor to the central basin, and (right) to the distant tors above the West Dart valley, are very fine.

Pass through the gateway, then immediately through gateway 8 (right); walk along the west side of the fence. Below, right, is a small subsidiary valley backed by a conifer plantation; ahead, left, is the Hameldon Beech Hedge, descending from the Beacon to the valley below. More clearance heaps appear ahead, and the way (now a traceable path) descend to a miry patch and follows an old wall down to the subsidiary valley floor, where a feeder of Broadaford Brook is forded by the track. A wide hunting gate (9) opens upon the continuing way beside another old wall (outer boundary of the Hatchwell enclosures) right; from here a short ascent brings the track to its junction with the main Track 23 at the lanehead gate on Gore Hill near Hatchwell Corner.

TRACK 25

SHERWELL CHURCH PATH: BABENY (WEST TERMINUS) – WIDECOMBE-IN-THE-MOOR VIA SHERWELL, AND BRANCH TRACK FROM ROWDEN
$3\frac{1}{2}$ miles

Route according to tradition received by the author from the late Ruby French and her cousin Peter Hannaford, both of Higher Sherwell.

It should not be assumed that, as a result of the episcopal dispensation to the eastern Ancient Tenement dwellers of Babeny and Pizwell (see p. 223) that both used the main Church Way (Track 23) to Widecombe: certainly those of Pizwell did, but the Babeny people used a more direct route.

The first settlement beside the 'Shir' or 'Shere' (the 'bright') wellspring of water in the valley of Lake Weir Stream is of great antiquity; it was later named Middle Sherwell to distinguish it from the subsequent Higher and West Sherwell farms. A path from Middle Sherwell to Widecombe existed in pre-Conquest times and made an ideal route for the tenants of Babeny and West Sherwell; it was joined on Church Hill by a branch from Higher Sherwell and, much further east on the route, by one from Rowden. Babeny, lying just within the Forest, consisted formerly of three farms, as also did Sherwell, whose dwellers had certain rights and privileges by virtue of their hamlet's status as an ancient 'vill' of Widecombe; at Rowden were once two hamlets of medieval origin, so that church-bound traffic on the old Sherwell Path is likely to have been not inconsiderable.

Following the Track (eastward). See Map on p. 242.
It is emphasized that cars may be parked at neither Sherwell nor Babeny and that the walker must plan a route of approach from some

higher point on the Ollsbroom-Sherwell road, where verges are wide enough for parking, or from the car-park at Dartmeet (672733), from where Babeny can be reached by following the East Dart riverside path (left bank).

A right of way exists through the Babeny home enclosures that allows the walker to visit the impressive ruin of one of its former longhouses. Follow Track 25 from here. Cross the modern farm drive below and enter Rit Lane below Babeny Green. The lane, a gem of times long past, is a part of the ancient inter-tenement route; it runs southward to Babeny Steps and clapper bridge site (both on East Dart) to reach the tenements of Brimpts and Huccaby; a short way down the lane appears the medieval clapper bridge over Walla Brook*; there is now no public access from Rit Lane to the bridge, which must be approached from the further, east bank of the brook along a well-marked path from the Sherwell road; this crosses Lake Weir Stream on a small clapper. Next walk to Middle Sherwell. Track 25, leaving the farm court, crosses the modern road and enters upon the open moor beside the north enclosure wall of a house named 'Hornets' Castle', from where it lies in a gully. (This is overgrown, and walking is easier along the verge.) On the further, south side of the enclosure is the path from Higher Sherwell, which for so long was the home of smallholder cousins Peter Hannaford (d.1982) and Ruby French (d.1985); it starts literally at their front gate and reaches the moor beside the south enclosure wall of Hornets' Castle; it then makes diagonally over open ground towards another enclosure, right, but before reaching this bears slightly left to ascend Church Hill (Pl. 43). Pass through a gap in a transverse, prehistoric reave (made obviously to admit the path). The gully carrying the Babeny/Middle Sherwell branch now converges with the Higher Sherwell path, and the combined ways follow a reave ascending from the head of the gully. Make for the clear dip in the Church Hill crest ahead, and Cathanger Rock will appear, right; also in sight when the reave is reached is a pointed, set stone, an important waymark on this track; it stands 300 yards west of Cathanger Rock and is known locally as 'Little Boy'.†

---

* The bridge carrying the tarmac road from Sherwell to Babeny is modern and was built over the ancient ford beside the ruins of Babeny Mill. When Walla Brook was in full flow, pedestrians would have used the clapper bridge and Rit Lane.

† Now that the Sherwell settlements are no longer held by moormen, the growth of bracken and gorse on Church Hill is practically unchecked; the waymark is therefore invisible from below when the bracken is at full summer growth.

The small tor named Cathanger Rock (Pl. 44), first recorded and described by the author in *High Dartmoor*, is the northernmost of those on Corndon Down and derives its name from the former sett of the wild cat beneath the protective, over-*hanging* canopy of the tor. It is in an advanced state of ruin, its clitter on the west slope of the down being known as Charlie's Rocks. Beyond it is seen the northernmost of the several cairns from which Corndon Down is named – the 'cairn down'. Views are splendid, extending north-west beyond the central basin from North Hessary Tor to Hangingstone Hill, a skyline punctuated by the major heights of Great Mis Tor, the Beardown range, the Longaford-Whiten Tors ridge and Cut Hill. Southward rises the great hill-chain from Pupers to Eylesburrow.

On cresting Church Hill above Little Boy, the long line of the Hameldon Beech Hedge appears in the distance. The path is now stranded for a short way, but all strands cross the hill crest to a wide, muddy hollow (a pool in wet weather). When the strands unify beyond the hollow, the path points to the Honeybag-Chinkwell ridge beyond the vale of Widecombe. The reave ascending Church Hill from Sherwell meanwhile continues on a more northerly course, but the track bears away right, descends from the hollow wide and clear and runs parallel to a bracken-covered reave nearby, right; the Corndon Tors are now visible, also a large area of the Moor's eastern highlands, with the gentle heights of Rowden Ball and Dunstone Down in the intermediate distance, crossed by Track 24. Ahead is a large hawthorn tree, and near it a copious spring (I have never known it dry); the path here veers left and brings into view the gate of Pepper Lane beside the road to Cator Gate; becoming a shallow, sunken way, it reaches the road on the south side of a disused quarry, now a grassy hollow and a convenient car-park. The Cator road runs for some distance at the east foot of Corndon Down and passes the fine old longhouse of Corndonford: the date 1718 above the porch signifies the rebuilding of a house basically of a much earlier date.

Westward from Pepper Lane gate: cross road beside disused quarry; follow clear track to large thorn tree; bear right at spring; aim always for dip in hillcrest; at muddy hollow bear left; follow nearby reave on right. Note Cathanger Rock, left; pass Little Boy; roofs of Sherwell appear below (see Pl. 43).

At the time of writing, Pepper Lane gate is kept locked. The lane traverses the property of Mrs B.J. Lind of West Shallowford, who is kindly willing for readers to climb the gate and pass through the lane;

if a party of walkers intends to do this, Mrs Lind asks that the party leader telephone her beforehand on (Widecombe) 036-42-267.

Pepper Lane is deep and shady; it bends sharply right at the foot to pass the modernized longhouse of West Shallowford, then immediately left to join a tarmac road descending to the shallow ford on the West Webburn river, a cool, beautiful spot enriched by old grey walls, the ancient ford beside the bridge – a modern clapper of three openings with parapets – and a flourishing crop of crowfoot and water buttercups.

Climb the hill from the bridge (past East Shallowford Farm) for a third of a mile. Enter a wide, ungated opening between walls, left; the stony way here is French's Lane (Pl. 45). Follow it to the lanehead gateway on the south slope of Rowden Down 180 yards above. Slotted gateposts are common in this locality, and a stone cut and slotted *in situ* is seen on the ground above the lanehead gate, abandoned during working due to flaw. From the gate ignore the path directly ahead and follow the track bearing right – the wall diverges from it and reappears later; it is well defined and becomes sunken. The rounded summit of the down, above left, is known as Rowden Ball; a small rockpile appears just below the summit, and Wind Tor and Dunstone Down are visible ahead; thus the view embraces the greater length of Track 24, stretching from Church Hill on Corndon Down to Dunstone Down above Widecombe. When the wall reappears, right, follow it down to the Ponsworthy-Postbridge road. The track remains sunken and its continuation on Dunstone Down is clear, also its junction with the Rowden branch converging with it from enclosures (left) beyond the road. Cross the road; the precise line of the track has been obliterated by a small quarry working, but it then ascends the down eastward as a sunken way beside a reave.

Branch Path from Rowden

Look west of the old longhouse of Rowden, one of two former farming hamlets, North and South Rowden. The line of the Rowden branch of Track 25 is followed by the tarmac road passing the farm and reaching a junction with the Ponsworthy road at Rowden Cross. Crossing this, it enters a completely overgrown, impassable lane running between field hedges; its emergence onto the open moor is seen at the south-east corner of a cornditch wall, where an ancient opening has in later times been in-filled by crudely placed stones. Ascending Dunstone Down, the path gradually converges with the main track and, united with it, reaches the crest of Dunstone Down a few yards south of the (tarmac) Southcombe road. Just east of the crest a large set stone stands on the right (south) side of the road; this is known as Two Crosses – a reference not to stone crosses but to an adjacent intersection of two moorland ways here: the Hameldon ridge-crest path arrives from Langworthy Hill, left, intersects the Southcombe road beside the guide-stone and continues past Wind Tor (right) to Higher Dunstone; the same path also intersects Track 25 (prior to its joining the Southcombe road), hence two 'crosses', or crossways. The view from here of the eastern highland tors beyond the vale of Widecombe is remarkably fine.

Southcombe Gate stands at the head of the steep descent to the Widecombe-Buckland road. Pass Southcombe Farm and turn left at the T-junction below. Widecombe Church, backed by magnificent tors, appears ahead in all its architectural dignity; to reach it, church-bound travellers from Babeny, Sherwell and Rowden had barely a further half-mile to go. Due to easy gradients and walking terrain, Track 25 is an excellent and most enjoyable route to follow.

TRACK 26

CUMSTON-DOCKWELL: THE ANCIENT WAY FROM HEXWORTHY TO SOUTH BRENT $9\frac{1}{2}$ miles
BRANCH TO MOOR CROSS FOR TOTNES $14\frac{3}{4}$ miles

Route according to traditions received by William Crossing and by the author from the late Newman Caunter of Dunnabridge and the late John Spencer of Plymouth.

The manor of South Brent became the property of the newly founded abbey of Buckfast in 1018. A market in the town and a fair on Brent Down under Brent Hill were established by 1350 – the market perhaps earlier. Although no early documentation is known relating to the granting of the market, its long-standing existence is suggested by this excerpt from Gregory Wall's *Portrait of South Brent*: 'On 2nd August 1639, a lease was granted to Symon Shephard of South Brent for all fairs and markets within the town and borough of Brent and drift of Brente Moore (Petre leases DCR 196).' It would appear from the Toll Board, now affixed to the Toll House in Church Street, that by Victorian times Brent market was only bi-annual, for above the listed rates is the heading 'Markets Last Tuesday in February and August' and 'Fairs Last Tuesday in April and September' – showing the unusual custom of holding a bi-annual fair, Brent being a noted pony fair.

Among the medieval Ancient Tenements established beside the West Dart river in the Dartmoor central basin were Huccaby and Hexworthy, together mustering eight farms; the medieval Cumston Farm above the south side of the Double Dart Gorge, and Sherberton Ancient Tenement (three farms) proximate to Hexworthy, brought this total to no fewer than twelve farms. It is hardly surprising, therefore, that there were well-defined tracks connecting the farming

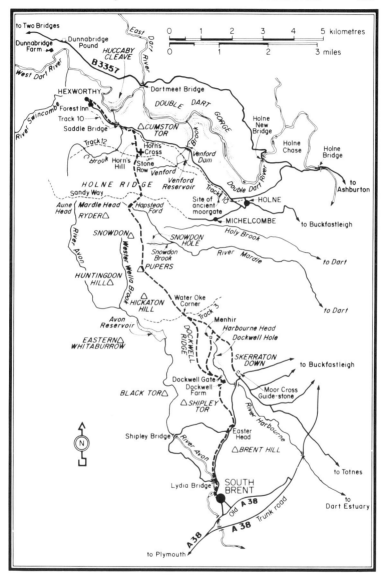

Track 26

hamlets with extensive peatbeds and with the market and fair of South Brent. The former ran via Skaur Ford and Sandy Ford (see also p. 149) on O Brook to Skaur Gut and Aune Head; the latter, the subject of this chapter, ran eastward from Hexworthy to cross O Brook at Saddle Bridge, where it was joined by the track from Huccaby via Week Ford; mounting Cumston Tor Hill, it was next joined by the track from Cumston Farm and, reaching the hill crest, it swung right to climb Horn's Hill intersect Track 12 at Horns†.

A South Devon town and port of great importance from Norman time onward was Totnes; moormen travelling from the central basin to the town would have followed Track 26 to Water Oke Corner (Dean Burn) and there branched left to Sandy Gate and Moor Cross. The guide-post at Moor Cross is described on p. 188, but the continuing route to Totnes passes from the Dartmoor border-country (where it is outlined here) into the Dart lowlands and therefore cannot be included.

Track 26, attaining to its greatest height on Pupers Hill at 1,500 feet, thereafter pursues a course of easy gradients as one of the best defined of all south Dartmoor's ancient tracks, a joy either to ride or to walk. Description begins here at Cumston Tor beside the Hexworthy-Holne road, with which connecting tracks from the central basin are mentioned above; Dockwell Gate terminates the moorland portion of the main South Brent route, while Sandy Gate and Moor Cross lie on the Totnes branch, the moorland portion of which is shown by *Greenwood* as far as Pupers Hill.

Following the Track (southward)
Cumston Tor (OS 'Combestone' – but old maps, including *Besley*, and local pronunciation give 'Cumston') should be visited on account of its numerous rock basins and for the view seen from it of Dartmeet and across the Double Dart Gorge. A convenient car-park exists beside the tor at 670718, reached by the Hexworthy-Holne road.

Track 26 is a well-defined, grassy way climbing Horn's Hill south of the road. The hill is a northward spur of Holne Moor, and its smooth terrain was adopted by prehistorc man as a site for hut circles, a large field system (bisected by the track), burial cairns and (east of the track) a stone row (see p. 147). From the plain of Horn's Hill, views northward over the central basin are panoramic, with the Warren House Inn conspicuous on the high shoulder of Watern Hill features of the valleys on either side include, left, the Venford reservoir

32 Track 20: Descent to South Zeal. The village lies spread below with South Tawton and its fine church tower beyond: Ramsley mine chimney-stack, right.

33 Track 21 terminal: Rattlebrook tin mine. Beyond the relics rises Green Tor.

34 Track 22: Powder Mills clapper bridge – Cherry Brook. A nineteenth-century replacement of an earlier bridge linking the track on either bank. On the right hillside is a wheel-house of the old gunpowder factory.

35 Track 22: Travellers' Ford – Cowsic. The Lych Way makes a diagonal ascent as a sunken track from the hillside opposite (centre) to the camera point.

36 Track 20 (foreground) intersects the Graveyard, a ruined triple stone row of the early Bronze Age with grave at the upper end.

37   Track 21: Tavy crossing A – Hill Bridge. The Lych Way descends
to the bridge from the hillside extreme right. Salmon ladder in the
foreground.

38   Track 22: Tavy crossing B – walkers approaching Corpse Lane
pass along a medieval sunken way (one hedge removed) towards
Coffin Wood.

39–40 Track 22: Tavy crossing C – near Standon Steps. Gateway 4 (paved) is in a breached medieval wall; 5 appears below (right) near wooden rail of bridge. Willsworthy Lane is seen ascending the west bank. *Inset*: Medieval chapel window, Higher Willsworthy.

41 Track 23: Runnage clapper bridge – Walla Brook (East Dart). Note the raised way and recessed wall. Buildings (near left) are of Ancient Tenement of Runnage.

42   Track 23: Pizwell. These granite homesteads, recorded in 1260, form the west terminal of the main Church Way. The walker leaves Pizwell Green to approach Pizwell Steps on Walla Brook (East Dart).

43   Track 25: Church Hill. The guide-stone 'Little Boy' has been passed and the roofs of Sherwell, ancient vill of Widecombe, appear below.

44 Track 25: Cathanger Rock. The overhang or 'hanger' of the main pile was a traditional sett of the Dartmoor wildcat.

45 Track 25: French's Lane. Note the great antiquity of the hedges.

46 Track 26, Totnes branch: Moor Cross guide-stone. The track approaches from the gate and descends past the 'T' (for Totnes).

47 Track 26: Upper Mardle Valley. The Cumston track descends from Holne Ridge (right) to Hapstead Ford, where its south bank approach is visible.

48 Track 27: Headland Warren House. Geese on the original track. This keeps to the river's left bank to reach Headland Bridge, where it intersects Track 28 (*below*).

49 Track 28: Looking east from Challacombe Down. The track descends to Headland Bridge and intersects Track 27. Beyond the pass road it runs below Hookner Tor to Grimspound (extreme right) and Grims Lake Head to reach Natsworthy Hill. The light powdering of snow helps delineate the track.

(of Paignton Urban District Council) and, right, the relics of Hexworthy Tin Mine in the O Brook valley and several leat channels following the hill contours; ahead, before a further climb to Holne Ridge, the way crosses the plain and intersects Tracks 12 at Horn's†. PUDC bond-stones appear in the locality, and the ascending track passes close beside one as it curves left to ease the gradient and rounds the bowl-like hollow of Brockley Bottom; here, as often on the Moor, the track has acted as a barrier to the spread of heather where it verges a large tract of this tough, wiry plant. Beyond a small scattering of rocks a branch track mounts the steep of the hill, right; ignore this and continue the oblique ascent (left), this time through the midst of a large heather patch; Brockley Bottom and the reservoir are now far below. The track is stranded for a short way, but becomes clear in swinging left to cross a wide earth 'bridge' over a gert between two fallen trees. This is the deep Ringleshutes Gert, below which are the remains of the nineteenth-century Ringleshutes Mine. A shallow gert, right, continues the line of the deeper, beyond which the track swings right to pass over a dip in the hillcrest between two PUDC stones 40 yards apart on the Venford-Mardle watershed.

Views from this elevated ridge are very fine; the majestic, rolling hills of Mardle country rise ahead, Ryder (right) their peer. Undulating, right to left from Ryder, are Snowdon, Pupers – with its three rockpiles – and Wallaford Down. The Moor's eastern highlands form an impressive range away to the left, and the line of the track southward over Mardle country is seen crossing the east flank of Snowdon; the Teign estuary and Teignmouth also are visible. The track now veers to the left to descend into the Mardle valley in line with the east end of Wallaford Down. It shortly intersects the Sandy Way, then bears right (towards Middle Pupers) and fords a streamlet in a shallow gert near a group of thorn trees (left), before passing through a sunken way to approach Hapstead Ford on Mardle (Pl. 47). A useful visual guide to the ford is the stony track approaching it on the further bank of the river.

The Mardle valley, although relatively near civilization, seems somehow remote; gentle and sunny of aspect, it is watered by the sparkling little river that once was the head of Holy Brook, until it (Mardle) 'cut back' and beheaded the brook. Hapstead Ford lies admidst tin-streaming works; cross; follow the stony right-bank track which (noticed above) curves gradually to regain the overall southerly direction of the track. The little valley of Holy Brook now appears below, and the track, stranded, passes a domed feather-bed mire containing a voluminous spring and runs towards a scattered group of thorn trees ahead; above, right, is the great bulk of Snowdon and below, left, the deep Mardle and Holy Brook valleys, peninsulated by the lowly Scorriton Down and backed by pleasant views over the south-east border-country. The course of Holy Brook can be followed visually below Holne village and the wooded mount of the Iron Age Hembury Fort, and points towards Buckfast Abbey's tower and Buckfastleigh's hilltop spire.

The track passes above the main group of thorn trees and approaches a small transverse gully; beyond this, where it remains stranded, is the deep indentation of Snowdon Hole. The rocks and incision of Gibby's Beam are above, and the headmire of Snowdon Brook is on the plain below; the strip of good ground between them narrowly confines the track and reliably pinpoints the route. The deep working of Gibby's Beam was a part of Huntingdon Mine in the Wester Wella Brook valley, over a century ago. Not far ahead, a re-entrant divides Snowdon from Pupers Hill; a streamlet from a small mire courses through it and is crossed by Track 26 at a stony fording place. The track bears right to ascend Pupers and, for the last time on its southward course, is again stranded. To dispel doubts about direction, ascend to the rounded hill crest ahead; in a short way, a conical rockpile will appear, right of the rounded crest: make directly for it – it is Middle Pupers, and the rounded crest first seen on the ascent is Inner Pupers. From the rocks notice the small pile on the west spur of Pupers Hill – Outer Pupers, and the high Whitaburrow ridge in the south-west climbed by Track 3 on the verge of Pipers Beam. Also visible are Beacon Rocks, the Aune (Avon) valley, Shipley Tor and Dockwell Ridge. In the south is a feature most helpful to the walker in open country, a reave followed by the track; it can be seen at a distance approaching the few wind-blown trees struggling to survive at Water Oke Corner, where it terminates and leaves the main track to disappear over the horizon, whilst the Moor Cross branch track runs for some way parallel to the outer wall of the Water Oke enclosure. Follow the reave south from Middle Pupers, for some distance on the right of the track; 500 yards beyond Pupers, cross obliquely the green track between Lyd (OS 'Lud') Gate and Huntingdon Warren; a mile further, at the southern extremity of a plain (the reave is now left of the track) ford the (flowing) Hayford leat at sunken approaches. A gentle ascent now begins of the east flank of

Grippers Hill, and the Water Oke trees are near ahead. The view of the eastern highlands from here, topped by Rippen Tor, is impressive. About 100 yards west of the Corner (i.e. of the enclosure wall, left) the way intersects Track 3 (see p. 72) and makes a steady ascent of Grippers Hill. Branching from it before the Corner is the track crossing Water Oke Plain to Sandy Gate and Moor Cross, which is detailed on p. 261.

From the east shoulder of Grippers Hill the track appears wide and clear in crossing the foot of Parnell's Hill above Smallbrook Head, where it dips into a slight hollow, and is seen in each direction as a wide, grassy way. South of the hollow it brings into view the knobs of Black Tor (Avon), overlooked by Beacon Rocks and Dockwell Ridge; this lengthy ridge runs southward beyond a visible standing stone on Smallbrook Plains (right) – one of a line of unmarked bond-stones between Brent and Dean Moors. Descending southward from Smallbrook Plains, the track passes another bond-stone in the series and gives a pleasant view of Harbourne Head (left), a green basin where the headmire is restricted to the banks of the stream and where a track crosses to link the two branches of Track 26. The wooded reach of the valley in the enclosed lands downstream is Dockwell Hole, now inaccessible to the public.

Dockwell Ridge now looms above the track, which crosses a small gert; eastward, the Moor Cross branch is seen following a wall to Sandy Gate. The main track reaches another, larger gert that drops (left) to the valley floor. Rounding the head, the way bears right to ascend the south-east foot of Dockwell Ridge; from here are seen the large (southern) cairn on Parnell's Hill and, below it, the Harbourne Head menhir known as the Longstone: Skerraton Down rises beyond; southward lies the border-country dominated by the near eminence of Brent Hill.

The track descends from Dockwell Ridge to approach the wide Dockwell Stroll formed by the converging cornditch walls of Yalland Warren (right – now a farm) and, left, Dockwell. Enter the stroll and pass through Dockwell Gate, near which a millstone has been incorporated in the wall (left). In Dockwell Bottom the way intersects the original route of Track 16 (route B); here the ancient stroll turns abruptly left and is densely overgrown as it leads to the fine old longhouse of Dockwell. Pass the stroll and follow the well-defined track converging with an enclosure wall ahead. At the enclosure corner is a gate bearing a no-access notice; from here onward to a gate below the Shipley-Buckfastleigh road the track was formerly an enclosed lane, and it is so shown by *Spencer*; the west hedge of the lane, however, has been removed and the enlarged field ploughed, but signs remain near the gate to show where the old west hedge was demolished. Follow the remaining east hedge, left to the gate. The hill summit crossed by the Shipley road here is known as Easter Head, and from the gate, the track verges a small roadside green and reaches the road 280 yards south-west of Gingaford Cross, where it branches left to pass the Lutton farming settlements and Splatton and enter South Brent town centre through Church Street.

South Brent is a pleasant, miniature town, compact and practically unspoilt. Tradition brings St Petrock to South Brent, a zealous Welsh preacher of the Christian Gospel in the sixth-century West Country, where numerous churches are dedicated to him in Devon and Cornwall. Tradition even takes him to Buckfast, which abbey anciently held the manor and church of South Brent – the latter, with its fine Norman tower and font, bearing his dedication. Gregory Wall writes in *Portrait of South Brent*: 'Brent Church possibly existed as a small chapel at about the time Petrock roamed the area. As it was a wooden structure nothing would remain ... Once Christianity had become established in the area under the influence of Buckfast Abbey, a Saxon cruciform church was built ...' The researches of Dom John Stéphan of Buckfast revealed the former presence of a chapel dedicated to St Michael on the summit of Brent Hill; a charter of 1374 (Register of Bishop Brantyngham of Exeter) gives licence for the celebration of Mass in the chapel by the abbot and monks of Buckfast.

And so the medieval moorman from Hexworthy, Cumston or Huccaby could drive his beasts to market, or the fair, along the Dockwell track and up to Brenthill Down; if of a sober disposition, he could also attend Mass in St Michael's Chapel before descending to the town for an evening of conviviality. A degree of over-conviviality contributed to the tragic end of a Hexworthy moorman attending Brent Fair, whose glazed eyes could not detect the many defects of the horse he had been persuaded by a dishonest dealer to buy, giving his own in part-exchange. Sobriety returned during his homeward ride over the breezy, high hills, and he was overcome by fear of his wife's reaction to the disastrous transaction. Leaving the old track, he branched right to reach the deep, sinister mine-working and pool in the Aller valley; here he removed the horse's halter and hanged himself therewith from a tree, fearing eternal disfavour less than an angry wife. Hence, Hangman's Hollow below the Holne road at 675715.

Branch Track via Moor Cross to Totens

This track enters the border-country at Sandy Gate (Skerraton Down) and is described now only as far as Moor Cross at the foot of Sandy Lane on the Shipley-Buckfastleigh road. Thereafter the route lay through original packhorse lanes via Moorshead Cross, Zempson Cross, Dean Cross and Rattery to Totnes town. *Besley*, although giving no details of the border-country route, shows the moorland portion as an almost straight line northward from Moor Cross, past Watern Oke to Pupers, from where its northern continuation is unmapped.

The branch leaves the main track south of the ford on the Hayford leat (p. 258) and gradually converges with the Water Oke enclosure wall; intersecting Track 3, it becomes slightly sunken in crossing a shallow gully ascending from the south corner of the enclosure, and runs due south-west at about 40 yards from the wall. Half a mile beyond the south corner of the large Lambs Down newtake (containing the little Water Oke enclosure), the track meets another coming over Lambs Down (left) from Cross Furzes and making for Skerraton Down Gate at the head of the down. Before reaching the junction, fork right into a wide, green branch pointing towards the transverse wall of Skerraton Newtake; the gate stands at the higher opening in the wall, but the green way – that is, the Moor Cross branch – makes for the lower corner and continues as a stony road to Sandy Gate.

A feature of some interest close by should be visited. Take another green way forking right from the track and descending towards the Harbourne Head basin. Ahead is the tip of the Longstone, a fine Bronze Age menhir almost 9 feet in height and bearing on one side the incised arrow of the early OS surveyors. The view from the menhir, right to left, is of Three Burrows, Wacka Tor, Brent Fore Hill, Dockwell Ridge, Beacon Rocks and, beyond the bulky outline of Brent Hill, a huge stretch of the South Hams between the visible Erme and Avon estuaries. Dockwell Farm and the wooded Dockwell Hole are below, showing the course of the little Harbourne; the early sixteenth-century traveller Leland came here and wrote, 'Harbertoun Water cometh out of a well-spring.' The path now followed from the Moor Cross branch track to the menhir crosses the head-basin and joins the main Track 26 at the south-east foot of Dockwell Ridge.

The visitor to Harbourne Head on a day of sunshine and azure skies will appreciate the beautiful and predominantly sunny aspect of South Devon. Undulating towards the blue band of the English Channel are the teeming little hills of the South Hams and, its indentation traceable on the landscape, the course of the River Harbourne reaching out to the Dart estuary under the distant, sentinel height of Dittisham's Fire Beacon Hill – the view from which point extends northward far over Dartmoor to Cut Hill and is detailed in *Historic Dart*.

To rejoin the Moor Cross track, walk 400 yards slightly east of south to the wall corner below. The track follows the wall to Sandy Gate and enters Sandy Lane; this very rough road descends for half a mile to a lower gate, 50 yards beyond which is the Moor Cross road junction (Pl. 46); see also p. 188.

TRACK 27

ANCIENT ROAD FROM BLACKATON AND CHALLACOMBE MEDIEVAL VILLAGES TO LIAPA MOORGATE (FOR ONWARD JOURNEYING TO CHAGFORD AND MORETONHAMPSTEAD) $3\frac{1}{2}$ miles

Route according to tradition received by the author from moormen William White of Barramoor and Jack Irish of Grendon.

East of the Warren House Inn on the B3212 highway, a branch road arrives at Challacombe Cross from Widecombe; a scenic pass through the hills, it was cut as recently as 1874 by landowner Frederick Firth and follows the upper West Webburn valley. $3\frac{1}{4}$ miles south of the junction, the branch road is joined at Lower Blackaton Cross by a road from Postbridge via Runnage and Grendon which, east of Grendon Top Gate is based on Track 23. Below this portion of the ancient way at Blackaton Bridge flows Broadaford Brook, beside which the village of Blakedon Pipard existed 750 years ago, its decay doubtless caused by the terrible scourge of the Black Death in 1348. The village included a manor house with chapel where, in 1299, lived Hugo and Muriel de Bollay, and about a dozen longhouses and cots; later, in the post-plague era, other tenements, or smallholdings, sprang into being. The next neighbouring village was Challacombe in the West Webburn valley, where another dozen or so farmers toiled on the stony land and grazed their flocks on Challacombe Down. Not only was intercourse between the two farming communities necessary, but access to their nearest market town, Moretonhampstead, would have been essential to their livelihood. In retracing the road of these moormen of the Middle Ages from villages to market, I have been great assisted by a still living tradition delineating the route from Challacombe and Headland to Moor Gate. The lower, shorter portion

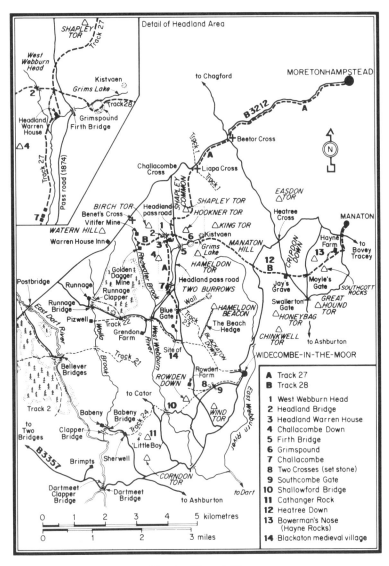

Tracks 27 and 28

between the two villages is detailed here according to my interpretation of relics and indications in the field which I believe indicates a logical inter-village route.

TDA 95 of 1963 and 40 of 1908 may be consulted by readers seeking further information on Blakedon, whilst an historical account of Challacombe appears in *High Dartmoor*.

The 1874 road from Lower Blackaton Cross to Challacombe Cross is here referred to as 'the pass-road'.

Following the Track (northward)

If using a car between Blackaton and Challacombe, park it on the ample roadside space near the Challacombe entrance track. If driving to Challacombe, park on the ample roadside space near the Challacombe entrance road at 696796.

Blakedon Pipard village. From Blackaton Cross drive for a third of a mile along the pass-road. Park. Enter a gate (left) and follow a short track between stones set kerb-fashion. Within a few yards it passes between two longhouses; in each ruin the position of the central passage can be seen, and the southern house (left) has two square stones remaining of the porch foundation, leading into the central passage. Return to the road; a large modern barn standing on the east (higher) side has regrettably been built on the site of the de Bollays' manor house and chapel. Drive to a minor crest at the head of the Broadaford Brook valley; a transverse wall – its higher portion is the Hameldon Beech Hedge – reaches the road at Blue Gate, where now only gateposts remain, and an old way is seen approaching the gate from the brook's right bank (left of the road) – all clear evidence that this portion of the pass-road follows a very ancient way. 55 yards south of Blue Gate, inside an enclosure (left), is a ruin I have identified in *High Dartmoor* as one of the *Blakedon* tenements. (The only remaining working tenement today is Lower Blackadon Farm above the right bank of Broadaford Brook.) An access gate to the enclosure is nearby.

North from Blue Gate the old way becomes a ditch between the wall (left) and the road-verge, and access from it to enclosures is in one place marked by a pair of slotted gateposts; the pass-road has here been built above the level of the ancient track. Near Challacombe, a modern slip-road, locally known as 'Straight Mile', was made by Firth to connect the pass-road with Grendon Bridge; at the junction occurred a fork in the ancient way. The left branch curved towards the valley floor, its line shown today by the curving wall corner (left); now intersected by Straight Mile, it entered the Challacombe enclosure where a choked, sunken way is visible; running to a ford on the river, it climbed as a lane to the south end of Challacombe village but today is *strictly a no-access route*. The right branch of the fork remained on slightly higher ground until bending to approach Challacombe Bridge on the West Webburn river; from the bridge it reached the main village street (joined further south by the lane mentioned above). A car should not be driven into the Challacombe entrance track.

Challacombe village. The manor of Challacombe is recorded in Domesday Book (1088) and the manor mill of 'Churlecombe' in 1303, its site being on West Webburn's left bank above the bridge, where in 1774 there still existed a gristmill. Walk across the bridge and turn left to see the ruin of old Challacombe, the longhouse of the community's principal farm in medieval times; it was abandoned when the twentieth-century farmhouse was built nearby. Another house nearer the bridge served the Challacombe miners as a cider-house. Turn about; walk northward along the track past Challacombe Cottages – built originally for miners – through a large grass enclosure in Challacombe Bottom (on the river's right bank) and enter upon the open moor at the east foot of Challacombe Down. Mining pits appear everywhere, and on the hillside ahead is the large gert known as Scutley Gully. Beyond this a track branches right to cross the river on a small girder bridge and reach the scant remains of Challacombe Mine, including a wheel-pit built for a 20-feet waterwheel.

Return to the main track under the steep of the down, where the south boundary wall of Headland Warren runs straight up the hillside. It is, or was, a rabbit-proof wall and contains two integral vermin traps, the lower only 200 yards above the track. Some 350 yards ahead, Track 27 crosses the river on a clapper bridge of seven imposts, which was built in mining days as a convenient crossing for the workmen; alongside is the ancient ford which on the upper reach of a small river would have been quite adequate to the needs of travellers – though it is possible that a small clapper footbridge preceded the miners' bridge. Ruined buildings, pits, mounds and tracks soon proliferate, for the workings of Headland Mine – a subsidiary venture of East Birch Tor Mine (as were those of Challacombe Mine) – are confusingly mixed with the relics of the former rabbit-warrening establishment there. The mound of

Challacombe Down, Hameldon's ridge and Hookner's rockpiles now overshadow the ruggedly beautiful valley; the huge gerts of Headland Mine cleave both valley-sides, one under Hookner Tor being the large, mire-filled gert noticed on p. 274.

The track now enters the enclosures of Headland Warren; it passes the warren carrion pool (left) supplied by the river, runs between the front door of the house (Pl. 48) and the warren garden and meets Track 28 at Headland Bridge. *No right of way exists on this portion of the old road, and the walker must follow the signposted footpath.* This leads past the circular ruin of an ash-house and immediately behind the old kennel court of the warren, its single dog-kennel cave being visible.

Continue to Headland Bridge (a single-opening clapper), where Track 28 crosses the infant river and is clearly indented on each valley-side. Track 27 continues ahead (north-east) through a sunken way choked by heather, disused since the building of the pass-road. Pass the north-east side of a small enclosure (the 'miners' garden') and notice the way heading towards a dip in the hill crest – the 'Head-land' – beyond. Continuing sunken and, on nearing the crest, grassy and free from heather, it is an altogether picturesque old way, especially when viewed southward as it drops between the huge hills into the deep Webburn valley, where its continuing line under Challacombe Down is plainly seen.

Enter the pass-road and walk for 150 yards uphill to a well-defined path seen descending (left) from Bush Down and ascending, right of the road, to Shapley Common. Turn right into this – it is the original Track 27; although now only a narrow path due to more than a century of virtual disuse, it is clear and direct. In climbing, it gradually diverges from the wall (right) dividing Hookner Down from Shapley Common. A backward glance brings a really fine view of the boldly shaped hills above West Webburn.

The rockpiles of Shapley Tor (left) and Hookner Tor (right) are now seen in detail, with the bold spur of King's Barrow and the long Hameldon ridge beyond Hookner. The way approaches a concave 'bay' in the outer wall of Coombe Newtake (ahead) and joins a broad, transverse grass track from which a branch enters Coombe Newtake and descends to East Vitifer Mine and West Coombe hamlet. Turn left. At the north end of the wall-bay, take a path branching left from the grassy track, to Shapley Tor. Although not in itself of unusual interest and consisting only of a scattering of low rockpiles mostly on the north slope of the tor, it affords very fine views, especially over north-east Dartmoor; from it, Track 27 is clearly seen continuing northward.

Rejoin the main track beyond the tor; pass two tinners' gerts and a slab tilted against a large bedrock; here turn right towards a gate in Coombe Newtake, then left before reaching it. Beyond the deep bowl of Coombe Head, right, lies the Barramoor valley, a scene finely backed by Easdon Tor. Track 1 is seen in the valley as a farm drive running from Liapa (now called 'Moorgate') Farm to the B3212 road, beyond which its line is in places visible crossing the Lettaford fields.

Continue beside the wall (of Liapa Newtake) down to a narrow opening between it and a small enclosure: this is an ancient stock-pound, sited at the junction of Tracks 27 and 8 (Moretonhampstead branch) for handling animals at the foot of the high moor (700833). The short lane so formed is in direct alignment with the B3212 road east of its right-angle bend – the original Moreton branch of Track 8 – and the two ancient ways unite for 150 yards to reach the site of Moor Gate (cattle-grid) where a toll house named Byhead Turnpike once operated. At the gate, and old lane – it can be seen from Track 27 when descending to the stock-pound – branches right to North Bovey, but it is now impassable.

From Moor Gate the line of the medieval road from the mountain villages of Blakedon and Churlecombe to Moretonhampstead market coincides, together with the Track 8 branch, with the modern highway.

TRACK 28

MINERS' PATH: MANATON – WEST WEBBURN TIN
MINES   5 miles

NOTE: Redwater Brook rises below Benet's† to become the first tributary of the West Webburn river; the phrase 'West Webburn Tin Mines' includes the mines in both valleys but not those north of the B3212 in the Bovey valley.

The history of tin-mining in the upper valleys of Redwater Brook and the West Webburn river is a long one. Some of the men lived comparatively near at Challacombe and Postbridge, or at Cape Horn near Vitifer Mine; others, with further to walk from border towns and villages such as Chagford, North Bovey and Manaton – even Moretonhampstead, would lodge during their working week in the mine 'barracks'. The principal mines were the Birch Tor & Vitifer and the Golden Dagger, both in the Redwater valley and at work until well into the present century; Headland and Challacombe Mines in the main West Webburn valley worked on a smaller scale and for a shorter period, both closing down before the turn of the century.

Neighbouring mines, also short-lived, were the West and East Vitifer and the Bush Down; a path branches north-west from Track 28 at Grimspound, crosses the Headland pass-road and runs over Bush Down to the sites of the two last.

Miners walking from Moretonhampstead to the Redwater valley would follow the Postbridge road (the B3212) as far as Moor Gate, where they would join Track 27. The path from Manaton to the Redwater valley is treated here as the main track, chiefly because of its scenic attributes and variety.

It would be impossible to say when the men of Manaton first began to work tin in the Bovey, Redwater and West Webburn valleys, but it is likely to have been not later than the thirteenth or fourteenth century. A bell in the parish church of St Winifred in Manaton was dedicated in *c.*1440 to St George, patron saint of England and of Manaton's Guild of tinners. Many tinners would, of course, have worked much nearer to their village, but the richer deposits of ore in West Webburn country are likely to have drawn men from the border villages long before the Industrial Age mechanization of the mines. William Crossing (*Guide*) writes in 'Tracks near Challacombe' (his T47) that, 'In this locality are several ... paths, mostly formed by the miners', and that one 'led from the enclosed lands in Manaton parish to Headland and Vitifer. It ran through Grim's Pound, the wall of which was broken down in two places.'

Finally, it can be said that this delightful walk through Dartmoor's eastern highlands is as attractive as any in the entire region.

Following the Track (westward). See map on p.264.
Park near Manaton Green (749812), where the fine church of St Winifred in the centre of this ancient borderland village makes a good starting point for the walk. Much of the fabric dates from the early fifteenth century; the rood screen, built *c.*1509, is of startling beauty and contains panel paintings of twenty-nine saints, of whom all but two have been identified. Alongside the church stands, in true Devon fashion, the fine old church house of 1597, now a private residence named 'Church Cottage'.

For the West Webburn miner leaving Manaton church after Sunday service, a visual reminder of his challenging Monday morning walk was inescapable, even from within the church porch. Sit on the granite bench here and look out to the hills, where the miners' track is seen mounting the ridge between Southcott and Hayne Rocks and disappearing towards distant Hameldon.

Walk south from the green, cross the Heatree-Bovey Tracey road and notice some slotted gateposts; at a lane junction named Sandy Meadow, turn right and descend to Hayne, a former moorland farm. The farm court was served by a leat from Hayne Brook falling to a dipping well and passing over granite steps into an escape channel. These features, seen from outside the entrance gate, are beside a grass track entering a copse on the left of the house. This was the original route of Track 28; crossing the Hayne leat on a clapper cart bridge and passing through a rockfield, it now meets with the public path (which must be followed by the walker) in the copse beyond the private grounds of the house. Very little of the original route will be missed, its junction with the public path occurring near a gate at the further edge of the copse. The track swings right here and is clearly defined as it ascends steeply to the hill-crest dip between Hayne Rocks (right) and Southcott Rocks (left).

Each rockpile is widespread and should be visited, Southcott being the higher. At Hayne Rocks comes a surprise in the form of an extraordinary rock pillar on the tor's north slope, detached from the main pile. This is Bowerman's Nose, a name perhaps attributable to the proboscis of a former moorman of the locality named John Bowerman, who was buried at North Bovey in 1663. More fanciful origins, such as are commonly attached to natural phenomena, may be discounted. Noel Carrington (1777-1830), poet of Dartmoor, wrote:

> ... High it towers
> Above the hill's bold prow, and, seen, from afar,
> Assumes the human form; a granite god!
> ... The hamlets near
> Have legends rude connected with the spot ...

There are fine views from both Hayne and Southcott Rocks over Dartmoor's eastern border-country, and an impressive torscape breaks upon the vision from the west side of the ridge. Left, above the great hollow of Houndtor Combe, are the tors of Rippen, Grea and Great Hound, whilst ahead are Holwell Rocks, Chinkwell and Honeybag Tors. The track, now clearly defined, traces a slight zigzag and bears left towards Moyle's Gate on the North Bovey-Ashburton road; crossing the road, it follows the newtake wall (left) in climbing Cripdon Down. (Ignore the DNPA yellow spot route on the south side of the wall as indirect and irrelevant to Track 28.) From Cripdon Down notice the jaggedly serrated crest of Honeybag Tor nearby (left). Descend to the Chagford-Ashburton road; cross; beside the junction is Jay's Grave, where a mound (remarkably, always flower-bedecked) indicates the resting place – according to ancient custom in unhallowed ground at a crossways – of a suicide named Kitty Jay in the early years of the nineteenth century.

Enter the gate beside the grave and follow the lane, from where the true proportions of the vale of Widecombe will be apparent. Old House Hill and Hameldon's far-flung ridge rise ahead beyond Heatree

Down, and a spring or autumn walk through the lane, which verges a copse, can be a delight. At the west end of the copse is a gatepost drilled (but not perforated) to take a timber bar, the opposite post having only small drilled holes and broken irons. Heatree Down now rises at the right hand, and as the path crosses the foot of the down, a romantically beautiful view opens of the vale of Widecombe, with the impressive 120-foot tower of the 'Cathedral of the Moor' piercing the great cleft in the land. The path then drops to the gate beside the Chagford-Widecombe road, crosses it and enters Natsworthy Gate opposite. Next is the approach to the wide, open spaces of the Hameldon massif.

On the left of the gate, and beside a sandpit once in regular use, is the 'Pit' Stone, a bond-stone of the Natsworthy manor estate, which was acquired by the Duke of Somerset (the stone is marked 'PIT' and 'DS') in the mid-nineteenth century. The green way forward intersects Track 1 and fords the (flowing) Heatree leat before following the crumbling newtake wall bordering the plantations, right. The crags of Auswell Rocks and Honeybag Tor rise on the left, backed by the twin bosses of Hey Tor, while Hameldon dominates the scene ahead. Follow the green way ascending Manaton Hill and, on leaving the wall-corner, the tip of a standing stone will appear above the shoulder of the hill. Beyond a fork in the track (take the right branch) the wall forms a concave 'bay'. The mass of Old House Hill (left) thrusts a green spur into the vale, while the circular outline of the prehistoric Berry Pound and the deep incision of the upper East Webburn in Hollake are near. Approaching the crest, the walker can look (left) at the shining river on Natsworthy Plain, from where it enters the vale. Tors too numerous to mention appear in the south-east while Easdon Tor (right) is backed by the north-east border-country.

Take a path branching left to the standing stone: this commemorates a tragic event of 1941, in which five British airmen lost their lives when their plane crashed into a mist-enshrouded Manaton Hill. The date and airmen's initials are engraved upon the massive, 6-foot-high stone which was erected by Mr Alec Kitson of Heatree House and Mr Charlie Hannaford of Natsworthy. Next, ignoring a wide, green way climbing directly from the stone, follow a narrow green path to rejoin Track 28. On cresting the hill, notice that the tors seen previously in the east now sink low; the prominent cairn of King's Burrow is on the right, and numerous tall wooden posts standing on the smooth, heathery hilltop plain are remnants of those erected during World War II to prevent enemy aircraft landing.

Cross the plain and begin the gentle westward descent from the East-West Webburn watershed, where the track touches the 1,600-foot contour. The high line of Shapley Common runs northward from Hookner Tor (ahead), then the deep Headland trough between Hookner and Birch Tors comes in view. Also seen (right) is a standing stone not far from King's Burrow – one of a line of bond-stones marking the boundary between North Bovey and Manaton parishes. Rocks on the high land above the left side of the track are those of the small but elevated Hameldon Tor. Notice, beyond the headmire of Grims Lake (right), a group of set stones protruding above the heather. These constitute the remains of Hookner Down kistvaen and may be reached by crossing the shallow valley (of Grims Lake). Do not cross until directly opposite the kistvaen, as Grims Lake Mire is inconveniently wet above that point; the kistvaen has a remaining cover of two slabs and a retaining circle some 19 feet in diameter.

Recross Grims Lake and rejoin the track. The Monday morning miner would have been cheered along his way on sighting the Warren House Inn, directly ahead on Watern Hill – as well as by the thought of the Birch Tor Inn in the valley below. This name was borne by Headland Warren House during the middle years of the nineteenth century, when the enterprising warrener Jan Roberts offered cider, ale and rabbit pie to the miners. His signboard read:

> Jan Roberts lives here,
> Sells cider and beer,
> Your hearts for to cheer;
> And if you want meat
> To make up a treat
> Here be rabbits to eat.

As the path descends, the rock-strewn north slope of Hameldon Tor is near (left) and the marshy hollow of West Webburn Head below, right. Also visible, to the right of the huge mining gerts (blasted out in the mid-1800s by gunpowder and, later, dynamite), is the continuing track, ascending from Headland Bridge and now marked by telegraph poles. Challacombe Down appears as a huge, hump-backed mound with a wall ascending to its crest; on its north slope is visible, on a clear day, the prehistoric triple stone row. Also now coming into view is the enclosure wall of prehistoric Grimspound.

This village of the early Bronze Age attracts many thousands of visitors each year. The pound encloses a part of the course of Grims Lake (for the convenience of the villagers), the remains of twenty-four stone huts, some with protective entrance passages (once roofed), and a few animal pens. Much of its attraction lies in its situation between two lofty tors and the outline and contours of the surrounding land. The restored hut, on the south side of the path bisecting the pound, was probably that of the village chieftain; not far from it is the massive, paved gateway, once closed with huge timbers and paved to prevent a quagmire resulting from the tramping hooves of animals driven in and out of the pound at the foot of Hameldon's steep slope. Although overshadowed by the big tors, the village lies high enough to provide a glimpse of the central basin beyond the Bush-Challacombe Downs col and of Track 28 continuing across the flank of Hookner Tor (Pl. 49).

The wide gaps in the pound wall are the consequence, over the ages, of the passage of pedestrian miners and mounted moormen. From the lower gap, branch right, cross Grims Lake and follow the path across Hookner's flank. (The left path running beside Grims Lake descends to a small parking space on the Headland pass-road above Headland Warren.) Notice the rocks of Birch Tor ahead and, below, the thatched roof of Headland Warren House, now a farm, an enclosed area of garden and a huge, mire-filled gert of Headland Mine. Cross the pass-road (see p. 265) and follow the path descending to the valley floor. Near Headland (clapper) Bridge, it is intersected by Track 27, crosses the bridge over the infant West Webburn and ascends the hill opposite beside the upper wall of the large warren home-meadow, the entire enclosing wall of which was of impressive, rabbit-proof construction: the labour involved in the masonry is appreciable. In a tinners' gully near the wall are the cover- and side-stones of a granite vermin-trap, discovered by the author in 1976.

Ascend the track to the col; a branch path leads (left) to the Challacombe stone row; this is uncommon in consisting of *three* parallel alignments, running for 528 feet. The upper end is terminated by a large blocking stone, and there are signs of an intermediate grave, also of one formerly at the north end of the row which was destroyed during excavation of the huge gerts here.

Rejoin the main track descending to the Redwater valley; near it (left) is the deepest of the gerts, Chaw Gully, a 50-foot-deep incision in this mineral-rich land. At a slight bend, a branch path runs (left) down the valley to Golden Dagger Mine, where a large wheelpit, ruined buildings, buddles and stamping-floors remain. The main track crosses Redwater Brook on a cart clapper bridge and enters the working area of the Birch Tor & Vitifer Mine, where similar relics remain. Here the miners would remove the boots that had borne them to work along such moorland paths as Track 28, and change into boots with perforated toes to let out the water they had so often to stand in when working.

Long walks, tiring work, a hard life: little wonder that the Birch Tor and Warren House Inns were well patronized, there to colour the miners' evening hours with cider and beer, their 'hearts for to cheer'.

Bibliography

MAPS

Road maps in *Britannia published by John Ogilby Esq His Majesty's Cosmographer London Printed by the author at his House in Whitefriars 1675*

*Map of the Duke of Bedford's Land c.*1760

A Map of the County of Devon, 1765, Benjamin Donn, Thomas Jefferies, London

Ordnance Survey Map of England and Wales, Sheet 90, one inch to one mile, first edition 1809, London

Map of the County of Devon from an Actual Survey, C. & J. Greenwood 1827, Greenwood, Pringle & Company, London

Map of Dartmoor, H. Besley, undated mid-nineteenth century, marked 'entered Stationers' Hall' but not so recorded, H. Besley & Son, Exeter

Spencer Maps, A collection of annotated 6-inch maps presented to the author in 1952 by John Spencer of Plymouth

Map of Devon, 1787, John Cary

A New Map of Devonshire, John Cary, 1818

BOOKS

A Perambulation of the Antient and Royal Forest of Dartmoor and the Venville Precincts, Rev. Samuel Rowe (J.B. Rowe, Plymouth, 1848)

Papers of John Andrews (1750-1824), Attorney-at-Law of Modbury, ed. R. Hansford Worth (*TDA* 73 of 1941)

Transactions of the Devonshire Association for the Advancement of Science, Literature and Art (Exeter)

The Mines of the Granite Mass, Atkinson, Burt & Waite (Exeter Industrial Archaeology Group of the University of Exeter, 1978)

A Description of the Part of Devonshire bordering on the Tamar and the Tavy Mrs A.E. Bray, (John Murray, London, 1836)

The Ancient Stone Crosses of Dartmoor and its Borderland, William Crossing (J.G. Commin, Exeter, 1902)

Guide to Dartmoor, William Crossing (*Western Morning News*, Plymouth, 1909)

High Dartmoor: Land and People, Eric Hemery (Robert Hale, 1983)

Walking the Dartmoor Waterways, Eric Hemery (David & Charles, Newton Abbot, 1986) (No direct reference)

The Metalliferous Mingin Region of South-West England, H.G. Dines HMSO, London, 1956)

Industrial Archaeology of Dartmoor Helen Harris (David & Charles, 1968)

General View of the Agriculture of the County of Devon, Charles Vancouver (2nd edition, 1813, Board of Agriculture, London)

Throwleigh, Emmie Varwell (Sydney Lee, Exeter, 1938)

Monastic Life in Medieval England, J.C. Dickinson (A. & C. Black, 1979)

The Woollen Industry of South West England, K. Ponting (Adams & Dart, 1971)

Christian England, David L. Edwards (Collins, 1981)

English Monasticism Yesterday and Today, E.K. Milliken (Harrap, 1967)

Buckfast Abbey, published at the Abbey, Dom John Stéphan (19th edition 1977)

Tavistock Abbey, H.P.R. Finberg (Cambridge University Press, 1951)

Saint Michael of the Rock, Revd P.A. Apps (Lydford Parish Church Council, 1983) Numerous papers on Dartmoor Stone Crosses in *TDA*, E. Masson Phillips

St Peter's Church Meavy, Rosemary Thomas (1970)

Battles Royal, H. Miles Brown (Libra Books, 1982)

Devon and Exeter in the Civil War, E.A. Andriette (David & Charles, 1971)

Story of an Ancient Chapel, Revd J. Rawson (J.G. Commin, Exeter, 1920)

The Little Book of Lydford, M. & S. Wootton (3rd edition, 1981)

The Archaeology of Dartmoor from the Air, Dartmoor National Park Authority (Devon Books, 1985)

The Making of the English Landscape, W.G. Hoskins (Hodder & Stoughton, 1955)

Portrait of South Brent, Gregory Wall (G. Wall, South Brent, 1982)

English Provincial Posts, Brian Austen (Phillimore, 1978)

Devon & Cornwall – A Postal Survey 1500-1791, D.B. Cornelius (Reigate Postal Historical Society, 1973)

The Faber Book of Poems and Places, Ed. G. Grigson (Faber & Faber, 1980)

Glossary

Adit Horizontal tunnel driven by miners to drain a mine-working, or provide access to a vertical shaft.

Ancient Tenement Farm in the central basin established in Norman times (or earlier) with rights of turbary and pasture in return for stock-ranger duties performed for the lord of the soil.

Ash-house Small circular building in or near a farm court, built entirely of stone – including the conical roof – containing a hatch facing the farmhouse kitchen door. Kitchen refuse, hot ashes from the fire and farmyard dung were tipped through the hatch. Opposite this was a door for the periodic removal of the rich compost for spreading as fertilizer on the land.

Barrow Archaeological term for 'cairn'.

Blowing house Medieval workshop for processing tin-ore. The remains of some today contain relics of furnace, water-wheel pit, drop-stamps, mortar stones and mould stones in which tin ingots were cast.

Bond-stone Boundary stone, sometimes unmarked, sometimes inscribed with initials of parish or land-owner.

Bottom Valley confining a stream, but less deep than a cleave or hole.

Bronze Age Period of pre-history *c.* 1950-500 BC.

Bury Artificial mound built for the colonizing of rabbits on a warren.

Cache Place of concealment for tools and tin ingots, constructed by medieval tinners.

Cairn Local name for a circular prehistoric mound formed of stones heaped above an interment. Many are sited on prominent hill-tops.

Clam Wooden footbridge.

Clapper Bridge Method of bridging streams by laying imposts (large stone slabs) on piers from bank to bank. Spans are spoken of as 'openings' and clappers vary from a single opening to formerly very large structures of four or even five openings. Most are medieval, some much later.

Cleave Valley with steep sides, a gorge.

Clitter Scattered rockfield below a ruined tor, ice-transported during the Ice Age.

Col Ridge connecting two peaks or summits.

Combe Valley closed at one end.

Cornditch Ditch dug on outer side of enclosure wall, the earth being thrown behind the wall to create a bank. Thus deer could not jump into the enclosure but any that entered through an open gate could leap outwards. In short, a ditch to protect the corn.

Cross, granite, medieval Rough-hewn from solid granite by monks and erected by them to function as Christian way-marks. Post-medieval crosses were erected in certain places to mark land boundaries. All such crosses mentioned in the text are shown by the symbol † following the name.

DNPA Dartmoor National Park Authority.

Dolmen Neolithic (*ie* pre-Bronze Age) burial chamber built with large stone uprights and a slab roof.

Driftway Wide space between enclosure walls to permit the driving of herds.

Featherbed (i) see 'Granite bedding'; (ii) a mire that undulates when trodden on.

Fen The peat (or blanket) bog areas of north and south Dartmoor.

Field system Prehistoric field-plan marked out by reaves. Medieval fields were similarly marked out and are usually recognizable because less decayed and proximate to the remains of longhouses.

Forest of Dartmoor Central area of the granite upland covering 56,000 acres and including the northern and southern fens and central basin. Since 1337 the chase of forest of the Duke of Cornwall, therefore historically a hunting ground rather than an area of dense woodland. The original boundary between the forest and the perimeter commons (apportioned to the border-country parishes) was laid down in a physical perambulation in 1240.

Gert Deep cutting made by miners to expose a vein of tin: sometimes known as a 'gully' or 'gulf'.

Granite bedding Solid granite platform, often found on tor summits and in river beds.

Gulf See 'Gert'.

Headmire Mire feeding the head, or source of a stream.

Headweir Weir deflecting stream water into a leat channel.

Hole Small gorge.

Hunting gate Narrow gateway in an enclosure wall of sufficient width to admit a horse and rider.

Hut circle Circular stone remains of prehistoric dwelling, originally thatched.

Impost See 'Clapper Bridge'.

Iron Age Period of pre history *c.* 500 BC-AD 50.

Jurat See 'Stannator'.

Kistvaen Stone chest for burial of human remains in the Bronze Age, usually by cremation.

Lake Tributary stream of which the source, drained by tinners, may once have been a tarn.

Leat Artificial channel contouring hillsides to carry water by gravity.

Logan stone Rock pivoted upon another at a fine point of balance caused by weathering, and capable of being rocked.

Longhouse Traditional Devon farmhouse with central passage dividing human from animal quarters. Many medieval longhouse ruins remain on Dartmoor, most of them emptied by the Black Death in 1348.

Menhir Celtic – tall stone; prehistoric monument usually associated with burial.

Mire Valley swamp.

Moorgate Access gate to open moor at head of border-country lane.

Mortar stone See 'Blowing house'.

Newtake Land taken in from open moorland.

Orthostat Large stone slab, sometimes of considerable width, set vertically in the ground. The walls of prehistoric and medieval enclosures are often formed of orthostats.

OS Ordnance Survey.

Peneplain Elevated plateau in the fen areas forming the upper reach of a Dartmoor main river. From it, the river drops steeply into its middle reach basin.

Pool (i) Area of standing water (e.g. Knattaburrow Pool); (ii) Mire (e.g. Raybarrow Pool, Ducks Pool); (iii) Eroded hollow in peat (e.g. Cranmere Pool, Dinger Pool).

Pound Enclosure for animals, usually circular.

Reave Boundary bank of earth and stones; some are prehistoric, some medieval.

Retaining circle Circle of small set stones surrounding a Bronze Age interment.

Rock Basin Natural hollow produced on tors by weathering, and in rivers by erosion.

Roundhouse Circular building in which a horse operated a revolving mill-stone for crushing cereals, apples and gorse. The remains of roundhouses are found on many Devon farms.

Slotted gateposts Granite posts slotted to receive lateral poles, precursor of the hinged gate.

Slotted Post-stile Rustic stile consisting of lateral poles supported by small stone uprights similar to slotted gateposts, and often provided with a step on either side to assist in mounting the stile.

Stannary (Latin *Stanum* Tin) The highly organized medieval tin industry of Dartmoor.

Stannator Area representative attending the administrative and disciplinary Stannary courts. Also known as a 'jurat'.

Steps Set of stepping stones in a stream, invariably having a specific name: most are found alongside a ford and bridge. Stone steps built into walls usually are unnamed.

Stone circle Open-air temple of the Bronze Age.

Stone row Monumental row of set stones leading from a Bronze Age interment to a terminal stone. The longest in Britain, two and a half miles (4 km) in length, is in the Erme valley on southern Dartmoor.

Stroll Driftway leading from moorgate to open moor.

Tare and feather Method of cutting granite after *c.* 1800 by inserting punches (tares) into pre-drilled holes, kept in position by tiny iron blades (feathers) and hammering on the tares.

TDA Transactions of the Devonshire Association for the Advancement of Science, Literature and Art.

Tinner Medieval worker in tin.

Tinners' house Medieval tinners' work-a-week shelter: a tiny house with wolf-proof cupboard and fireplace.

Tor (also Rock) Celtic *Twr*, Cornish *Tour* a rockpile; most have been ruined by Ice Age conditions and weathered in vertical partings and horizontal jointings.

Vermin trap, granite Miniature granite tunnel, built and sited by warreners to protect buries from predators. The tunnel had a false floor which, when trodden on, released slate shutters imprisoning the animal.

Warren Rabbit farm; some are of medieval foundation, Ditsworthy and Trowlesworthy on southern Dartmoor being the oldest. Sporting warrens were established from the late eighteenth century onward by landowners for sport and for replenishing their larders.

Waste Term peculiar to south Dartmoor. It indicates a former open tract of moorland, later enclosed.

Index

This is the first paperback edition of the definitive guide to Dartmoor's most important and hitherto uncharted historic tracks. The moor's traditional travel routes have been shrouded in mystery and many of them were in danger of being lost altogether. Through meticulous research and intensive field work over decades to clarify doubtful portions of the routes, Eric Hemery, acknowledged as Dartmoor's leading writer, established the historical background to the 28 tracks described here. His painstaking study led him to take issue with the Ordnance Survey over such fictions as 'Abbot's Way' and 'Drizzlecombe' and he presents convincing arguments to support his findings.

An important feature of track-routing throughout the book is the use of recorded evidence from experienced moormen, present and past, for route details. In every case such evidence was personally communicated to the author and may be regarded as irrefutable.

Sixteen trans-moorland tracks occupy part 1 of the book and twelve inter-moorland tracks, part 2, many of which had not been previously researched before the first publication of this book. Detailed maps and illustrations allow readers to follow in the steps of monks, merchants, tin miners and others who over the centuries established safe ways across the treacherous moor.

Cover photograph (by the author): a wild area of north Dartmoor showing the ancient Cut Lane

GB £ NET   +013.99

ISBN 0-7090-6075-0

01399>

£13.99 net

9 780709 060758